GREAT RACEHORSES OF THE WORLD

Roger Mortimer
and
Peter Willett

 LONDON MICHAEL JOSEPH

First published in Great Britain by
MICHAEL JOSEPH LTD.
52 Bedford Square
London, W.C.1
1969

Set and printed in Great Britain by
Ebenezer Baylis & Son Ltd., The Trinity Press, Worcester, and London
and bound by James Burn, Esher.

7181 0625 3

CONTENTS

Foreword

Acknowledgements are due to: Allen F. Brewer, Jr., for plate 26; *The British Racehorse*, for plates 3, 9, 12, 15 and 16; Central Press Photos, for plate 23; Rex Coleman, A.R.P.S., for plate 31; Fiona Forbes, for plate 33; *Herald & Weekly Times Ltd*, Melbourne, for plate 28; The New York Jockey Club, for plate 2; W. W. Rouch & Co. Ltd., for plates 5, 7, 8, 10, 11, 14, 17, 18, 19, 20, 21, 22, 24, 27, 29, 30 and 32; *Stud & Stable*, for plate 1; and Winants Bros, Inc., Maryland U.S.A., for plate 25.

FOREWORD

Controversy is liable to surround any selection of well-known horses classified under a particular heading, since inevitably widely differing views exist as to their qualifications for inclusion. The authors of this book do not claim that their selection embraces all the greatest horses in world racing history; they do consider that all the horses they have chosen have valid claims to greatness in one respect or another. This distinction is implied in the title, for they have refrained deliberately from calling the book "The Greatest Racehorses of the World".

The horses included were chosen because they possessed qualities which made them of special interest to the authors; it is hoped that they will prove of equal interest to the readers.

West Australian

West Australian, who carried off the "Triple Crown" in 1853, was the last, and unquestionably the best, of the four Derby winners owned by Mr. John Bowes. The other three were Mündig (1835), Cotherstone (1843) and Daniel O'Rourke (1852). A member of the Jockey Club, Mr. Bowes owned horses for over fifty years and until John Scott's death in 1871, he remained a patron of that trainer's famous Malton stable.

Mr. Bowes was a son of Lord Strathmore but was unable to succeed to the title as he was born nine years before his parents married. Although extremely shy, and in later years a recluse, he always possessed a shrewd idea of the value of money, and unlike many men of his era who took up racing at an early age, he substantially increased his fortune, despite a kindly but expensive habit of hiring the Variétés Theatre in Paris for the benefit of his wife, a not noticeably talented French actress.

Mr. Bowes was still at Cambridge when Mündig won the Derby. He was just twenty-one at the time and Mündig had been entered for the Derby by his trustees, one of whom was the Duke of Cleveland. When Mündig's merits became apparent, the trustees had the impudence to back Mündig at long prices for themselves without telling Bowes or offering him a share of the commission. Bowes was justly indignant when he heard of this, but he had a strong hand and he played his cards well. He summoned his trustees and after some ignoble attempts at bluff on their part they were compelled to transfer to him their most favourable bets when he threatened to have his horse scratched. "What an owdacious young 'un!" was John Scott's admiring comment on the situation.

Bred by his owner, West Australian was by Melbourne out of Mowerina, by Touchstone. Melbourne, virtually the only male line

descendant of Trumpator, had sired a very good horse called Sir
Tatton Sykes that was owned by the great jockey Bill Scott, John
Scott's brother. After one particular satisfactory gallop Bill Scott,
not a noticeably devout man as a rule, had gone down on his knees
and thanked God "for at last having given me the hell of a horse".
Sir Tatton Sykes won the Two Thousand Guineas and the St.
Leger in 1846 and would have won the Derby too, had not Bill
Scott, who rode him, been hopelessly drunk. Melbourne also sired
Blink Bonny, who won the Derby and the Oaks in 1857, and two
good fillies, Canezou and Cymba, respective winners of the One
Thousand Guineas and the Oaks. Mowerina, dam of West
Australian, was out of Emma and was thus a half-sister to Mündig
and a full sister of Cotherstone.

When West Australian arrived at John Scott's stable from Mr.
Bowes's place, Streatlam, as a yearling, it was swiftly recognized
that he possessed exceptional merit. Sam Wheatley, who had
trained for the Duke of Cleveland, declared that he had never seen a
finer yearling. Straightaway he backed West Australian for the Derby
and never hedged a penny. In fact West Australian was not all that
easy to train, as he always carried a great deal of flesh while a weakness in his feet caused recurrent lameness. Because of this he did not
see a racecourse till the Newmarket Houghton Meeting in October.
In the Criterion Stakes he ran idly and was beaten half a length by
Speed the Plough, with Filbert third. It was the one defeat in his
racing career. During the same week he reversed that form in the six
furlong Glasgow Stakes, winning by two lengths from Filbert with
Speed the Plough third.

During the month of August, John Scott had tried West
Australian very highly with Longbow, a four-year-old that had just
won the six furlong Stewards Cup at Goodwood with 9 st. 9 lb.
When the morning came for this trial to take place, the rain was
teeming down and it was put off till the afternoon. The local touts
thought it had been put off till another day and none were present
when West Australian, ridden by Sim Templeman and receiving
only 21 lb., beat Longbow, Frank Butler up, with remarkable ease.
Mr. Bowes at once departed for York, where he caught the fast train to
London and backed West Australian to win him £30,000 in the Derby.

As a three-year-old West Australian stood 15 hands 3 inches and
was described as "a yellowish bay, rather long in the body with a
low stealing action". He did not run before the Two Thousand

Guineas, which he duly won by half a length from a very good horse called Sittingbourne belonging to the Duke of Bedford.

At this stage of his racing career Mr. Bowes rarely visited a racecourse and he could not be persuaded to journey to Epsom to see West Australian, commonly known as "The West", perform in the Derby. "The West", ridden by Frank Butler wearing the jacket and cap worn by Bill Scott on Cotherstone, started a 6–4 on favourite in a field of twenty-eight and the sporting public of Yorkshire were on him to a man. The crowd was gigantic and the sun shone from a cloudless sky. Approaching Tattenham Corner there were only three horses that seemed to hold a chance, Cineas who was the leader, West Australian and Sittingbourne. Cineas was going so easily that he looked sure to win, but approaching the final furlong the other two closed on him and in a tremendous finish "The West" won by a neck from Sittingbourne with Cineas, a head away, third. West Australian was John Scott's fifth Derby winner and Scott rated him by far the best horse he had ever trained. The great bookmaker Davis had a terrible race and could only just settle. He only had £200 left when he went to Ascot a fortnight later but luckily for him won £12,000 on the opening day of that meeting.

By the autumn "The West" had reached his peak and before an admiring Yorkshire crowd he won the St. Leger in the commonest of canters, thereby becoming the first horse to win the "Triple Crown". "I only touched him with the whip once and I was glad to get him stopped", observed Butler afterwards.

West Australian finished the season with a couple of walk-overs. As a four-year-old he ran three times, winning a Triennial Stakes at Ascot, the Ascot Gold Cup in what was then record time, and a sweepstakes at Goodwood by twenty lengths. The Goodwood race concluded his racing career. He was then sold for 5,000 guineas to Lord Londesborough who retired him to the stud at Tadcaster at a fee of 30 guineas. When Lord Londesborough died, "The West" was bought for 4,000 guineas by the Duc de Morny and on the Duc's death he passed into the hands of the French Emperor. Neither in England nor in France was he a success as a sire but through Solon, Barcaldine and Marco, Hurry On is descended from him in tail-male. Hurry On sired three Derby winners, Captain Cuttle, Coronach and Call Boy, as well as the Gold Cup winner Precipitation who sired the 1946 Derby winner Airborne and is grandsire of the 1964 Derby winner Santa Claus, a son of Chamossaire.

Lexington

It has rightly been stated that the evolution of the British Thoroughbred has been supported by two pillars, the General Stud Book and
the annual volumes of "Races Past". The former supplies the
pedigrees of brood mares and their foaling records; the latter the
evidence of the racecourse test upon which the selection of the most
suitable animals is based.

Towards the close of the last century the bloodstock industry both
in Australia and the United States was passing through a phase of
rapid expansion and Australian and American horses were being
imported by Great Britain in considerable quantity. This became a
matter of some concern and the Advertisement to Volume XVIII of
the General Stud Book, published in 1897, contained the following:
"The importation of a number of horses and mares bred in the United
States of America and in Australia, a few of whom will remain at studs
in this country, may have some effect on stock here, but the pedigrees
of these horses, though accepted in the Stud Books of their own
country, cannot in all cases be traced back to the thoroughbred stock
exported from England from which they all claim to be, and from
which, no doubt, they mainly are descended; these animals are, therefore, in these cases, marked with reference to their own Stud Books".

The General Stud Book was then the property of the Weatherby
family. The editors of the Stud Book felt that the measures so far
taken were inadequate, as indeed they were, and sought the advice of
the Stewards of the Jockey Club. As a result the following qualifica-
tion was made for admission to the General Stud Book: "Any animal
claiming admission should be able to prove satisfactorily some eight
or nine crosses of pure blood, to trace back for at least a century, and
to show such performances of its immediate family on the Turf as to
warrant the belief in the purity of its blood."

Early this century anti-betting legislation nearly killed American racing. There was no market for racehorses in the United States and the Turf authorities in this country began to be nervous that American horses, many of dubious origin, would be dumped in England by the thousand. The result was a notice in Volume XXI of the General Stud Book, published in 1909, that ran as follows: "The Editors beg to inform subscribers that, since the last Volume of the Stud Book was published, they have had cause to consider the advisability of admitting into the Stud Book horses and mares which cannot be traced to a thoroughbred root, but which have fulfilled the requirements given in the preface to Volume XIX. They have decided that, in the interests of the English Stud Book, no horse or mare can be admitted unless it can be traced to a strain already accepted in the earlier volumes of the Book."

This measure, however, was deemed insufficiently stringent and at a Jockey Club meeting in 1913 Lord Jersey, Senior Steward the previous year, put forward a proposal that was found acceptable and was included in Volume XXII published later that year. This regulation stated: "No horse or mare can, after this date, be considered as eligible for admission unless it can be traced without flaw on both sire's and dam's side of its pedigree to horses and mares themselves already accepted in earlier volumes of the Book."

This regulation, commonly known as the "Jersey Act", caused fierce resentment in the United States where it was held that the English were less concerned with maintaining the purity of their Stud Book than with the protection of their export trade; and that to accomplish this they had not scrupled to stigmatize the majority of horses bred in America as "half-bred". No doubt self-interest played its part in the passage of the "Jersey Act"; at the same time the American Stud Book was known to be inaccurate in some respects and this was admitted by certain responsible critics in America. The main cause of the trouble was the great American sire Lexington, who appeared in the pedigree of so many American horses. Lexington was in fact descended in tail-male from the first winner of the Epsom Derby, Diomed, who had been exported in his old age to the United States. Lexington, though, had doubtful elements on the dam's side of his pedigree which barred him from the Stud Book under the "Jersey Act".

Foaled in 1850, Lexington was by Boston out of Alice Carneal, by Sarpedon. He was bred in Kentucky by Dr. Elisha Warfield who had retired from medical practice, due to ill-health, at the early age of forty and devoted the rest of his life—he was seventy-eight when he died in 1859—to bloodstock breeding. He was clearly a practical man of business as he advertised the services of his stallion, Tup, for "$22 cash, or bricks at $4 per 100; beef on foot at $15 per hundred-weight; whiskey at $2 per gallon". There is no denying that the pedigree of Alice Carneal is open to very considerable doubt. Some sources have also queried the origins of Boston, and it has even been suggested that Timoleon, Boston's sire, was at stud under three different pedigrees within a period of eight years!.

Boston was so called because he was won in a card game of that name, the winner being Mr. Nathaniel Rives, the loser Mr. John Wickham, a well-known Virginian attorney. Boston proved extremely difficult to train in his early days and in fact was returned to the man who had broken him with the suggestion that he (Boston) should be castrated or shot, preferably the latter. Eventually Boston became more tractable and it was possible to train him, but he remained ill-tempered and was always inclined to make a meal of any horse that endeavoured to pass him in a race. He continued to run until he was ten years of age and was only beaten five times in forty-five starts. He was a great stayer, equally good on firm ground or on soft, and thirty of his victories were in four-mile heats. Horses were expected to be tough in those days and Boston, who was leading American sire in 1851-52-53, as well as being a successful sire of trotters, began his stud duties while his racing career was still in progress. For instance in 1841, when he was eight years of age, he covered forty-two mares in the spring and then raced in September and October. In 1842 he ran in the spring and the autumn and fitted in some stud duties in between. He was stone blind and terribly emaciated when he died in January 1850. Lexington was born shortly afterwards.

Lexington was bay in colour and stood 15.3 hands. He had a narrow blaze on his face, while his fore and hind feet, pasterns and a small portion of his hind legs were white. He began his racing career under the name of Darley and carried the colours of Dr. Warfield, but in fact he was a partnership horse, the other partner being a negro trainer, a former slave known as "Dark Harry". Darley's first experience of racing came in May 1853 in the one mile Association Stakes for three-year-olds, run in heats. He won both his heats most impressively. Only four days later he won the Citizens Stakes, two-mile heats. He ran in three heats and won them all with ease. Among those who saw him win was Mr. Richard Ten Broeck, who was very well-known in the racing world and owned horses, trained by J. B. Pryor at Natchez, in partnership with Mr. Adam L. Bingaman. In "The History of Thoroughbred Racing in America" Mr. William Robertson wrote: "Ten Broeck looked the perfect prototype of the old Mississipi riverboat gambler. In fact during one phase of his life, he was." Certainly Ten Broeck had had an eventful life and his family, an old and distinguished one from Albany, New York, had severed all connection with him after he had left the U.S. Military Academy at West Point under a somewhat murky cloud. At all events Ten Broeck bought Darley for the modest sum of $2,500 and shortly afterwards Darley's name was changed to Lexington.

It was intended that Lexington's first major objective should be the Great State Post Stake, to be run at Metairie, New Orleans, on April 1st, 1854. However in the meantime Mr. Louis Smith of Alabama, who disliked Ten Broeck, challenged Lexington to a match with a four-year-old filly called Sally Waters. At Metairie Sally Waters had put up some fast times in two-mile heats against another of Ten Broeck's horses. The match against Lexington was to be run over three miles and the terms of the contest stated: "Match for $8,500— $5,000 on Sally Waters against $3,500 on Lexington". Although Lexington had never been tested over three miles and furthermore had been let down since he last ran, Ten Broeck felt unable to resist what he rightly judged to be favourable odds. The match took place on December 2nd and on a muddy track Lexington won in straight heats.

The Great State Post Stake, run on April 1st 1854 was a curious event that was intended not only to stimulate regional rivalry, but to be the most valuable race yet run. The conditions stated: "Subscription at $5,000 each; $1,000 to each starter, if not distanced, the remainder to the winner. Each State subscribing to be represented by the signatures of three responsible gentlemen, residents of the said State, the majority of whom shall name the horse to start. Four-mile heats".

In the end only four States mustered a candidate. Lexington represented Kentucky, while Mississippi, Alabama and Louisiana were represented by Lecomte, Highlander and Arrow. Except for Highlander all the runners were by Boston. The going was extremely heavy, which suited Lexington who won in straight heats, the first in 8 minutes 8¾ seconds, the other in 8 minutes 4 seconds. Lecomte had never previously been beaten.

A week later, though, on very much faster ground, Lecomte had his revenge in the Jockey Club Purse, four-mile heats. In the first heat Lecomte led from the start and beat Lexington, who was very distressed at the finish, by half a dozen lengths. The time of 7 minutes 26 seconds beat the previous record by 6½ seconds. After a rest, Lexington rallied and fought back gamely in the second heat but Lecomte mastered him after three miles and drew clear to win by four lengths in 7 minutes 38¾ seconds. Lexington was never again defeated.

Excuses were subsequently made on Lexington's behalf. It was said that he was "fed indulgently" after the Great State Post Stake before the decision had been made to start him in the Jockey Club Purse. It was also alleged that a spectator, evidently a supporter of Lecomte, had run on to the course during the second heat and had instructed Meichon, Lexington's jockey to pull up; and that Meichon had obliged him by doing so. This story seems somewhat unlikely since Meichon was an experienced jockey.

Ten Broeck did not relish being beaten and his reaction to Lexington's defeat was to challenge Lecomte's owner, General Wells, to another match, $10,000 a side, but the General showed scant sign of interest. Ten Broeck, therefore, had the following inserted in a newspaper called "Spirit of the Times":

"Although the mistake made by the rider of Lexington in pulling up at the end of three miles in the recent four-mile race at New Orleans, was witnessed by thousands of persons, I believe it has not been referred to in print except in the last number of your paper. As Lexington will probably follow the fashion in making a foreign tour, I propose the following as his valedictory: I will run him a single four miles over the Metairie Course at New Orleans (under the rules of the Club) against the fastest time at four miles that has been run in America for the sum of TEN THOUSAND DOLLARS—one-fourth forfeit. Two trials to be allowed, and the race to be run between the 1st and 15th of April next. Arrow to be substituted if Lexington is amiss.

"Or, I will run Lexington over the same course, four-mile heats, on the Thursday previous to the next Metairie April Meeting, against any named horse, at the rate expressed in the proposition subjoined.

"Or, I will run him over the Union Course, at New York, the same distance, on the third Tuesday in October. The party accepting the last race to receive TWENTY FIVE THOUSAND DOLLARS to twenty thousand dollars or to bet the same odds if Lexington travels to run at New Orleans. The forfeit to be FIVE THOUSAND DOLLARS, and to be deposited with Messrs COLEMAN & STETSON, of the Astor House, when either race is accepted. If the amounts of the last proposition are too large, they may be reduced one-half, with forfeit in the same proportion. The first acceptance coming to hand will be valid— subsequent ones declined; and none received after the commencement of the races at the National Course in New York, the 26th of next month.

R. Ten Broeck. May 30th, 1854."

Not surprisingly Ten Broeck's statement resulted in a flood of comment and criticism, interspersed with a number of challenges. General Wells truculently announced that he would run Lecomte against "any horse in the world, any day, any distance, for any amount of money". Messrs Calvin Green and John Belcher, both of Virginia, declared acceptance of Ten Broeck's first proposition, the race against time. Later on Belcher proposed to match Red Eye, a potentially brilliant but unreliable son of Boston, against Lexington with certain changes in the conditions, but this particular challenge was declined.

In the meantime Lexington travelled up to New York, but his campaign in the Atlantic States never took place as he got loose at exercise one morning, galloped into a field and injured a leg. This story, incidentally, was received with scepticism by the many people who disliked and distrusted Ten Broeck. Lexington returned home and began his preparation for the assault on the four-mile record of 7 minutes 26 seconds. The Metairie track was specially prepared and it was agreed that Lexington was to be permitted not only a flying start, but pacemakers as well. The day selected was April 2nd and no other racing took place that afternoon. At 3 p.m. Lexington, carrying 7 st. 5 lb. and ridden by Gilpatrick, went down to the post accompanied by his pacemakers, Arrow and Joe Blackburn, the latter of whom proved not good enough to be able to assist Lexington at all.

Lexington covered the first mile in 1 minute 47¼ seconds. This was considered dangerously fast and orders were yelled at Gilpatrick to take a pull. The second mile was run in 1 minute 52¼ seconds, the third in 1 minute 51½ seconds and the final mile in 1 minute 48¾ seconds. Thus the full time was 7 minutes 19¾ seconds, beating the previous best by 6¼ seconds. The result of the race was received with the utmost enthusiasm by the thousands present, as the test had aroused tremendous interest and for days horse-lovers and gamblers had been pouring into New Orleans. Lexington's record, by the way, stood till 1874.

Undeterred by Lexington's triumph, the bold General Wells entered Lecomte in the Jockey Club Purse on April 14th, a race in which Lexington was to run, and bet Ten Broeck an additional $2,500 on the result. Lexington had been a bit footsore after his race against time, but had swiftly recovered. Lecomte, though, had had a touch of colic a few days before the race and the probability is that he was not at his best. He certainly proved no match in the first four-mile heat, Lexington winning very easily in 7 minutes 23¾ seconds. Lecomte was a very tired horse in the closing stages and General Wells withdrew him from the second heat, leaving Lexington the victor.

Lexington never ran again. He had been having trouble with an eye and there were ominous signs that the other eye was becoming affected as well. Like his sire, he became stone blind. In 1856 Ten Broeck transferred his racing interests to England. While he was there he met the American breeder, Mr. Robert Aitchison Alexander, and sold him Lexington for $15,000, at that time the biggest price ever paid for an American horse. Installed at the Woodburn Farm, near Medway, Kentucky, Lexington lived till he was twenty-five and became one of the greatest sires in American racing history. "The Blind Hero of Woodburn" was champion sire in American no fewer than sixteen times, fourteen in succession. Altogether he got some 600 foals, 40% of which proved winners, a remarkably fine record. His very first crop of runners included the best colts in the country, Norfolk, Asteroid and Kentucky, all of whom were out of mares by Glencoe. Norfolk and Asteroid were never beaten, while Kentucky's solitary defeat was at the hands of Norfolk. Lexington's stock won $1,159,321 on the American Turf and his daughters made admirable brood mares. Foxhall, who won the Cambridgeshire, Cesarewitch, Grand Prix de Paris and the Ascot Gold Cup was out of a Lexington mare.

Lexington's story must conclude, as it began, with the "Jersey Act". That Act had not been retrospective and American strains that were already in the Stud Book were permitted to remain so. This was fortunate, as three American horses that had come to England in the 1890s exercised a profound effect on thoroughbred breeding in this country. Americus sired Americus Girl, whose descendants, from Mumtaz Mahal onwards, include some of the most brilliant performers in English racing history. Rhoda B became the dam of the Derby winner Orby, while Sibola won the One Thousand Guineas and became the grandam of Nearco. Americus, Rhoda B and Sibola all had Lexington in their pedigrees.

The absurd side of the "Jersey Act" became apparent in 1914 when Durbar II won the Derby. Durbar was out of Urania, by Hanover, whose sire Hindoo was out of Florence, by Lexington. Durbar therefore was barred from the Stud Book for being out of a Hanover mare, whereas Orby, also out of a Hanover mare, was included. In 1940 M. M. Boussac won the Two Thousand Guineas with Djebel, who was not eligible for the Stud Book as his sire Tourbillon was out of a mare by Durbar II. After the war the stock of Tourbillon and Djebel were immensely successful in European racing and numerous important events were won by so-called half-breds. The situation became embarrassing in 1948 when the Two Thousand Guineas was won by My Babu and the St. Leger by Black Tarquin, both barred by the "Jersey Act" from the Stud Book.

The writing was now very clearly on the wall and the Advertisement to Volume XXXI of the General Stud Book, published in 1949, contained the following:

"In July, 1948, the Publishers referred to the Stewards of the Jockey Club the question whether steps should now be taken to broaden the scope of the Book so as to allow for out-crossings with certain strains which at present were not admissible. The Stewards appointed a Committee to take evidence and report upon the point, and the report given to the Jockey Club at their December meeting stated that some modification was advisable in the qualifications at present required.

"The Publishers, therefore, give notice that as from this date the conditions which have governed admission continuously since Volume XXII are rescinded.

"Any animal claiming admission from now onwards must be able to prove satisfactorily some eight or nine crosses of pure blood, to trace back for at least a century, and to show such performances of its immediate family on the Turf as to warrant the belief in the purity of its blood."

Thus the conditions and wording of 1901 were brought back. The stigma of illegitimacy had been removed from a vast number of American horses and their descendants, Lexington among them. The repeal of the "Jersey Act" came just in time to save English racing from looking ridiculous, as within fifteen years the Derby was won four times, and the St. Leger four times, too, by horses that would not have been allowed in the Stud Book had the Act remained in force.

Gladiateur

Gladiateur was one of the greatest racehorses ever to grace the Turf, and so much more besides. He was one of only eleven horses in the whole of racing history to have secured the imaginary Triple Crown conferred by victory in the Two Thousand Guineas, the Derby and the St. Leger. He is the only horse in the whole of racing to have won the English Triple Crown and in addition the Grand Prix de Paris, for long the greatest race in France. But even that is not all; Gladiateur also was French, and in 1865, the year of his Classic triumphs, that was a fact whose significance could hardly be exaggerated.

For thirty years before the advent of Gladiateur the French had been striving to develop a fully competitive racing and breeding industry under the contemptuous eyes of the English, the creators of the thoroughbred. English complacency was expressed by the editor of the General Stud Book, who referred to this foreign competition and concluded; "With the advantages this country already possesses, and so long as horse racing continues to be followed up with spirit by her men of rank and opulence, there can be little to apprehend."

Such arrogant pride invites a fall. The French steadily improved their standards by judicious selection and rigorous application of the racecourse test, and none was more judicious or steadfast in pursuit of progress than Count Frederic de Lagrange. The only son of one of Napoleon's Generals, Lagrange inherited a fortune on the death of his father in 1836 and multiplied it by skilful investment in a variety of industrial enterprises, while maintaining a leading position in Parisian society and becoming a founder-member of the French Jockey Club. In 1857 he bought the entire stud of Alexandre Aumont, one of the most successful pioneers of racehorse breeding in France, and entered into a short-lived partnership with Baron

Nivière which was known as "the big stable". The French breeding industry was poised to challenge British supremacy. Lagrange pursued his racing ambitions systematically. With the superbly laid-out and equipped Dangu Stud as his nursery, he divided his horses in training between England and France, with the astute Englishman Tom Jennings in overall command at Phantom Cottage, Newmarket. In 1864 Lagrange won both the English and French Oaks with Fille de L'Air. This wonderful filly was bred at Dangu, but her sire Faugh-a-Ballagh was English. There was no such consideration to temper French rejoicing over the resounding victories of Gladiateur the following year because both his sire, the French Derby winner Monarque, and his dam, Miss Gladiator, were themselves bred in France.

In view of his own parentage and that of his owner, it is no wonder that Gladiateur was hailed by the chauvinistic sections of the French Press as "The Avenger of Waterloo".

Miss Gladiator was a cripple who could not be trained and one of the most extraordinary features of the career of her brilliant son was that he was intermittently lame and could not be given an orthodox preparation for any of his races. His dam trod on him when he was a foal and as a result he had such an ugly swelling on his off-fore joint that the stable vet wanted to fire him when he came in to be broken at the Count's stable at Compiegne as a big, rangey, raw-boned yearling. Lagrange would not agree without consulting Jennings, and Jennings, summoned from Newmarket, emphatically turned down the suggestion of firing and ordered normal training routines for Gladiateur. Events proved the trainer completely right, for the enlargement never affected the horse in any way, and it was navicular disease that was the cause of his chronic unsoundness.

Sheer fighting spirit and love of racing enabled Gladiateur to rise above his physical disability. As soon as the green van used for transporting him to race meetings was brought into the yard he pricked up his ears and was impatient to enter it, and from that moment until the race was over he seemed to forget his unsoundness. Nor did Jennings modify the normal severe training methods on account of Gladiateur's infirmity. The colt was put through the mill from the time he went into training. Jennings was a firm believer in yearling trials, and the twenty-five or more yearlings that Lagrange used to send into training each autumn were always tried before Christmas in Compiegne forest. As the forest rides were not wide enough to take more than four or five horses abreast, the yearlings used to be galloped in a series of eliminating trials until the best had been discovered and brought together in a final trial.

Gladiateur, Le Mandarin, Gontran and Argences were the finalists in the autumn of 1863. Lagrange and Jennings had their usual bets of a new hat on the result, Lagrange choosing Gladiateur and Jennings Le Mandarin. Jennings proved correct as Le Mandarin won the trial narrowly from Gladiateur, with Gontran third and Argences fourth. Two years later Gontran, Le Mandarin and Argences occupied the first three places, in that order, in the French Derby. Surely these must have been the four most distinguished horses ever to take part in a yearling trial. Jennings himself was in no doubt about the class of this group of yearlings, for he backed Gladiateur for the Derby before and after the trial.

Gladiateur did not appear until the Newmarket Second October Meeting as a two-year-old because he was such a big, backward colt and was already suffering from the recurrent lameness which was to dog him throughout his career. His first race was the Clearwell Stakes, for which he was backed down to 7-4 and won by a length from Joker and a field of no special distinction. He ran again in the Prendergast Stakes later at the same meeting, but could only dead-heat with Longdown, who was to finish fourth in the Derby, for third place behind Bedminster and Siberia, though Jennings afterwards claimed that he should have won easily if his jockey Edwards had not lain miles out of his ground. His third and last appearance as a two-year-old was in the Criterion Stakes at the Houghton meeting, in which he was unplaced behind Chattanooga. It was a culpable error by his trainer to run him, as he was coughing badly at the time.

During the winter Gladiateur was so lame that he was blistered on both fore-legs. This kept him in his box for the whole of January and much of February, which left Jennings with little time to get him fit for the Two Thousand Guineas. Jennings was determined to get a line to the three-year-old form and accordingly ran Argences, much against the wishes of Lagrange, in the Newmarket Biennial at the Craven meeting. Although Argences was only fourth, the form was considered good enough and Gladiateur satisfied his trainer when he gave Argences a stone in a gallop the following day and beat him as he liked. Four days before the Guineas Jennings tried Gladiateur again, this time with Le Mandarin as his chief opponent, and

Gladiateur gave away 18 lb. and won easily. Nevertheless, Gladiateur was still only half fit when he ran in the Guineas. Taking
advantage of the lax rules then in force, Jennings did not send him
into the paddock but saddled him behind the Ditch, whence the
bush telegraph signalled a message that he was "an ugly great
coach-horse". He was allowed to start at 7–1 and, owing to his lack
of condition, had the hardest race of his life to beat Archimedes by a
neck, with Liddington, Zambesi and Breadalbane all in a bunch
immediately behind.

Gladiateur enjoyed a period of relative soundness between the
Guineas and the Derby and for once Jennings was able to give him a
practically uninterrupted preparation. Jennings subjected him to one
searching trial when he set Gladiateur to give the brilliant Fille de
L'Air 8 lb. over the full distance of 1½ miles. This put Gladiateur
at a disadvantage of 25 lb. compared with the weight for age and
sex scale then in force, but he beat the filly with ease. The result of
the trial suggested that Gladiateur could have won any Derby that
had ever been run, but in the event he met second-rate opposition at
Epsom after Liddington had gone lame and The Duke had succum-
bed to an attack of equine flu. He started favourite at 5–2, and the
only danger to him was the over-confidence of his short-sighted
jockey Harry Grimshaw, who was dozing quietly back in tenth
place rounding Tattenham Corner and might never have woken up
to the fact that Christmas Carol was making the best of his way
home far ahead of him if Jem Goater on Brahma had not shouted to
him to get a move on. As soon as Grimshaw was alive to the danger
and shook him up Gladiateur tore through the middle of the field
and won easily.

Although Gladiateur had started favourite, English pundits took a
little time to attune themselves to the realization that a foreign
horse had actually beaten the best horses that England could put into
the field for the Derby. They also had to stifle memories of the ill-
feeling aroused by the in-and-out running of Fille de L'Air the
previous year, as Lagrange's filly had finished down the course when
favourite for the Two Thousand Guineas and had been the target of a
hostile demonstration after she turned the form upside down in the
Oaks. In time admiration for a great horse overcame prejudice.
"When Gladiateur gallops the other horses seem to stand still",
stated a racing writer; and the Prince of Wales gave a large
dinner party for Lagrange at which Lord Derby congratulated

the Count in a speech full of courtesy and goodwill towards France.

A crowd estimated at 150,000 turned out to pay their respects to a horse who had become a French national idol when Gladiateur ran in the Grand Prix de Paris. There were some good horses in the field, including Vertugadin and Gladiateur's own stable companions Gontran and Le Mandarin, but Gladiateur outclassed them, coming from eight lengths behind Vertugadin at the final Longchamp turn to win on the bit.

At Goodwood he beat Longdown by forty lengths in the Drawing Room Stakes and walked over for the Bentinck Memorial Stakes the next day. The contemporary thinking was that it was a mistake to run a St. Leger horse at Goodwood, but normal rules did not apply to Gladiateur and Jennings preferred to run him on the perfect Goodwood going rather than give him the same amount of work at home. Gladiateur's bouts of lameness were becoming increasingly frequent and severe. The intention was to send him to York in the middle of August for the Great Yorkshire Stakes, but he was so lame the previous weekend that not only had any hope of sending him to York to be abandoned, but his chances of taking part in the St. Leger seemed extremely slim.

Something like panic set in at Phantom Cottage, because Jennings had already made arrangements to back Gladiateur for the St. Leger. Tom Jennings junior, the son of the trainer of Gladiateur and later a successful member of the same profession himself, left an account of his father's hectic activities in the days that followed: "Father feared the big bet he had asked his commissioner to put on the horse whilst attending York races would be lost. In the gig he drove to Peterborough, 42 miles away, and caught the train to York, arriving at Harkers Hotel in time for dinner and the St. Leger call-over held there. As Father had no runners at the meeting his appearance created a mild sensation, Gladiateur being favourite at 5–4. Through his commissioner, Mr. Henry Morris, the original bet was laid off and, being unable to get a bed at Harkers, Father caught the mail train about 3.00 a.m. at York to Peterborough where he had stabled the horse and gig. After a quick breakfast he drove back to Newmarket.

On his arrival at Phantom Cottage, Father was met by the head man who blurted out that the colt's leg was quite well again and that he had given him two sharp canters that morning. Father made a quick decision. He repeated his previous day's journey to York via

Peterborough, ensured that his bet was put again on Gladiateur (at 5–4 against) and returned home as before.

Altogether Father did 168 miles in his gig with the same horse and had two night train journeys with the certainty that even if Gladiateur won the St. Leger the two transactions would leave him £500 out of pocket."

Gladiateur still was not out of the wood. He alternated almost daily between reasonable soundness and moving in very gingerly fashion, and was so sore and lame on the Saturday before the St. Leger that Jennings was in two minds about sending him to Doncaster.

He was not much better when he reached the course, and went so feelingly in a canter on the Town Moor on the Monday that Ben Bartholomew, who had watched the exercise, went straight home saying: "I won't stop to see that horse break down."

In the event Gladiateur won quite easily by three lengths from the Oaks winner Regalia, but did so virtually on three legs. That he started again for the Doncaster Stakes two days later was due to a misapprehension. Jennings was sure that he would be given a walk-over, but at the last minute the number of Reginella went into the frame. Then Jennings would have been only too pleased to withdraw, but the high-couraged Gladiateur got so excited during the preliminaries of a race that he might have been difficult to control if he had been disappointed. No harm was done as Gladiateur won in a canter and was no lamer when he pulled up than when he started.

In spite of all his vicissitudes, Gladiateur had not yet finished for the year. He won the Prix du Prince Imperial (later the Prix Royal Oak or French St. Leger) at the Longchamp autumn meeting and beat his old rival Longdown, whose owner Mr. Spencer must have been a glutton for punishment, by forty lengths again in the Newmarket Derby. Finally he was called upon to carry 9 st. 12 lb., an impossible weight for a three-year-old, in the Cambridgeshire. All the same Jennings was convinced that he would have been in the first three if Grimshaw's defective eyesight had not led him to commit another grave error of judgment. Jennings watched the race well down the course and was horrified to see Gladiateur 100 yards behind the leader and well out of it as he passed him. "Where were you at the Bushes?" he asked Grimshaw afterwards. "Oh, I was lying in a good place, about half a dozen lengths from the front," was the jockey's reply.

Gladiateur had six races as a four-year-old and won them all. He was allowed walk-overs for two races at the Newmarket Craven Meeting, which was fortunate because he was becoming permanently unsound as the navicular bones in his forefeet became more inflamed. He went over to France to win the Grand Prix de l'Imperatrice and La Coupe, and returned to give the most spectacular performance of his career in the Ascot Gold Cup. The ground at Ascot was terribly hard and Grimshaw was given orders to lie up with the leaders as far as the paddock turn, and then take him very quietly down the hill into the Swinley Bottom so as to spare his forelegs. Poor Grimshaw erred once more. Far from lying up with the leaders, he had Gladiateur forty lengths behind the pacemaker Breadalbane passing the stands, and then nearly pulled him up going down the hill so that he was fully 300 yards behind the leader in the Swinley Bottom. At that stage Admiral Rous, on the stand, turned to Lagrange and expressed doubt whether Gladiateur could win from that position. "Mais, monsieur l'amiral, c'est absolument certain", Lagrange coolly replied. And so it was; when Grimshaw gave Gladiateur his head the great horse closed the gap in a manner that had to be seen to be believed, sprinted past the leaders and scorched up the straight to beat Regalia by forty lengths, while Breadalbane was so utterly exhausted that he was pulled up.

Gladiateur had one more race, the Grand Prix de l'Empereur (now the Prix Gladiateur) over nearly 4 miles at Longchamp on October 7th. He won easily by three lengths, ridden by George Pratt, because Grimshaw, a likeable man and a good jockey within the limitation imposed by his short sight, had been killed when his dog cart was overturned on the road at Newmarket.

Gladiateur retired from the Turf with an aura of invincibility. Those critics who had earlier decried him as an ugly coach-horse professed to find him a magnificent specimen of the thoroughbred in the days of his greatness. He was a bay with black points, standing 16 hands 1 inch, with a large plain head, a beautifully arched neck, powerful sloping shoulders, very muscular fore-arms and second thighs, and a deep girth. Unfortunately his achievements at stud did not match his deeds on the racecourse, for he failed to pass on his own speed, stamina and spirit to his progeny. He sired only one horse who showed signs of true class and he, a colt named Hero, broke a leg at exercise on Newmarket Heath after only one race.

He was at stud in England and France at various times. When

Lagrange sold most of his bloodstock at the time of the Franco-Prussian war Gladiateur was bought by Mr. Blenkiron of the Middle Park Stud for 5,800 guineas, which was 200 guineas less than the sum paid two years later by the German government for Breadalbane, the horse that Gladiateur had run literally to a standstill in the Gold Cup.

He died in 1876 as a result of chronic navicular disease, though some said he died of old age. For the cynics had always claimed that the phenomenal record of Gladiateur in the Classic races could never have been achieved by a genuine three-year-old. Indeed William Graham, the brash whisky distiller who owned Regalia, lodged objections to him before and after the St. Leger on the grounds that he was really a four-year-old. The Stewards rightly refused to consider these objections since Gladiateur had been properly registered with the required veterinary certificate.

Nevertheless the victories of Gladiateur, and of many other French-bred and owned horses during the next decade, continued to rankle in the minds of many Englishmen who could not reconcile themselves to the end of the supremacy of the British-bred racehorse. Jennings once came to blows with Mat Dawson over the assertion of the respected doyen of Newmarket trainers that "the French horses and everyone connected with them should return to their own country"; and Lord Falmouth, the most successful owner-breeder of his day who won the Derby with Kingcraft and Silvio, urged the exclusion of French horses during the Jockey Club debates over what was called the "reciprocity issue".

Thus Gladiateur was not only a racehorse of consummate greatness, but also a portent. His career marked the achievement by the French racing and breeding industry of parity with the English, a status which it has maintained, within various swings of the pendulum, ever since. No horse could be more richly entitled than Gladiateur to commemoration by a bronze statue placed immediately within the main gates of Longchamp. Nor, to the eternal credit of the French, is there any chauvinism there; for the legend on the granite plinth simply identifies Gladiateur without a word of reference to his incomparable record on the Turf.

Kincsem

One of the greatest race fillies of all time was undoubtedly Kincsem. In four seasons she ran fifty-four times and was never beaten.

Foaled in 1874 at the Hungarian National Stud at Kisber, Kincsem was bred by Mr. Ernest de Blascovich, then a young man in his twenties, and was by Cambuscan out of Waternymph, by Cotswold. At this period the Hungarian Jockey Club was responsible not only for the conduct of racing, but in addition its "Commission of Nine" controlled the importation of thoroughbreds into the country. The Commission's first official agent was Mr. Francis Cavaliero, an Italian by birth but an expert on racing and breeding in England, whence most of the imported horses came.

Cavaliero gave 5,500 guineas for Captain J. White's Cambuscan, a son of Newminster. Cambuscan had been second in the Two Thousand Guineas, fourth in the Derby and third in the St. Leger. He stood for eight years in Hungary but only got ninety-eight foals. In addition, Cavaliero had imported both the sire and the dam of Waternymph. Cotswold, originally named Tithonus, had belonged to Lord de Mauley and had run unplaced in the Derby in 1856. As a four-year-old he was second in the Royal Hunt Cup at Ascot with 6 st. 7 lb. and subsequently won seven races of scant significance, their total value amounting to only £602. The Mermaid, dam of Waternymph, won the £160 King John Stakes at Egham as a two-year-old and the following season was fifth in the Oaks. Her first foal, Waternymph, bred and owned by Prince Esterhazy, won the Hungarian One Thousand Guineas and was bought as a four-year-old by Mr. de Blascovich. Waternymph's first produce was a filly by Ostreger called Hanat that won the Hungarian Oaks in 1875. Kincsem was her second foal.

It was Mr. de Blascovich's custom to sell all his yearlings privately in a bunch and the leading owners of the day were annual visitors to his stud at Tapioszentmarton. Among those that came to see the yearlings in 1875 was Baron Alex Orczy, bearer of a name later well-known in England through the authoress of the "Scarlet Pimpernel". Mr. de Blascovich asked the modest sum of £700 for his seven yearlings and the Baron agreed at once to pay that price. However he firmly refused to take over Kincsem and another filly on the grounds that they were common and unattractive. Kincsem was a liver chestnut without a single white hair on her and with large brown spots on her quarters. She may never have been handsome judged by the highest standards, but she grew into a fine upstanding filly standing 16.1 hands, while her conformation was difficult to fault. From her earliest days she galloped with her head held very low and she bitterly resented any attempt by her rider to check this habit.

Blascovich decided to keep Kincsem himself and she was sent to be trained by Robert Hesp. Born in England in 1823, Hesp was the son of a prosperous saddler and after a period of apprenticeship at Malton, in Yorkshire, he went out to Hungary to take up the post of huntsman with Prince Batthyany's hounds. In the Hungarian war for liberation against Austria, he saved the life of Count Edmund Batthyany, son of Prince Gustav Batthyany, owner of St. Simon. Hesp managed to make his way through the Austrian lines with Count Edmund posing as his valet. Later Hesp, who must have been a remarkable and resourceful character, became head of the Hungarian Secret Service and a highly successful spy. In true James Bond fashion he once swam the Danube with documents of the highest secrecy and importance attached to his head. As soon as the war was over, Hesp relinquished espionage and once again hunted Prince Batthyany's hounds. He took up training in 1873 and immediately made a success of that profession. In all he trained the winners of fourteen classic races. He died in 1887 in Vienna, leaving five sons and four daughters. One of his grandsons was at one time head lad to the late George Lambton at Newmarket.

Kincsem had a strenuous time as a two-year-old, winning ten races on ten different courses. She won in Berlin, Hanover, Hamburg, Doberan, Frankfurt and Baden-Baden in Germany; in Sopron and Budapest in Hungary; and in Vienna and Prague in Austria. Bearing in mind the somewhat crude facilities for travel that existed in central Europe in those days, it was indeed fortunate

that Kincsem liked nothing more than a lengthy journey by train.
The moment she saw her train she began to whinny with pleasure,
and once she was sure that her lad and the cat who went everywhere
with her were in too, she invariably settled down in obvious con-
tentment. The only occasion that she gave trouble in transit was at
Deauville on the way back from Goodwood. Her cat could not be
found when she left the ship and she refused to enter the train. For
two hours she stood on the dockside calling for her cat. Eventually
the cat heard her voice, came running to her and jumped on her
back. Kincsem at once entered the train and lay down. Her lad
Frankie apparently had no surname and invariably signed himself
"Frankie Kincsem". Under that name he did his military service and
under it was buried.

Like many great horses Kincsem was a "character". One cold
night she noticed that Frankie had no rug. She somehow pulled
her own rug off and put it on Frankie. From that day onwards she
would never wear a rug at night. If one was put on her, she always
managed to get it off and drop it on Frankie, even if Frankie was
already submerged under a stack of blankets. Whenever she won
a race, Mr. de Blascovich always gave her a bunch of flowers that
she liked to have placed in her head-band. On one occasion he
was late arriving with his flowers and she refused to permit her
jockey to unsaddle her until he was there. She would only eat oats
from her owner's estate and drink water that she was accustomed
to as well. Once at Baden-Baden the water brought with her ran
out and she refused to drink a drop for three days. In the end water
was found from an old local well that had the same earthy tang
as the water she was used to at home.

As a three-year-old Kincsem won seventeen races. These
included the Two Thousand Guineas at Pozsony; the One
Thousand Guineas, the Oaks, the Autumn Oaks and the St. Leger
in Budapest; the Derby and the Emperor's Prize in Vienna; the
Grosser Preis at Baden-Baden; and the Grosser Preis at Hanover.
The Emperor Francis Joseph, who liked steeplechasing but was
inclined to be bored by the flat, never missed an opportunity of
seeing Kincsem run and after each success he used to send for Mr.
de Blascovich and congratulate him.

As a four-year-old Kincsem began by winning nine races between
April 21st and the end of May, the distances varying from a mile
to two miles. She was sent to England in July to compete in the

Goodwood Cup but unfortunately the eagerly awaited battle between her and Verneuil did not take place, as Verneuil met with a mishap on the eve of the race and could not run. A French horse trained by Tom Jennings, Verneuil had won three long distance races at Royal Ascot that year, including the Gold Cup, and had not been headed for a yard in any one of them. In his absence Kincsem won the Goodwood Cup with ease. She was ridden in the Cup by Michael Madden, who rode her in forty-two of her races. He was not a great rider, but honest. His son Otto won the Epsom Derby on the 100–1 outsider Jeddah.

After Goodwood Kincsem won the Grand Prix de Deauville without difficulty, but she then had a narrow squeak at Baden-Baden, dead-heating with Prince Giles the First. However she won the run-off in a canter. As a five-year-old she won twelve more races, including the Grosser Preis at Baden-Baden for the third year running. Her fiftieth victory was in the Grosser Preis at Frankfurt. Her glorious career ended when she won the Hungarian Autumn Oaks in a canter by ten lengths for the third year running, conceding her opponents two stone.

Unfortunately Kincsem's stud career was a brief one as she died on her thirteenth birthday. However, although she had produced only two sons and three daughters she was an immensely influential brood mare. Her daughters and the progeny of her daughters won two Hungarian, three Austrian, one German, one Italian, two Roumanian and two Polish Derbys; six Hungarian, three Austrian and one German Oaks; one French, one German and five Hungarian St. Legers; five Hungarian and five Austrian Two Thousand Guineas; and three Hungarian One Thousand Guineas. All over Europe Kincsem's descendants founded great families, but two terrible European wars, to say nothing of risings and revolutions, have taken a fearful toll, and sad to say there are very few members of them left.

St. Simon

In April 1883, half an hour before the Two Thousand Guineas was run, Prince Batthyany dropped dead in the stand at Newmarket on the short flight of steps that led to the Jockey Club luncheon room. He was known to be suffering from a weak heart, and his death may well have been due to the excitement engendered by the fact that Galliard, a son of his beloved Galopin, winner of the 1875 Derby, was very much expected to win, and in fact won, the Two Thousand Guineas. The Prince, by birth a Hungarian, had come to England in his early twenties and had chosen to remain there, fascinated by the life that was then open to a young man with plenty of money and sporting tastes. He became to all intents and purposes a naturalized Englishman and was elected to the Jockey Club in 1859. He maintained his training establishment in appropriately princely style, the horses' clothing being of scarlet, while the lads were arrayed in dark blue livery and tall hats.

The Prince's horses came up for sale at Newmarket in July and it occurred to the Duke of Portland that he would like to buy Fulmen, who had proved himself a good two-year-old but because of the Prince's death had not yet run at three. The Duke was then twenty-five years of age. In 1879, when an ensign of modest private means in the Coldstream Guards, he had succeeded to the title on the death of an eccentric first cousin once removed whom he had never seen, inheriting a fortune that made him one of the richest men in England. He had taken up racing in 1880 and had wisely selected as his trainer the celebrated Mat Dawson, a man of great eminence in his profession, as shrewd a judge of men as he was of horses, and though a Scot, indifferent to the acquisition of wealth.

Before the sale the Duke and Mat Dawson went to look at Fulmen and both of them liked him very much. In the next box was a two-year-old called St. Simon, to whom they also took a fancy. It was eventually agreed that the Duke would bid up to 4,500 guineas for Fulmen, but Mat insisted that if Fulmen could not be bought for that price, the Duke was to bid for St. Simon. It so happened that Fulmen was sold for 500 guineas in excess of the Duke's bid and accordingly the Duke bought St. Simon for 1,600 guineas, a purchase that was to prove in due course a most wonderful bargain. The underbidder was the Duke of Hamilton, whose horses were trained by Richard Marsh. According to Marsh, the Duke of Hamilton would certainly have gone on bidding if only some know-all friend had not whispered in the Duke's ear that St. Simon was really a cripple. St. Simon did in fact have a dressing on his hocks, but Mat had made sure that this was really of no significance.

After the sale, Mat sought out his brother John, who had trained for Prince Batthyany and whom he had been unable to find before St. Simon entered the ring, and asked him if he thought St. Simon was worth the money. John replied quite truthfully that he did not know very much about him. In the spring he had tried him against a five-year-old called Rout, and St. Simon had beaten him easily, but as Rout had gone wrong afterwards and had been unable to run since the trial, he did not know the precise value of St. Simon's performance. After this conversation, Mat returned to the Duke of Portland and made a courtly bow. "I think," he said, "I may congratulate Your Grace on a good morning's work." Mat's view was reinforced not very long afterwards when Rout, restored to health, won the Prince of Wales's Cup at Kempton Park, a good five furlong sprint, carrying 8 st. 2 lb.

Galopin, sire of St. Simon, was a medium-sized bay horse by Vedette, a son of Voltigeur. Ridden by a deaf jockey called Morris, he had won the Derby comfortably enough in the end, although at one point Morris was taking matters altogether too easily and George Fordham had yelled at him, "Go on, Deafie," to warn him that Claremont was getting desperately close. Galopin, who was not engaged in the St. Leger, did not run as a four-year-old as the strain of watching him in a race was bad for his owner's heart. At the stud he attracted little patronage to begin with, but he gradually established his reputation and by the time of his death he had been champion sire on three occasions, the last time at the age of twenty-six. He got very plump in his old age and was said to look like a well-fed shooting cob.

St. Angela, dam of St. Simon, was by King Tom, runner-up in the Derby and twice winner of the Goodwood Cup, while her grandam was a half-sister of the Derby winner Little Wonder. Undistinguished on the race course, she was sixteen years of age when St. Simon was foaled and had previously produced nothing of racing merit. It may be for that reason that St. Simon was never entered for the Derby or the St. Leger.

St. Simon was extremely fat when he joined Mat Dawson's stable and his action in the first few canters he was given was more suited to a rabbit than a racehorse. That very successful trainer Robert Peck, thinking that maybe the Duke was disappointed with his purchase, offered him an immediate profit of 400 guineas. The Duke, however, replied that no better advice to retain the horse could have been given than the offer Peck had made.

After a very short time St. Simon began to display swift and remarkable improvement. All his engagements had been rendered void, according to the rule that then existed, by the death of his nominator, so he was entered for the Halnaker Stakes and the Maiden Plate at Goodwood. He won them both with singular ease. He then went on to win without the slightest difficulty the Devonshire Nursery at Derby and the seven furlong Prince of Wales's Nursery at Doncaster. At Doncaster he carried top weight of 9 stone and was opposed by a strong field that included St. Medard, second in the Two Thousand Guineas the following spring. Nevertheless he was fifty yards clear at halfway and eventually won by that distance. Mat had two other good two-year-olds in his stable that season, Harvester and Busybody.* The following year Harvester dead-heated in the Derby with St. Gatien, while Busybody won the Oaks. After Doncaster St. Simon was galloped with these two and beat them so easily that Mat Dawson thought they must have trained off. That was far from being the case, though, as Busybody soon afterwards won the Middle Park Plate in decisive style. After the Middle Park, Mat wrote to his old friend the Rev. John Welby, saying: "I know you love a really good horse. I hope you will come to the Houghton Meeting to see St. Simon. He is certainly the best two-year-old I have ever trained—he will possibly make the best racehorse that has ever run on the turf."

* Harvester and Busybody left the stable when their owner, Lord Falmouth, gave up racing at the end of that season.

At the Houghton Meeting it was arranged for St. Simon to take the field in a 500 guineas Match, run over six furlongs, against a very fast two-year-old called Duke of Richmond belonging to the Duke of Westminster. This contest aroused the utmost interest and the partisans of the two participants drove to the racecourse sporting either the yellow of the Duke of Westminster or the Duke of Portland's black and white. In the paddock St. Simon, a well-grown brown colt that combined power and quality to an unusual degree, seemed to tower over his opponent who was neat and well-proportioned but slightly on the small side, a mere pony in Mat Dawson's opinion. John Porter, Duke of Richmond's trainer, instructed Tom Cannon "to jump off and cut the beggar's throat from the start". Mat gave precisely the same orders to Fred Archer who partnered St. Simon. Before they had gone two furlongs St. Simon led by fifty yards. Archer dropped his hands once victory was assured and at the winning post St. Simon was only three-parts of a length in front, a margin which certainly failed to represent the true measure of his immense superiority. "That's the best two-year-old I have ever seen in my life," was Mat Dawson's only comment. The following season Duke of Richmond ran second in the Royal Hunt Cup with 8 stone; second in the Wokingham Stakes with 8 st. 11 lb.; and second in the Stewards Cup with 8 st. 10 lb.

As a three-year-old St. Simon stood 15 hands $3\frac{1}{4}$ inches but was so perfectly proportioned that he was frequently judged to be smaller than he really was. His profile was markedly concave, while his shoulders were so sloped as to give the impression that he was short in the back. From hip to hock his length was exceptional, and he was higher at the croup than at the withers. He was a splendid doer and the fortunate possessor of an exceptionally robust constitution. Exuding vitality—Mat Dawson was fond of saying he had never known a horse so full of "electricity"—he was highly strung, inclined to be irritable and to sweat freely. At all times he required gentle and patient treatment. The lad that looked after him once observed: "It's all very well to talk of the patience of Job, but Job never had to do St. Simon." The Duke of Portland himself admitted that doing St. Simon was a task not only difficult, but dangerous. When at the stud at Welbeck St. Simon was looked after by a man called Lambourn, who had many tricky quarters of an hour with him, but being both brave and extremely powerful, always got the better of him in the end. Chapman, at one time the stud groom at

Welbeck, wore a wig. One day it fell off and St. Simon pounced on it and shook it like a rat. A cat that was given to him as a companion was immediately seized by St. Simon, who threw it up against the ceiling of his box and killed it.

Mat Dawson advised the Duke not to give St. Simon too strenuous a second season and to retire him at the end of it, declaring that he would then make a really outstanding stallion. The advice was accepted and accordingly the Gold Cup at Ascot was made St. Simon's sole important objective. In the spring St. Simon, who, when fully extended, was said to resemble a greyhound rather than a horse, was inclined to work somewhat sluggishly. On Dawson's recommendation, Archer gave him a touch of the spur one morning. The effect of this was both instantaneous and startling. St. Simon at once took charge of Archer, dashed headlong through another trainer's string of horses and disappeared from view. Archer managed to get him under control at the entrance to Newmarket town and there the Duke and Dawson eventually found him in a somewhat shaken condition. Archer was convinced he had never been so fast in his life. "As long as I live," he said, "I will never touch that animal again with the spur; he's not a horse, he's a blooming steam engine."

St. Simon's first appearance as a three-year-old was in a most extraordinary and irregular affair that was described as a "Trial Match", but was certainly not a match since four horses took part, while it could hardly be called a trial since the result of it was published in the Racing Calendar. The Duke had come to an agreement with M. Lefevre to try St. Simon with Tristan, a really good six-year-old whose victories included not only the Ascot Gold Cup, the Gold Vase and the Hardwicke Stakes, but also the six furlong July Cup. The distance was a mile and a half, there was no prize or money involved, and Tristan conceded St. Simon 23 lb. To ensure a true gallop the Duke also ran Iambic and M. Lefevre Credo. Wood rode St. Simon as Archer was unable to do the weight. The "Trial" took place half an hour before the first race on the last day of the Second Spring Meeting at Newmarket and St. Simon drew clear from the Dip to win as he pleased by six lengths. Looking back on this unorthodox contest, it is important to remember that in those days racing was still primarily a sport and not a business. Nowadays it is hard enough in all conscience to induce the owner of a good horse to take on another good one even when there is a rich prize to be won. The notion of racing a top-class horse for nothing bar sport and amusement is unthinkable by modern standards.

St. Simon was given a walk-over for the Epsom Gold Cup. In the Gold Cup at Ascot he met Tristan again and this time he beat him by twenty lengths. It was suggested that Tristan must have trained off, but he came out the very next day and won the Hard-wicke Stakes. St. Simon then went up to Gosforth Park and won a Gold Cup there run over a mile. His final racecourse appearance was in the Goodwood Cup. He treated his opponents, one of whom had won the St. Leger, with complete contempt and won as he pleased by twenty lengths. Excluding the "Trial Match", he had won nine races worth £4,676. This does not look anything out of the ordinary on paper and may seem somewhat slender evidence on which to base a claim that he was the greatest racehorse of his century. It is important to remember, though, that he was never extended. After winning the Gold Cup at Ascot he galloped on for another mile before it was possible to pull him up; at Goodwood, after winning over two miles and five furlongs, he went right on to the top of Trundle Hill. He was equally formidable over a short distance as over a long one. Mat Dawson, who trained six Derby winners and a Grand Prix winner, once declared: "I have trained only one good horse in my life—St. Simon." Fred Archer, who rode another outstanding horse in Ormonde, never had the slightest doubt that St. Simon was the better of the two.

St. Simon was rested in 1885 and then took up stud duties at the Heath Stud, Newmarket, the next covering season. Later he was transferred to his owner's stud at Welbeck, remaining there for the rest of his long life. His stud fee was 50 guineas to start with, but rose to 500 guineas. During his stud career he covered 775 mares and got 554 in foal. It is a sign of his prepotency that all his foals were bay or brown bar a single grey filly that he sired in his old age from a grey mare. His stock were clean-winded, and when fit, needed very little work. Like their sire, they were for the most part highly-strung and free sweaters.

Right from the start he was outstandingly successful as a sire. His first crop of runners won 34 races worth £24,286 as two-year-olds and he was third that season in the list of successful sires. The next year he was champion sire and remained so for seven consecu-tive seasons. He was third in 1899, champion again in 1900 and 1901, second in 1902 and third in 1904. Altogether he sired the winners of 571 races worth £553,158. His classic winners were as follows: Persimmon (Derby and St. Leger); Diamond Jubilee (Two Thousand Guineas, Derby and St. Leger); St. Frusquin (Two Thousand Guineas); La Flèche (One Thousand Guineas, Oaks and St. Leger); Memoir (Oaks and St. Leger); Aimable (One Thousand Guineas and Oaks); Mrs. Butterwick (Oaks); La Roche (Oaks); Semolina (One Thousand Guineas); and Winifreda (One Thousand Guineas).

St. Simon was twenty-seven years of age when he dropped dead at Welbeck one morning when returning from exercise. His skin was preserved at Welbeck and his skeleton was presented to the Natural History Museum, South Kensington.

Ormonde

Asked to choose between the two greatest horses he rode, Fred Archer was inclined to give St. Simon slight preference over Ormonde. This judgment was probably correct on the balance of the evidence, and as Ormonde began racing in 1885, only one year after the retirement of St. Simon, there had been no long passing of the years to lend enchantment to the jockey's view of the older horse. On the other hand, Archer's opinion was not universally accepted. Ormonde's trainer John Porter, a biased witness perhaps, wrote of Ormonde in the preliminary notes for his memoirs: "He was a giant among giants, and I do not think we ever saw his equal as a racehorse." Richard Marsh, who could claim to be an absolutely neutral witness, wrote in his book *A Trainer to Two Kings*; "I have seen all the best horses of the last fifty years, and I suppose I would be justified in saying that Ormonde was the best of all. I say that simply because he was the best horse in an exceptionally brilliant year for three-year-olds." Porter, by implication, and Marsh, more explicitly, laid their fingers on the essence of the case that could be made out for Ormonde. St. Simon, though possessing the superior merit of complete soundness in wind and limb, never ran in a Classic race and met few top class rivals; but Ormonde won the Triple Crown in one of the finest vintage years in the history of the British Thoroughbred. George Lambton said that St. Simon educated the public as to what a high class horse should be and helped them to appreciate the greatness of Ormonde.

Comparisons of unbeaten horses may be invidious, but the relative merits of St. Simon and Ormonde were debated so eagerly at the time that it is scarcely possible to do justice to Ormonde without referring to the question. Like many another great horse, Ormonde had a background that was in some respects romantic, even inauspicious. He was bred by Hugh Lupus Grosvenor, first Duke of West-minster, who had built up the most powerful stud in the country at Eaton Hall, in Cheshire, had won the Derby already with Bend Or and Shotover and was to breed and own another Triple Crown winner, Flying Fox, before his death at the turn of the century. Ormonde was by Bend Or, and so had a perfectly orthodox Classic pedigree as far as his sire was concerned. However, Polly Agnes, the grandam of Ormonde, had been so small and delicate as a foal that she had been given by Sir Tatton Sykes to his stud groom James Snarry on condition that she was removed from the famous Sledmere Stud immediately. Snarry kept Polly Agnes to breed from, and was rewarded when she produced Lily Agnes, who was described as a "light-fleshed, ragged-hipped, lop-eared filly", and was affected in the wind, but was also a first class stayer who won no fewer than twenty-one races including the Northumberland Plate, the Doncaster Cup and the Ebor Handicap.

For her fourth stud season, 1880, Lily Agnes was sent to Eaton Hall to be mated with Doncaster, the sire of Bend Or. There the stud groom, Chapman, took a great fancy to her and persuaded his employer to buy her, with the result that she became the property of the Duke of Westminster for £2,500 plus two nominations to Bend Or, whose fee was £200. The following season Lily Agnes was mated to Bend Or and produced Farewell, winner of the One Thousand Guineas in 1885, and then returned to the same stallion to produce Ormonde.

Ormonde was an extraordinary foal. His dam carried him a month beyond the normal time, and when he was foaled his mane was already three inches long. He was terribly over at the knees, and in his early days Chapman described him as a "three-cornered beggar that might be anything or nothing". When he did begin to develop on the right lines his appearance improved rapidly. He looked a high class colt when he left Eaton to go into training, and Porter wrote to the Duke of Westminster from Kingsclere that he was the best colt he had ever sent him. He had a short but muscular neck, excellent bone, a straight hind-leg and exceptionally powerful quarters. Two years later, when Ormonde was at the height of his fame, the Duke of Westminster rode Ormonde in two sharp canters on the Downs at Kingsclere, and, though an expert horse-man, confessed that Ormonde's propelling power was so great that he felt he was going to be pitched forward out of the saddle at every stride. Ormonde had a most equable temperament and was a wonderful doer. His only faults were that he had very low withers and was none too good a mover in his slow paces. Archer said that you felt you were sitting on his neck until he began to stride out at the gallop.

Ormonde threw two splints below the knee during his first winter at Kingsclere, and Porter was able to do little with him in the early part of his two-year-old season. Consequently he did not go into serious work until August, and after a few gallops was tried with Kendal, who had won four races in succession including the important July Stakes at Newmarket. Ormonde gave 1 lb. to Kendal in the trial and was beaten by a length. He was not very fit at the time, but Porter had hoped that he would do better and decided to give him his first outing in the Post Stakes, instead of the Middle Park Stakes, at the second October meeting at Newmarket. The Post Stakes was the minor race, but Ormonde was opposed by an exceptionally fast filly in Modwena, who started at slight odds on, and established his class at a single blow when he beat her comfortably by a length. Ormonde was improving rapidly, and was an even easier winner of his remaining two races as a two-year-old, the Criterion Stakes and the Dewhurst Stakes, in spite of the fact that the opposition was strong on each occasion. This progress was maintained during the winter, and by the time Ormonde began his Classic preparation as a three-year-old Porter, who had won the Derby already with Blue Gown, Shotover and St. Blaise and so judged by the very highest standards, was convinced that he was a horse in a million. But it was also clear that the opposition he was going to meet in the 1886 Classic races was unusually strong. There was The Bard, the unbeaten winner of sixteen races as a two-year-old, a charming little colt whose chestnut coat was flecked with white hairs; and there was Minting, who had won the Middle Park Stakes in spite of getting unbalanced going down the hill into the Dip. Minting was in the Exning stable of Mat Dawson, the rugged Scotsman who trained six Derby winners and, like Porter, knew a good horse when he saw one. He gave Minting a searching preparation for the Two Thousand Guineas and shortly before the race told George Lambton: "When John Porter says he has a good horse, you may be certain he has a damned good one, but he does not know what I have got; when it comes to a matter of talking, Ormonde wins the Two Thousand, but, when it comes to a matter of racing, Minting will win."

The Bard missed the Guineas, but the field was still one of the best that have ever turned out for the race. The runners included Saraband, for whom Archer had accepted a retainer in all his races, and St. Mirin, who was to be the innocent cause of Archer's death. Coracle was started to make the running for Ormonde, but in the event his services were purely nugatory. Ormonde, ridden by George Barratt because Archer was not available, and Minting jumped off in front and disputed the lead the whole way. There was nothing between them until they began the descent into the Dip, where Minting began to roll and changed his legs, allowing Ormonde to draw away and win by two lengths, with the rest of the field outclassed.

Influenced partly by the crushing nature of Minting's Guineas defeat, and partly by the advice of Archer, who had ridden the horse in the Middle Park Stakes, that he would not be suited by the downhill gradients at Epsom, Dawson decided that it would be pointless to take Ormonde on again, and withdrew Minting from the Derby when it was evident that his redoubtable rival was going to Epsom fit and well. Instead Minting was sent to Paris for the Grand Prix, which he won easily. In his absence Ormonde and The Bard, who was running for the first time that season, overshadowed the other Derby runners. Saraband, like Minting, had been scratched, so Archer was free to take the mount on Ormonde. From Tattenham Corner Ormonde and The Bard drew out with the race between them, but whereas Ormonde was cantering, The Bard was under pressure to hold his place. As soon as Archer asked him for an effort Ormonde shot ahead to beat his gallant little rival decisively, and the judge, Mr. Clarke, said he had never seen an easier winner.

The excellence of Ormonde's achievement at Epsom was revealed by the subsequent performances of The Bard. The little chestnut was beaten only once more, and that was when he failed narrowly to concede 31 lb. to the very useful three-year-old Riversdale in the Manchester Cup three weeks after the Derby. The Bard's victories included the Goodwood Cup, for which he walked over, and the Doncaster Cup.

After the Derby the other three-year-olds who had begun the season with high hopes of Classic success carefully avoided Ormonde, who was left to enjoy his supremacy virtually unchallenged in his own age group. However he had Melton, the winner of the Derby and the St. Leger the previous year, to beat in the Hardwicke Stakes at Royal Ascot, and did so in effortless fashion. He had won the St. James's Palace Stakes earlier at the meeting. He beat St. Mirin by four lengths in the St. Leger to complete his Triple Crown triumph. Four more easy victories came his way at Newmarket in the autumn. In addition he was given a walkover for a private sweepstakes in which his opponents should have been Melton and The Bard. The previous day Ormonde had given 2 st. each to Mephisto and Theodore in the Free Handicap and won by eight lengths, and after that marvellous performance neither Lord Hastings, the owner of Melton, nor Robert Peck, the owner of The Bard, was willing to have his horse shown up.

Archer was on Ormonde's back for the last time when he walked over for the private stakes. That same autumn brought the tragedy of the brilliant jockey's illness and suicide after severe wasting to ride St. Mirin in the Cambridgeshire, and Ormonde had a new partner, Tom Cannon, in his races as a four-year-old. By then Ormonde had been afflicted by a tragedy of his own, though a less fatal kind than that of Archer. Indeed the trouble had manifested itself even before the St. Leger when, one morning on the Downs at Kingsclere, he gave unmistakable evidence that he was becoming a roarer. During the winter various remedies, including electrical treatment, were tried, much against the wishes of Porter, who declared that there was no cure possible in such cases and that it would be better to leave the horse alone. Porter was correct in doubting the efficacy of the treatment, and Ormonde was an incurable roarer by the time serious training was resumed in the spring; on the other hand, the treatment probably did no harm, because Ormonde gave clear evidence in his gallops that he had not lost his form. He did not run until Ascot, where he had his first outing in the Rous Memorial Stakes. He had to concede 25 lb. to the three-year-old Kilwarlin and Captain Machell, who managed the colt, told John Porter before the race that the horse had never been foaled who could give so much weight to Kilwarlin. Ormonde gave the lie to that opinion by winning in a canter by six lengths, yet Machell's had been no idle boast, for Kilwarlin went on to win the St. Leger after being left lengths at the start.

Ormonde's second race at the Ascot meeting was the Hardwicke Stakes over 1½ miles. Mat Dawson, having steered clear of Ormonde since the previous year's Two Thousand Guineas, decided that the opportunity was right to take him on again with Minting, as he could not believe that a roarer could possibly beat a horse of whom he still, and justifiably, had an extremely high opinion. "I shall beat you today," Dawson told Porter shortly before the horses were saddled, and Porter himself did not dare to be sanguine about the result. The race was one of the most exciting ever run, for it was only after a long drawn-out struggle and an almost unbelievable display of class and courage by both horses that Ormonde beat Minting by a neck. Ormonde's performance was all the greater since Barrett, who thought that he should have succeeded Archer as Ormonde's jockey, deliberately bored Phil into him as they were turning into the straight, and Ormonde came in with strips of skin torn off his hind-leg above the hock.

Ormonde was led in by his owner to a resounding ovation. Overcome by pride and joy, Westminster seemed unable to tear himself away from his champion, and led him twice round the paddock and half-way back to the stables before consenting to hand him over to his lad. If anyone wanted further proof of the greatness of Ormonde and Minting they could find it in the running of Bendigo, who was outclassed in finishing a poor third. Yet Bendigo had already won the Kempton Park Jubilee, was soon to win the first race for the Eclipse Stakes, and in the autumn was second in the Cesarewitch with 9 st. 7 lb. and second again in the Cambridgeshire with 9 st. 13 lb.

Ormonde had one more race, the Imperial Gold Cup at Newmarket, and won easily from his stable companion Whitefriar. Afterwards Porter suggested that Westminster should ride him in the procession through the streets of London which formed part of the Jubilee celebrations marking the fiftieth year of Queen Victoria's reign, assuring the Duke that he "would go quiet as a sheep". However Westminster demurred; instead Ormonde was boxed to Waterloo Station and led across Westminster Bridge and through the parks to Grosvenor House, where he was one of the main attractions of a gigantic garden party. Comporting himself with a dignity proper to the occasion, Ormonde consumed gifts of sugar and flowers and appeared thoroughly to enjoy the admiration of hundreds of guests.

Ormonde served his first stud season at Eaton in 1888, and the produce of that season included the top class horses Orme and Goldfinch. He was leased to Lord Gerard for his second season, but became seriously ill and got few mares in foal. Westminster then sold him to the Argentine for £12,000. He was not successful there and later, when he had been sold to the United States, became a very poor foal-getter.

Westminster was much criticized for selling such a great horse abroad. The Duke's reply was that Ormonde was a roarer and had roarers among his ancestors, and it was undesirable that he should perpetuate his infirmity in British stock. Some of Ormonde's progeny were affected in the wind, and others were not. Orme was perfectly sound, and it was through Orme that the influence of Ormonde was transmitted to the modern thoroughbred by means of the two powerful male lines of Orby and Flying Fox.

Ormonde gave a strange twist to his story on his last appearance in his native country. He spent some time in England while he was being transferred from the Argentine to the United States, and John Porter went to see his old friend at Netley. It should have been a happy reunion, but Ormonde, usually so mild-tempered, must have been bearing a grudge against his former trainer, because he went for him the moment he entered his box.

They had little chance to see Ormonde in the north; consequently he was surrounded by a large crowd, eager to appraise the champion, while he was being saddled for the St. Leger. One famous Yorkshire trainer had a long look at him, and exclaimed: "He looks like a damned great coach horse"; and added, as he turned away: "I wish I had one like him." Horses like Ormonde not only make the fortunes of a stable—they add a new dimension to the attractions of the Turf.

Carbine

Of the many great horses bred in New Zealand, the most famous is surely Carbine. Even though his racing career took place over seventy years ago, his wonderful victory in the Melbourne Cup remains the standard by which the major long-distance handicap events are gauged in Australia. In New Zealand, poker players still call a hand containing a pair of tens and a pair of fives a "Carbine" in memory of Carbine's remarkable achievement in winning the Melbourne Cup with 10 st. 5 lb. in a field of thirty-nine and in a time which then constituted a record.

Carbine was by Musket out of Mersey, by Knowsley. Musket, by Toxophilite, was bred in England by the eccentric and irascible Lord Glasgow, who thought nothing of the colt and with peremptory ruthlessness ordered him to be shot. The north-country jockey John Osborne pleaded for Musket and obtained for him a temporary respite. The situation, however, was saved soon afterwards as far as Musket was concerned by the death of Lord Glasgow. Sent to be trained by Alec Taylor senior at Manton, Musket proved himself a very useful stayer, among his victories being the Ascot Stakes and the Alexandra Plate at Ascot. In due course he took up stud duties at a fee of 40 guineas at the Bonehill Stud in Staffordshire. Possibly because his sire had been a breaker of blood-vessels while there was a record of wind infirmity in his dam's family, there was no unseemly rush to secure Musket's services. His first six seasons at the stud produced only sixty-five foals, his best winner being Petronel, who won the Two Thousand Guineas and the Doncaster Cup. While Petronel was still a yearling, Musket was sold to the Waikato Agricultural Company of New Zealand and he began his stud life in New Zealand at Fencourt, near Cambridge, in the fertile Waikato district which is the centre of New Zealand's dairy production.

Mersey, Carbine's dam, was also exported to New Zealand from England. She was by Stockwell's son Knowsley and was descended from Martha Lynn, dam of the 1850 Derby winner Voltigeur and ancestress of Lord Clifden, sire of Hampton from whom Hyperion is descended in tail male. Mersey's dam Clemence was a half-sister of the One Thousand Guineas and St. Leger winner Imperieuse. Mersey herself was also dam in New Zealand of Carnage, by Musket's son Nordenfeldt. After a distinguished racing career, Carnage was exported to England and eventually ended up in Germany.

Musket started off in New Zealand by covering half-bred mares, but he had not been there long before he was bought by Major Walmsley and Mr. T. Morrin, who installed him at the Sylvia Park Stud a few miles from Auckland, North Island. In seven seasons there he got about a hundred and thirty foals. Two of his best sons, Carbine and Trenton, were exported to England. Trenton, foaled in 1881, only came to England when he was in his fifteenth year. Nevertheless his name appears in the pedigrees of Gainsborough and of Buchan. Another of Musket's sons, Martini-Henry, appears in the pedigree of the 1949 Derby winner Nimbus.

Musket died in 1885, a month after Carbine was foaled. The following year, at the dispersal of the Sylvia Park yearlings, Carbine was bought for 620 guineas by Daniel O'Brien, a leading owner-trainer and an extremely bold gambler. Carbine's first appearance as a two-year-old was in the Hopeful Stakes at Christchurch and he duly won despite losing ground at the start. His next outing was in the far more important Middle Park Plate, also at Christchurch. He was again very slowly away but saved the day and his owner's money with a tremendous late run. Years later Freeman Holmes, who rode Manton in that race, recalled how "something that looked like a greyhound flashed past on the outside and that was Carbine. I realized in another stride that I wasn't in it; but I also realized that this Carbine must be more than an ordinary horse, for we had a high opinion of Manton, which was borne out the following year when he won the Derby."

Carbine had two more races in New Zealand, the Champagne Stakes and the Challenge Stakes at the Canterbury autumn meeting in Christchurch. He won them both and O'Brien then decided to run him the following season in Australia. Carbine's first major target was the Victoria Racing Club's Derby at Flemington. Here he

Plate 1 West Australian

Plate 2 Lexington

Plate 3 Gladiateur

Plate 4 Kincsem

Plate 5   St. Simon

Plate 6   Ormonde

Plate 7   Carbine

Plate 8   Persimmon

met with his first defeat, a reverse that was almost entirely due to the incompetent riding of his jockey, Derrett. It was widely believed that O'Brien lost a stack of money over Carbine's failure; whether this was the case or not, he decided to sell Carbine, who came into the sale-ring not long afterwards with a reserve of 3,000 guineas. At that price he was bought by Mr. D. S. Wallace who sent him to be trained by Walter Heginbotham. Mr. Wallace was something of a character. One night at dinner he was seated next to Lady Hopetoun, wife of the Governor of Victoria. Suddenly he exclaimed with considerable intensity: "Lady Hopetoun, I love you." Lady Hopetoun not surprisingly was rather taken aback, but Mr. Wallace quickly added: "I love you because you love old Carbine, and I love him, too."

Carbine's career thenceforth was typical of many high-class horses of that era in that he ran over all sorts of distances and frequently had a number of races in very rapid succession. It is tempting to compare the top horses of today unfavourably with Carbine and his like in respect of versatility and toughness, but it is essential to bear in mind that horses did not specialize over matters of distance in Carbine's time as they so often do now. It is arguable that a modern all-rounder would probably stand little chance against, say, a five or six furlong specialist. It must be remembered, too, when comparing the toughness of past and present horses, that in Carbine's time long distance races used to be run at a very much slower pace and were frequently, in fact, a dawdle followed by a sprint. In addition the upright style adopted by old-time jockeys reduced speed by offering the maximum wind resistance. By and large, races were probably considerably less exacting in the last century than they are now.

Carbine at least partially atoned for his unlucky defeat in the V.R.C. Derby by winning the Flying Stakes and the Foal Stakes at the same meeting. He then finished third in a sprint handicap to Sedition and Lochiel, an effort which he followed up by running second to Lochiel in the two and a quarter mile Australian Cup. However he then won the three mile Champion Stakes and two other races as well.

He moved on to New South Wales and at Randwick he was second to Abercorn, a very good four-year-old, in the mile and a half Australian Jockey Club Autumn Stakes. On the second day of the meeting, though, he put up one of his finest performances by winning the two mile Sydney Cup under 9 stone, the year older Abercorn, who was third, conceding him only 4 lb. He next won races over a mile, a mile and three quarters and two miles and a quarter, beating Abercorn on each occasion.

Carbine began his four-year-old season with three defeats. He was second to Dreadnought in the Caulfield Stakes, third in the Melbourne Stakes, and then with 10 stone on his back, he put up a great fight in the two mile Melbourne Cup, only to be narrowly beaten by the six year old Bravo who was receiving 21 lb. After that Carbine won the Flying Stakes, but in the Canterbury Plate he injured a foot and had to be pulled up.

Fortunately he made a rapid recovery and by the autumn he was in truly magnificent form. He won three races at Flemington and going on to Randwick he won four races in five days at the Sydney Cup meeting. These were the mile and a half Autumn Stakes; the two mile Sydney Cup in which he carried 9 st. 9 lb.; the one mile All Aged Stakes; the mile and three quarters Cumberland Stakes; and the A.J.C. Plate run over two miles and a quarter. No wonder he was idolized by the sporting public.

At five years of age he was as good as ever. He won twice in Sydney, and at Melbourne won the Melbourne Stakes. Then came his famous victory in the Melbourne Cup in which he carried 10 st. 5 lb., beat thirty-eight opponents, and won in the then record time of 3 minutes 28¼ seconds. Before the race he was very placid, almost lethargic in fact, and this was regarded as a favourable omen by those who knew him best. Bob Ramage, who invariably rode him for Mr. Wallace, always found him a wonderfully easy horse to manoeuvre and had him in a handy position from the start. Just below the distance a tremendous cheer went up from the 100,000 spectators as Carbine raced into the lead and with that wonderful low, daisy-cutting action of his, drew clear to win by two lengths and a half. Scenes of uninhibited jubilation then took place on a scale that has never been repeated on Flemington racecourse. Lovers of a good and gallant racehorse certainly had something to cheer about as Carbine was conceding the runner-up, Highborn, no less than 53 lb., a truly remarkable feat bearing in mind that five months later Highborn won the Sydney Cup with 9 st. 3 lb.

The Melbourne Cup represented the peak of Carbine's career, but he won several good races afterwards including the Essendon Stakes, Champion Stakes and All Aged Stakes, all at Flemington, and the Autumn Stakes at Randwick. Racing at Randwick without plates he got stuck in the heavy ground and was beaten in a race by Marvel, but later that afternoon he was plated and beat Marvel easily in the Cumberland Plate, a performance he repeated in the A.J.C. Stakes on the last day of the meeting. This proved to be Carbine's final appearance on the racecourse as his foot injury reasserted itself and it was decided to take him out of training. Mr. Wallace retired him to the Lerderberg Stud in Victoria where he was only moderately successful although his very first foal, appropriately named Wallace, proved an extremely good racehorse and later a successful sire. In the eleven seasons that Carbine's progeny raced in Australia, they won 208 races worth £48,624 in stakes.

In 1895 the Duke of Portland, wishing an outcross for his St. Simon and Donovan mares, bought Carbine from Mr. Wallace for 13,000 guineas. The sale coincided with one of the worst slumps that Australia has ever experienced. However, despite the general atmosphere of gloom and the near famine conditions that existed in some parts of Melbourne, over two thousand people went to see Carbine shipped aboard the "Orizata" and the great horse was given a wonderful farewell.

A big, powerful bay standing well over 16 hands, Carbine began his stud career at Welbeck at a fee of 200 guineas, a big one for those days and based less on his achievements as a sire in Australia than on his wonderful racing record for he had run 43 times, won 33 races and only once had been unplaced. He had won £29,476, a total which stood as a record till 1922. After four years in England his fee was reduced to 100 guineas and later to 50. By 1905 it was up to 200 guineas again, but in 1906 it came down to 98 and eventually to 48 guineas.

At Welbeck Carbine was ridden out daily by Jack Cunningham, who had accompanied him to England. It snowed heavily during Carbine's first winter at Welbeck and the first morning he saw snow on the ground he declined to leave his box. The second morning he took a mouthful of snow, bounded out of his box and rolled for five minutes in the centre of the yard. He always disliked getting his ears wet and once, when saddled for the Melbourne Cup, he refused to leave his box on account of the rain. His trainer Heginbotham had to walk down to the starting gate holding his umbrella over Carbine's head. Following this incident Heginbotham had a leather protector

made, rather like a small umbrella which was attached to the bridle
to prevent the rain from falling on Carbine's ears. This odd contrap-
tion was sent on to Welbeck.

Carbine sired plenty of useful handicappers in England but he
could hardly be described as an unqualified success. By far the best
horse he got was Spearmint. Bred at the Sledmere Stud, Spearmint
had bad forelegs and Major Eustace Loder was able to buy him
cheaply for 300 guineas. Spearmint won the Derby in 1906 and
eleven days later the Grand Prix de Paris. It proved impossible to
keep him sound enough for racing afterwards. He sired the 1920
Derby winner Spion Kop and the 1922 St. Leger winner Royal
Lancer. Spion Kop in his turn sired the 1928 Derby winner Fel-
stead, but the Carbine male line has failed to survive in this country.
Spion Kop was sire of a horse of Lord Rosebery's called The
Bastard. Exported to Australia, where his name was delicately
altered to The Buzzard, he proved an outstanding sire and his
progeny won over £450,000 in stakes. Spearmint sired some notable
brood mares, in particular the famous Plucky Liège, dam of the
Derby winner Bois Roussel; the Grand Prix winner Admiral Drake;
the French Two Thousand Guineas winner Sir Galahad III; and
Bull Dog, a successful sire in America. Spearmint also got the dams
of the Grand Prix winner Comrade and the Oaks winners My Dear
and Brulette. Moreover his daughter Catnip appears in the pedigrees
of many famous horses as she is the grandam of that great racehorse
and highly successful sire Nearco. Catnip was a weedy sort of filly in
training and was sold to go to Italy in 1915 for £75.

Carbine died at Welbeck in his twenty-eighth year from a cerebral
haemorrhage. His skeleton was sent to the Melbourne Museum, his
skin to the Auckland Museum. In Government House in Wellington, the capital of New Zealand, there is a gold inkstand made from
three of Carbine's hooves.

Persimmon

The last horse to win the Epsom Derby and the Gold Cup was Persimmon, foaled in 1893. In 1945 Lord Rosebery's Ocean Swell won the Gold Cup, having won the Derby the year before, but his Derby victory was achieved in a war-substitute race at Newmarket. Persimmon was an outstanding success as a sire, Ocean Swell a notable failure.

Persimmon was bred and owned by the Prince of Wales, later King Edward VII, and was by the mighty St. Simon out of Perdita II, by Hampton out of Hermione, by Young Melbourne. Perdita II was bought for the Prince of Wales by John Porter, who was then his trainer, for 900 guineas. "You'll ruin the Prince if you go on buying these thoroughbreds", grumbled old Sir Dighton Probyn as he handed over the cheque on the Prince's behalf. In fact Perdita II proved a marvellous bargain. She bred two Derby winners, Persimmon and his own-brother, Diamond Jubilee, and altogether her offspring won twenty-six races worth over £72,000, a very big total for those days when the Derby was worth £5,540 to the winner.

Bred by Lord Cawdor, Perdita II had been raced by Mr. David Falconer, a jute merchant. She started her career in selling races but made considerable improvement winning the Great Cheshire Stakes twice and the Ayr Gold Cup. However her owner always reckoned her a jade and was far from reluctant to sell her. Persimmon was her fourth foal.

In appearance Persimmon was a lengthy bay, just a shade on the leg in his early days, with a bold head, slightly lop ears, perfect shoulder and immense power behind the saddle. He was thoroughly genuine but high-mettled and could be difficult when in the mood. He certainly did not have the savage temper, though, of his brother Diamond Jubilee. He was already regarded as a colt of outstanding promise when he joined Richard Marsh's stable in August 1894 and the following spring he soon showed his trainer that he possessed ability far above the average. His first racecourse appearance was in the Coventry Stakes at Royal Ascot which he won with impressive ease. Before Goodwood he was tried against a sprinter called Ugly, whom he beat without difficulty at level weights. As Ugly proceeded to win the Singleton Plate at Goodwood with 7 st. 7 lb., it was no surprise when Persimmon won the Richmond Stakes with ease.

Persimmon's only other race as a two-year-old was in the Middle Park Stakes in which he could only finish a moderate third behind Mr. Leopold de Rothschild's St. Simon colt, St. Frusquin, and Omladina, a very fast filly that had won the Champagne Stakes at Doncaster. Persimmon had in fact been coughing not long before the Middle Park and Marsh had not wanted to run him. He was overruled, though, by the Prince's racing manager, Lord Marcus Beresford. The race could have done Persimmon considerable harm but luckily Jack Watts had the sense to drop his hands as soon as he realized Persimmon had no hope of defeating St. Frusquin.

Persimmon was slow to come to hand in the spring and Marsh wisely took him out of the Two Thousand Guineas. St. Frusquin on the other hand was fit to run for his life by April. He won the Column Produce Stakes at the Newmarket Craven meeting and followed that up by winning the Two Thousand Guineas from Love Wisely, a good horse that later won the Ascot Gold Cup.

Towards the end of April Persimmon really began to thrive but his first Derby gallop was a disturbing fiasco. He was always labouring and eventually trailed in four lengths behind a moderate animal called Safety Pin. "A nice sort of Derby horse", dryly observed Lord Marcus Beresford. Marsh could offer no explanation for Persimmon's wretched display but four days later he galloped him again, this time with entirely satisfactory result. The final gallop took place in front of the Prince and Princess of Wales and of the Duke and Duchess of York. Persimmon did all he was asked in delightfully smooth manner and it was clear that it would require a really good horse to beat him in the Derby.

It was planned for Persimmon to travel by train from Dullingham Station to Epsom. Usually he was a tractable, easygoing traveller but on this all-important occasion he took it into his head to be awkward and stubbornly refused to enter his box. The situation was verging on the desperate when two horse specials had left Dullingham without him and with only fifteen minutes left before the final one departed, he showed not the slightest sign of changing his mind. Marsh, distraught with worry and on the brink of apoplexy, then played his last card. He enlisted a dozen lusty volunteers and between them they more or less carried Persimmon into his box. Once inside, Persimmon realized the game was over and settled down quietly to enjoy his feed.

The weather was extremely sultry at Epsom and the course very hard and in somewhat rough condition. Persimmon had sweated up before he won at Goodwood the previous year and Marsh had marked him down then as a high-mettled colt that would always need careful handling. On Derby Day Persimmon was irritable and sweated freely, but perhaps fortunately for him and his backers, the preliminaries before the big race were conducted on far more free-and-easy lines than is the case today. He was saddled in Sherwood's stables close to the start and took no part either in the parade or in the canter in front of the stands. St. Frusquin was saddled in the grounds of the Durdans. St. Frusquin was a hot favourite at 13–8 on whereas Persimmon was a 5–1 chance.

With a quarter of a mile to go the issue, as expected, lay clearly between St. Frusquin and Persimmon. St. Frusquin, ridden by Tommy Loates, was on the rails and in the lead but Persimmon was gradually closing the gap. Just inside the distance Persimmon suddenly faltered and for a few strides it looked as if he was beaten. At this critical juncture Jack Watts, to his eternal credit, kept his head. He steadied Persimmon, got him nicely balanced and then drove him home as hard as he could to win a wonderful race by a neck. It needed both nerve and skill to act as Watts did so close to the winning post, and if Persimmon had then been beaten no doubt Watts would have been savagely criticized.

The crowd went wild with enthusiasm and delight and Marsh had the utmost difficulty in getting near Persimmon on whom Watts who was liable to suffer from melancholia when he was having trouble with his weight, was sitting as glumly as if he had finished last. Marsh slapped Watts briskly on the thigh and shouted at him, "Don't you realize you have just won the Derby for the Prince of Wales," and Watts then permitted himself the luxury of a faint and transitory smile.

The following month Persimmon and St. Frusquin crossed swords again, this time in the mile and a half Princess of Wales's

Stakes, a far more important race then than it is today. The Derby form worked out well and St. Frusquin, receiving 3 lb, won a splendid race by half a length. Persimmon did not run in the Eclipse Stakes which St. Frusquin won without difficulty. Unfortunately St. Frusquin went wrong shortly afterwards and could not compete in the St. Leger, leaving Persimmon with an easy task in the final classic which he won with any amount in hand by a length and a half from Labrador with Rampion a bad third. The betting was unusual for a classic; 11–2 on Persimmon, 6–1 Labrador, 66–1 Funny Boat, 200–1 Rampion, Dynamo, Love Lane and Chevele d'Or. Persimmon concluded the season by defeating the 1895 Derby winner Sir Visto in the Jockey Club Stakes of a mile and three quarters at Newmarket. That race was then worth £8,990, considerably more than the Derby and the St. Leger. In 1967 the Jockey Club Stakes was worth just over £2,000 to the winner and is no longer an event of any particular significance.

Good as he was at three years of age, Persimmon was even better at four. At three he had always looked a shade unfurnished; at four he had put on weight in the right places and was a truly magnificent specimen of the thoroughbred. His main target, and also his first outing of the season, was the two and a half mile Gold Cup at Ascot. A week before that event Marsh galloped him at home over the Gold Cup distance and Persimmon put up such a convincing performance that his trainer regarded him as near a certainty as there can be in racing. However there was a horse in the Cup that was genuinely fancied to beat him and that was Mr. J. C. Sullivan's Winkfield's Pride. Horses in those days were more versatile than they are today and Winkfield's Pride had proved himself a fine miler, winning both the Lincoln and the Cambridgeshire. However that shrewd judge Captain Machell was confident that Winkfield's Pride, who had been highly tried at home, could make all the running and win and his confidence was shared by the horse's trainer, Robinson. The evening before the race Robinson told Marsh he thought Winkfield's Pride was sure to beat Persimmon. "The faster your horse makes the pace", replied Marsh, "the further mine will win."

Persimmon looked magnificent in the paddock. "When Persimmon was stripped for the Ascot Cup", recorded that great trainer George Lambton, "he stands out in my memory as the most perfectly trained horse I ever saw, and on that day it would have given my two heroes, St. Simon and Ormonde, as much as they could do to beat him."

Winkfield's Pride proved no match for Persimmon, who drew clear to win in the final quarter of a mile to beat his rival by eight lengths. Love Wisely was a moderate third. Captain Machell walked up to congratulate Marsh afterwards. "I don't know what sort of horse yours is," he said. "I did not think it possible for you to beat me, but you beat Winkfield's Pride as if he had been a common hack."

It was next decided that Persimmon would run in the valuable Eclipse Stakes, run over a mile and a quarter at Sandown. The Ascot course had ridden very hard and during that brilliant summer the going all over the country continued to be firm. This caused Marsh a certain anxiety and in any case it is by no means easy to train a horse for a race over two and a half miles and then bring him back to half that distance. However Marsh concentrated on sharpening up Persimmon's speed and worked him on the tan over five and six furlongs.

Persimmon started at 100–12 on in the Eclipse and won comfortably by two lengths from Velasquez. His Gold Cup-Eclipse Stakes double remained unequalled until his son Prince Palatine achieved it in 1912. Golden Myth brought off the double in 1922.

The Eclipse was Persimmon's last race. Two consecutive races on hard ground proved more than he could stand; he threw out two spavins, one on each hock, and it was decided to retire him to the stud forthwith at a fee of 300 guineas. He proved an immediate success, his first crop of runners including the famous filly Sceptre who won every classic bar the Derby. He also got Keystone II and Persola, who both won the Oaks; Prince Palatine and Your Majesty, winners of the St. Leger; and Zinfandel who, like Prince Palatine, won the Gold Cup. Unfortunately he broke his pelvis at the comparatively early age of fifteen. He was four times champion sire and equally successful as a sire of brood mares.

Sceptre

Nature has sometimes shown herself oddly capricious in her distribution of famous horses, and never more so than when she decreed that Sceptre and Pretty Polly, probably the two greatest fillies ever to run in England, should be foaled within two years of each other. Their careers in training actually overlapped for two seasons, those of 1903 and 1904, but they never met, and their retirement left the racing critics in complete disarray. Hardly had they finished saying of Sceptre, after her victories in four of the five Classic races: "We shall never see her like again", than they were referring to the "peerless Pretty Polly", a blatant contradiction that seemed to disturb no one unduly.

The careers of Sceptre and Pretty Polly followed parallel courses in certain respects. They were both in training for four seasons. Sceptre ran 25 times and won £38,283 in first prize money; Pretty Polly ran once less and won £37,297. Pretty Polly sustained only two defeats in contrast to the twelve defeats of Sceptre; but it is arguable that Sceptre, who claimed one more Classic victory than Pretty Polly, should not have been beaten more than once or twice if she had been in the hands of a first class trainer and had the services of a competent jockey in all her races.

Richard Marsh, who trained Sceptre's sire Persimmon, wrote in his memoirs: "I do not find it easy to name the best filly or mare in my long career. It may have been Pretty Polly, to whom I rather incline, or again it may have been Sceptre, who I do not think had quite a fair chance through being trained and raced for the Lincolnshire Handicap as a three-year-old." Robert Standish Sievier, who owned and trained Sceptre for part of her career, remarked that they were too good to be compared. Sievier was probably right; comparisons in such cases are odious and inconclusive.

Unlike Pretty Polly, Sceptre had a superb Classic pedigree, as she was by Persimmon, regarded as an outstanding Derby winner and the best son of that greatest of stallions St. Simon, out of Ornament, a sister of Ormonde, one of the greatest racehorses of all time. She was bred by the first Duke of Westminster, who had bred and raced Ormonde, and but for the accident of the Duke's death in the winter of 1899, when she was a foal, she would have gone, like all the rest of the Westminster horses, to John Porter of Kingsclere, one of the most experienced trainers of Classic horses. Unfortunately the death of the Duke necessitated the dispersal of all his bloodstock by public auction and as a result Sceptre was submitted with the yearlings at Newmarket in the summer of 1900.

The first Duke's heir bought several of the Eaton yearlings at the dispersal, and intended to include Sceptre among his purchases, but he was thwarted by the determination of Bob Sievier. Sievier was the editor of a weekly racing paper called *The Winning Post* which included such scurrilous features as "Letters to Celebrities in Glass Houses". He was also a compulsive gambler on and off the race-course, and was no stranger to financial embarrassment, but his betting had prospered in the first half of the 1900 season and he made up his mind to invest in some of the Westminster yearlings. Accordingly he drew twenty-five £1,000 notes out of his bank in London and, on arrival at Newmarket on the evening before the sale, went straight to Mr. Somerville Tattersall, the head of the firm of auctioneers, and handed him the money with the information that he was a likely bidder. Tattersall protested that this procedure was quite unnecessary, but Sievier insisted. The banks were already shut, and Tattersall solved the problem of safe custody of such a large sum for the night by putting the notes in an envelope on top of the wardrobe in his room at the Rutland Arms.

In the morning Sievier made a close inspection of all the Eaton yearlings in the company of his trainer Charles Morton and an Irish vet called Peard. Early in the sale he bought one colt for 700 guineas and another, subsequently named Duke of Westminster, for 5,600 guineas. Several other lots were knocked down to the new Duke of Westminster. Then the filly by Persimmon out of Ornament was led into the ring. Apart from a mousey patch round her muzzle that had also characterized her sire, she was a good hard bay. She was flawless in quality and conformation except that she was rather straight in front, and turned one toe in slightly. Sievier opened the bidding at 5,000 guineas, the Duke's agent bid 5,100 whereupon Sievier countered with a bid of 6,000 guineas. So the bidding continued until it reached 10,000 guineas, 4,000 guineas more than had ever been paid for a yearling before. At this point the Duke's agent remained silent, and the filly who was to gain undying fame as Sceptre became the property of Sievier. "I was dubbed by some 'an ass', by the majority as 'mad', while a few kindly referred to the proverb of 'a fool and his money'. I should have gone much higher, for I had determined that Sceptre should be mine", wrote Sievier, who never lacked boldness when he was in funds, in his autobiography.

Naturally the first racecourse appearance of such a high-priced filly was eagerly awaited. In April Sceptre, Duke of Westminster and two other two-year-olds were tried with the five-year-old Leonid, whom Sievier had bought for 350 guineas after he had won a selling race at Lincoln. Sceptre won the gallop in a hack canter by six lengths from Duke of Westminster, who finished about two lengths in front of Leonid. This was clear evidence that Sceptre, at least, was something out of the ordinary, because she was meeting the five-year-old on about 2½ stones worse terms than weight-for-age. As a result she started a hot favourite for her first race, the Woodcote Stakes at the Epsom Summer meeting, and, although she negotiated Tattenham Corner none too well, she was an easy winner. The ground was on the firm side and she jarred her knees. She had to miss Ascot, but was sound in time to gain another easy victory in the July Stakes at Newmarket. Her only other race as a two-year-old was in the Champagne Stakes at Doncaster in September. When he saw her in the paddock Sievier was shocked to see that she had grown so thick a winter coat, when the autumn had hardly begun, that she had been trace-clipped. She ran far below her proper form in finishing third to Game Chick and Czardas, as she had beaten Czardas easily in the Woodcote Stakes.

By the end of the season Sievier was in financial difficulties and had to sell either Duke of Westminster, who had proved himself a fast colt and won the New Stakes at Royal Ascot, or Sceptre. He wanted to keep Sceptre and sell the colt, and hit upon the stratagem of asking 20,000 guineas for the colt and 15,000 for Sceptre, in the hope that potential buyers would come to the conclusion that he must think Duke of Westminster the better. John Porter, who was negotiating on behalf of his patron Mr. Gerald Faber, was not fooled for a moment, but he was aware that Faber preferred Duke of West-minster and would not accept the heavy responsibility of dissuading him. For this reason Duke of Westminster was sold and Sievier, to his immense relief, was able to keep the filly for a while longer.

At this time Sievier decided to train Sceptre himself as Morton, who had trained her as a two-year-old, had accepted the post of private trainer to Mr. J. B. Joel. For this purpose Sievier bought a training establishment at Shrewton and installed an American there as his assistant. Sceptre's first race as a three-year-old was to be the Lincolnshire Handicap. In later times running a three-year-old filly with a Classic programme in a mile handicap against older horses in March would have been unthinkable and even in 1902, when there was less tendency to keep high class horses in cotton wool, the policy was considered highly injudicious. Sievier had to make a business trip to Paris a few weeks before the Lincolnshire, and on his return was horrified to find Sceptre listless and off her feed. It transpired that the assistant had given her four severe gallops over a mile on succes-sive days during his absence and, although she gradually pulled round, she was not really herself when she ran in the Lincolnshire and suffered a head defeat by St. Maclou, who caught her in the last stride.

The assistant was promptly given notice and Sievier took sole charge of Sceptre's training. There could be no greater tribute to her courage and wonderful constitution than the fact that she recovered from this unpropitious start to her three-year-old season and survived the training methods of a man who, despite his unabashed self-confidence, was completely inexperienced. She began to improve rapidly in the final stages of her preparation for the first two Classic races. She beat the colts comfortably in the Two Thousand Guineas in the record time of 1 minute 39 seconds, and Duke of Westminster was unplaced. Two days later she also won the One Thousand Guineas in spite of twisting a plate at the start. As no farrier was present Sievier himself had to wrench off the twisted plate, and she ran in three plates only.

Probably Sceptre should have retired with the unique honour of having won all five Classic races, for her jockey Herbert Randall, who was in his first year as a professional after riding previously as an amateur, certainly rode an ill-judged race in the Derby. She was inclined to be restive at the start and lost some ground, whereupon Randall rode her hard all the way up the hill in order to join the leaders. She came round Tattenham Corner neck and neck with Ard Patrick, but her exertions in the first half mile had taken too much out of her, and she dropped back to finish fourth, while Ard Patrick went on to win by three lengths from Rising Glass. Two days later Randall rode a perfect race in the Oaks, waiting with Sceptre until reaching the straight and then bringing her along to win easily.

Rumours circulated that Sceptre had not tried in the Derby. The truth was that Sievier had backed her to win £33,000 in the Derby, and had to make special arrangements to draw the Oaks stake early in order to settle his Derby bets.

Sceptre was allowed no respite. From Epsom she was sent straight to Paris to run in the Grand Prix, in which Randall threw her chance away as surely as he had in the Derby. Evidently over-impressed by the reputation of the French jockeys for giving visiting riders a rough passage, he kept her on such a wide outside the whole way that she must have covered 50 yards more than any of her rivals, yet she finished only two or three lengths behind the winner Kizil Kourgan. After her reverse at Longchamp she returned home for the Royal Ascot meeting, at which she was beaten in the Coronation Stakes but won the St. James's Palace Stakes a day later. Randall's handling of Sceptre in the Coronation Stakes was the last straw as far as Sievier was concerned as, after being thrown at the start, he allowed her to become tailed off and then tried to make up all the ground in a furlong rounding the bend into the straight. He was not allowed to ride Sceptre again.

As at Epsom and Ascot, Sceptre had two outings at Goodwood and was beaten in her first race, the Sussex Stakes, and won her second, the Nassau Stakes. By then Sievier had decided that she was so thick-winded that she needed a tremendous amount of work, and her St. Leger preparation must have been one of the most strenuous ever given to a Classic filly. "She thrived daily on long gallops of all distances, eating her hay and corn with the same precision as her matchless action, putting on muscle, revelling in her daily work without intermission, and stumping up a horse a week," wrote Sievier. He had her to his entire satisfaction when he sent her to Doncaster, but less partial observers on the Town Moor were appalled to see her strip in such lean condition that she was practically skin and bone. She got through the St. Leger all right and beat Rising Glass, who had been second in the Derby, by three lengths.

But two days later she was badly beaten by Elba, who had been no match for her at all in the Oaks and the Nassau Stakes, in the Park Hill Stakes. The explanation was simply that she had just one more gallop left in her when she arrived at Doncaster, and she was finished for the season after the St. Leger.

It is quite a feat to win four Classic races and end up the season short of money, but Sievier managed it in 1902. Having refused an offer of £40,000 for Sceptre during the season, he found it necessary to send her to the Newmarket December Sales, where she failed to attract a bid at her reserve price of £24,000. Sievier took her home to Shrewton, but his hopes of keeping her through the next season depended on her landing a gamble in the Lincolnshire Handicap. This she failed to do when she finished fifth, carrying 9 st. 1 lb. and giving lumps of weight to all her opponents. She had to go, and before long her sale to Mr. William (later Sir William) Bass for £25,000 was completed. Sievier was a disreputable character in several respects. Afterwards he was involved in a slander case in which cheating at cards was one of the milder allegations made against him, and when it was over he was warned off Newmarket Heath. His redeeming feature was absolute devotion to Sceptre. If she had spent her whole career with an acknowledged Classic trainer, with John Porter or with Alec Taylor to whom she was sent by Bass, she would no doubt have suffered many fewer defeats; but it is questionable whether she would have been granted the opportunity to win all five Classic races; a record that Sievier proved she had the constitution if not the luck to achieve.

Sceptre won her first race, the Hardwicke Stakes at Royal Ascot, after joining the stable of Alec Taylor at Manton and then took part in a race which may still be regarded as one of the greatest in Turf history. Her opponents included Ard Patrick, her conqueror in the Derby, and Rock Sand, who had already won the Two Thousand Guineas and the Derby and was to capture the coveted though imaginary Triple Crown by winning the St. Leger. Rock Sand was made favourite to beat his two distinguished seniors, but he was in trouble early in the straight and Sceptre and Ard Patrick drew away with the race between them. Sceptre had a slender advantage entering the last furlong, but Otto Madden, a jockey who knew exactly where the winning post was, timed his final effort to perfection and got Ard Patrick up in the last few strides to win by a neck.

Several excuses were made for Sceptre. It was said that Taylor had not had time to get her fully to his liking; and that the going was terribly hard and not really suitable for a filly with her doubtful knees. The going was, indeed, so hard that the surface was slippery, and Sam Darling had fitted Ard Patrick's racing plates with rims which enabled him to keep his balance better than his rivals round the bends and come the shortest way home. These excuses may have had some validity. On the other hand there may not have been much the matter with the result, as a line through Rising Glass in the Derby and St. Leger the previous year indicated that there was little to choose between Ard Patrick and Sceptre.

The four-year-old season of Sceptre ended gloriously. She gave perhaps her finest performance when she met Rock Sand again in the Jockey Club Stakes over 1¾ miles at Newmarket in the autumn. On that occasion she gave the Triple Crown winner 7 lb. more than the weight for age and sex allowance and beat him easily by four lengths. She then won the Duke of York Handicap at Kempton Park, in which her victims included Our Lassie and Hammerkop, the first and second in that year's Oaks, and wound up with victories in the Champion Stakes and the Limekiln Stakes at Newmarket. That triumphant autumn campaign marked the effective end of her racing career. She stayed in training as a five-year-old, but failed to recapture her former brilliance and was beaten in all her three races—the Coronation Cup, the Ascot Gold Cup and the Hardwicke Stakes. By that time she had become a very finicky feeder, and the wise decision was made that she should retire.

For a great mare Sceptre changed hands an extraordinarily large number of times. In 1911 Sir William Bass sold all his bloodstock and Sceptre was bought by Mr. Somerville Tattersall for 7,000 guineas. In later years she became the property in turn of Mr. John Musker and Lord Glanely, and she was owned by Lord Glanely when she died in February 1926.

Like Pretty Polly, Sceptre was rather disappointing at stud. She had been barren for nine years before her death. She bred only four winners, of whom Maid of the Mist won three races and Maid of Corinth won two races besides finishing second in the One Thousand Guineas. On the other hand, also like Pretty Polly, she had a potent influence on the progress of the thoroughbred in the longer term. Maid of the Mist bred the Oaks winner Sunny Jane and the Two Thousand Guineas winner Craig an Eran; and in

1963 Relko became the first descendant of Sceptre in the direct female line to win the Derby—very soon after Pretty Polly's two descendants St. Paddy and Psidium had also won the most famous of Classic races.

Pretty Polly

If Sceptre was bred in the purple Pretty Polly, who was her junior by only two years and was a performer of equal or even greater brilliance, had relatively plebeian origins—origins, indeed, which could not possibly have been calculated to produce one of the outstanding fillies of all time. Gallinule, the sire of Pretty Polly, possessed plenty of speed and won three races as a two-year-old, but was both a roarer and a bleeder and lost all his form as his disabilities became more pronounced; and it was necessary to trace the pedigree of her dam Admiration back five generations in the direct female line to discover an animal of note.

The pedigree of Pretty Polly was so unpromising that it warrants some further description. Her sixth dam, an unnamed daughter of Pantaloon, was a half sister of Leamington, who won the Chester Cup twice and became a very successful stallion in America. Between Pantaloon's daughter and Admiration stretched a series of mediocrities of whom one, a filly of charm but excessive appetite, raced successively under the names of Sweet Pretty Pet, Chaperon and Fatty, winning two small races as Fatty at three years of age, and reverting to the name of Chaperon when she went to stud. Gaze, the dam of Admiration, ran only once and finished nearly last in a selling race. She was sold to "Mr. Cash" for only 7 guineas when she was submitted as a thirteen-year-old at the dispersal sale of the deceased trainer Robert Peck's bloodstock. "Mr. Cash" quickly repented of his purchase, and sent Gaze a few weeks later to Tattersalls Sales at Knightsbridge, where she was sold as a hack for 15 guineas.

Admiration, by the New Stakes and Chesterfield Cup winner Saraband, was bought by Major Eustace Loder, a serving officer in the 12th Lancers, for 510 guineas as a yearling in 1893. At first

Loder thought something of her, and ran her in the important Richmond Stakes at Goodwood as a two-year-old. She failed badly in that class, and had to descend to much more modest company to gain her first place, a second at Stockbridge the following year. She was then sent to Ireland, where she won a £50 handicap at Baldoyle. As a four-year-old she won a handicap at Leopardstown and dead-heated for another race, though she was relegated to second place in the run-off. She also ran several times over fences and was placed in a military steeplechase at Punchestown before retiring to the stud which Loder was forming at Eyrefield Lodge on the edge of the Curragh. There she proved a foundation mare in a thousand, for she bred a total of nine winners, while several of her daughters, including Veneration II, Miranda and Adula, besides Pretty Polly, became successful broodmares.

Sir Henry Greer, later Director of the National Stud, was convinced that Gallinule would make a good stallion in spite of his various infirmities and bought him for £1,000 for stud. This opinion was fully vindicated and it was largely on account of Greer's friendship with Noble Johnson, the stud manager at Eyrefield Lodge, that Admiration was sent to visit Gallinule in 1900 and in due course produced the chestnut filly foal who was destined to become famous as Pretty Polly. Incidentally, Gallinule got further Classic winners in Slieve Gallion, Night Hawk and Wildfowler.

Pretty Polly was lucky to survive to go into training. When she was being broken as a yearling and was being driven in long reins one morning on the Curragh she got loose and galloped along a narrow path with a high stone wall on one side and a forty-foot drop into a sand quarry on the other, doing two circuits of this perilous course before she allowed herself to be caught. On another occasion, when some of the other yearlings were being given a rough gallop over three furlongs before going into training, she was sent down to the start just to have a look, but when she got there she took charge of her lad and won the gallop, though she was carrying about 10 st. in contrast to the 8 st. carried by her companions.

However Peter Purcell Gilpin, who trained for Loder, was not particularly impressed by Pretty Polly when he came over from Clarehaven Lodge, Newmarket, to have a look at the Eyrefield Lodge yearlings. He found her almost too powerful-looking, which is surprising because she was delightfully feminine in appearance, with her lovely quality combined with an indefinable air of athleticism, when she was in full training. Nor did she reveal much speed when Gilpin first put her into strong work as a two-year-old. She moved in lethargic fashion until one morning she woke up and worked more satisfactorily with a fast colt called Delaunay. She was receiving 23 lb., but he had just won his first race at Manchester by five lengths, and there was more encouragement when he won again easily on the first day of the Sandown Park June meeting. Pretty Polly made her debut in the British Dominion Two-Year-Old Plate on the second day of the meeting, and as a result of her stable companion's win she was quite well backed at 6–1 though there was no stable confidence in her. No one was prepared for the electrifying turn of speed she produced. She left the gate like a flash of lightning and was soon many lengths clear of the rest of the field. As Charlie Trigg, popularly known as Hellfire Jack, had got the bird from the crowd for being caught napping in the previous race, he rode her right out to the finish, where Judge Robinson, notorious for his miscalculations of distance, estimated her winning margin very conservatively at ten lengths. Mr. George Thursby, who was third in the race on the next year's Derby second John o' Gaunt, thought she had won by nearly a hundred yards. No matter which estimate was correct, there was general agreement that she had given a brilliant performance; and although, with more restrained riding from the jockeys Halsey and Lane, she won her remaining races as a two-year-old by smaller margins, she swept the opposition aside almost with contempt in every case. She was kept busy enough, and by the end of the season had victories in the National Breeders Stakes at Sandown Park, the Mersey Stakes at Liverpool, the Champagne Stakes at Doncaster, the Autumn Breeders Foal Plate at Manchester and the Cheveley Park Stakes, the Middle Park Plate, the Criterion and the Moulton Stakes at Newmarket to her credit. In two of those races, the Champagne Stakes and the Middle Park Plate, she readily disposed of the next year's Derby winner St. Amant.

Pretty Polly had proved herself a marvellous two-year-old. Gilpin accounted for the amazing improvement over her home form that she had shown on her debut at Sandown Park by the fact that it had been very hot in the horse-box on the journey from Newmarket and she sweated profusely, a thing which she had never done on the gallops. The trainer ascribed her excellence to "electric dash", a quality which had also been attributed to another great horse, St. Simon. Nevertheless there were doubts concerning her stamina. One racing correspondent wrote during the winter: "Pretty Polly may take rank with the most brilliant sprinters we have known, but because of her breeding she cannot be another Sceptre, who is at her best over a distance of ground." Well, he was neither the first nor the last expert to be made a fool of by the thoroughbred.

Pretty Polly's first appearance as a three-year-old was in the One Thousand Guineas. In the paddock, where she paraded with her inseparable companion, the cob Little Missus, she was seen to have wintered well. She had filled out and grown a little, standing just under sixteen hands, and was very placid in her demeanour. In the race she made short work of her opponents, as William Lane took her to the front directly after the start and allowed her to make all the running and win in a canter by three lengths from Leucadia. The performance was so impressive that the former doubts about her stamina were forgotten, and only three other fillies were started against her in the Oaks, which she won just as easily, at odds of 100–8 on. She sailed through her next two races, the Coronation Stakes at Royal Ascot and the Nassau Stakes at Goodwood, in effortless fashion, and completed a Classic treble by beating the colts in the St. Leger. By that time she was such a public idol that she attracted a record crowd to Doncaster, where Little Missus caused a lot of amusement by cantering down to the start with Pretty Polly. The race itself was uneventful, as Pretty Polly strolled to the front on the last bend and went on to beat Henry The First in a canter, with St. Amant unplaced. Two days later she had another canter to win the Park Hill Stakes at 25–1 on.

Soon after the St. Leger meeting Eustace Loder decided to send Pretty Polly to run in the Prix du Conseil Municipal at Longchamp with the avowed intention of enabling her to treat the best French horses in the same summary fashion as she had beaten the best horses in England. William Lane, who had ridden Pretty Polly in all her previous races that season, had sustained such terrible injuries in a fall at Lingfield that his career in the saddle was terminated, but Danny Maher, the supreme exponent of the art of jockeyship of his time, was engaged for her. Even so, the expedition seemed to be ill-fated from the outset. She was held up at Folkestone by a storm in the Channel and eventually had a rough crossing. A special train had been hired to take her from Boulogne to Paris, and her travelling lad had been given £100 to grease the palms of railway officials and ensure that there were no delays on the journey. Unfortunately tipping on this liberal scale did not achieve its purpose. The private train was shunted into sidings repeatedly to let other trains through, and Pretty Polly was a tired filly when she arrived two days before the race.

Torrential rain fell on the eve, but the day of the race was sunny, with a touch of frost in the air, and the ground at Longchamp became extremely holding. This was by no means to the advantage of Pretty Polly for the Prix du Conseil Municipal, the principal autumn race—it was also called the Grand Prix d'Automne—in those days before the Prix de l'Arc de Triomphe existed, had a complex system of penalties and allowances which meant that she met all her opponents except Macdonald II on worse terms than weight for age and sex. However she was still considered practically certain to beat the best of the French horses, Macdonald II, who had been placed to Ajax in the French Derby and the Grand Prix de Paris; the danger, if there was one, was thought to be her English rival Zinfandel, a high class four-year-old who had been deprived of his chance of winning the Derby the previous year when his entry was rendered void by the untimely death of his nominator Colonel Harry McCalmont.

The result was one of the most debated upsets of racing history. The outsider Presto II, who met Pretty Polly on terms 13 lb. more favourable than weight for sex, detached himself from the rest of the field from the start and set a very strong gallop. Pretty Polly and Zinfandel followed him into the straight and at that point it was expected that the two English horses would pass the pacemaker whenever they wished. But nothing of the sort happened. Presto II kept up his gallop without any sign of weakening, the English horses could make no impression, and Presto II passed the winning post with 2½ lengths to spare from Pretty Polly, with Zinfandel half a length away third.

Presto II paid 66–1 on the Pari-Mutuel, although there were no more than eight runners. The result was received with consternation, not unmingled with bitterness, by most of the French spectators who, like the large number of English visitors, had supported Pretty Polly enthusiastically. One scrap of post-race dialogue on the Longchamp stands has survived and may be worth recording:

French Lady (sarcastically): "Ah, Ces Anglais!"

English Gentleman (acidly): "Madame, we didn't talk like that when Gouvernant was beaten at Epsom!"

(Gouvernant was a French horse who had started favourite for the Derby and finished unplaced behind St. Amant).

Then came the post-mortems. Some people said that Maher and Morny Cannon, who rode Zinfandel, had been so preoccupied watching each other that they had given Presto II too much rope, but Gilpin dismissed this accusation out of hand and gave Maher the ride on Pretty Polly again when she carried top weight to victory in the Free Handicap on her final appearance as a three-year-old. Gilpin attributed her defeat to the strains of the journey. Maher thought otherwise. He told George Lambton on his return to Newmarket that he did not think she was a true stayer, despite her victory in the St. Leger, and that the $1\frac{1}{2}$ miles in such heavy going at Longchamp had found her out.

The truth may have been that both these causes contributed to the defeat, and that an additional cause was the weight factor which was undoubtedly onerous for her in the muddy conditions. But the question of her stamina was to crop up again in circumstances equally controversial.

Pretty Polly gave one of her finest performances on her first appearance as a four-year-old in the Coronation Cup at Epsom. Although she had only two opponents, they were the good French horse Caius and Zinfandel, who went on to a meritorious victory in the Ascot Gold Cup. George Stern, on Caius, was instructed to repeat the tactics that had led to the defeat of Pretty Polly in the Prix du Conseil Municipal, and set an extremely hot pace. But he could never get Pretty Polly off the bit, and the filly took up the running soon after Tattenham Corner and went on to beat Zinfandel in a canter by three lengths. She had covered the $1\frac{1}{2}$ miles in 2 minutes $33\frac{4}{5}$ seconds, which was not only a course record but was nearly 6 seconds less than Cicero had taken to win the Derby the previous day and more than 4 seconds less than Cherry Lass took to win the Oaks a day later. Not until Mahmoud in 1936 did any Derby winner equal the time of Pretty Polly's first Coronation Cup.

The plan had been to run her in the Ascot Gold Cup that year, but a few days after her Epsom victory she trod on a patch of slippery ground when cantering up Long Hill at Newmarket and strained the muscles of her quarters. As a result she had to be rested until the autumn, when she returned to beat the dual Cambridge-shire winner Hackler's Pride in the Champion Stakes and win the Limekiln Stakes and the Jockey Club Cup. Those who idolized her declared that she had won the $2\frac{1}{4}$ miles Jockey Club Cup hard held by half a length from Bachelor's Button, but Danny Maher, who rode Bachelor's Button, swore that she was at the end of her tether and took her performance as confirmation of his idea that she did not stay. He told Lambton that Bachelor's Button would certainly have beaten her if he had had a pacemaker.

Bachelor's Button did have a pacemaker when they met again in the Ascot Gold Cup the next year after Pretty Polly had opened her five-year-old season with easy victories in the March Stakes at Newmarket and the Coronation Cup. The pacemaker was a horse that could not be ignored, for he was St. Denis, who had been third in St. Amant's Derby. St. Denis did his job well, going a great gallop for the first $1\frac{1}{2}$ miles. In the final furlong Bachelor's Button and Pretty Polly had the race to themselves, but, to the dismay of her legions of admirers, she could not show her brilliant speed and Bachelor's Button and Danny Maher prevailed by a length. The crowd were stunned into silence by the defeat of their heroine, and could not raise even a half-hearted cheer for the gallant winner.

All sorts of excuses were made for Pretty Polly; that she had had a large wart on her belly lanced a few days beforehand and was not herself; that Bernard Dillon, then the Clarehaven stable jockey, had not ridden her to orders; that she was upset by the oppressively hot weather and had been strangely reluctant to go onto the course from the paddock; that she had lost lengths when forced off a direct line by the tiring Achilles in the straight. The one explanation that her connections would not accept was that Maher had been right to cast doubt on her stamina. And, as at Longchamp, the evidence was inconclusive. Gilpin intended to run her again in the Doncaster Cup, but the ground on the Newmarket gallops was hard in the late summer and she jarred her off fore joint in her final gallop before the Doncaster meeting and any idea of running her again was abandoned.

Pretty Polly retired to the Eyrefield Lodge Stud. Although she bred four winners, she was rather a disappointment as a broodmare as far as her own offspring were concerned, though in the longer term she had a powerful influence and was the ancestress of the Derby winners St. Paddy and Psidium half a century later.

For all her surpassing brilliance, Pretty Polly was something of an enigma. Sweet tempered while in training, she became nervous and irritable at the stud. Noble Johnson wrote of her: "Polly was not the sort of animal you could take liberties with, and if anything went wrong, and she got upset, there was no knowing what might happen." This problem of her temperament, taken in conjunction with the problem of her stamina, makes her one of the most puzzling of all the great horses that have graced the Turf.

Lutteur III

It has been justly claimed that what Gladiateur, the "Avenger of Waterloo", accomplished for French horses on the flat by winning the Two Thousand Guineas, the Derby, the St. Leger and the Ascot Gold Cup, to say nothing of the Grand Prix de Paris in his own country, Lutteur III achieved for French steeplechasers by his victory in the 1909 Grand National. As Lutteur III was only five years old at the time it was a truly remarkable performance. After all, many present-day owners reckon a chaser is insufficiently mature for the National at seven although the fences are nothing like as severe as they used to be. Lutteur is the only five-year-old to have won the Grand National this century and only the fifth in the history of that race, the others being Alcibiade (1865), Regal (1876), Austerlitz (1877) and Empress (1880).

Lutteur III was bred in France by M. Gaston Dreyfus and was a chestnut by the English-bred St. Damien, a son of St. Simon, out of Lausanne. As a yearling he was bought by M. James Hennessy, a member of the famous Anglo-French family of brandy distillers, and was sent to Chantilly to be trained by Albert Jacquemin who at that period trained the majority of M. Hennessy's horses, particularly those in training for the flat. As a two-year-old Lutteur III was somewhat unpromising, being backward and distinctly on the slow side, but instead of getting rid of him his owner elected to retain him with the ultimate objective of making him a hunter.

However in the meantime it was thought expedient to see what Lutteur III could do as a jumper and as a three-year-old he was packed off to George Batchelor, whose stable was at Mesnil-le-Roi, near the training centre of Maisons-Laffitte. Batchelor had a very good eye for a horse and once he had seen Lutteur jump, he took a great liking to him and even began to have thoughts of Aintree at the back of his mind. It is certainly recorded that towards the end of 1907, after Lutteur had been cut, Batchelor showed him to some friends who were going round his stable and told them that one day Lutteur was likely to run in the National.

However Lutteur's first race, a steeplechase at Enghien in February 1908, was not a success. Ridden by Ernest Pratt, who was a brother of Frank and Willie Pratt and who was killed in 1915 in the Dardanelles, he ran deplorably. Pratt was disgusted with his ride and in forthright terms told Batchelor that Lutteur was no good and would never win a race. Jockeys are often indifferent judges; within a week Lutteur had won his first race and in a little over a year he had won the Grand National.

Lutteur's first victory was on March 7th in a steeplechase at Saint Ouen, the Prix du Pays du Caux. He was ridden this time by MacGough, who, like Pratt, was apprenticed to Batchelor. With the same jockey up Lutteur won at Auteuil on March 22nd. However his progress then met with a check as he injured a fetlock and had to be rested until September.

In later years M. Hennessy used to tell his family that the secret of Lutteur's success was the fact that he had been lightly raced at the start of his career. M. Hennessy's definition of "lightly raced" is a curious one. On October 17th Lutteur ran in a 3,100 metre hurdle race at Auteuil won by his stable-companion Cappiello. On October 24th he and Cappiello both ran in a 3,500 metre steeplechase at Auteuil, Cappiello again proving the winner. On November 5th they both turned out for another steeplechase over the same distance, Cappiello finishing second. On November 8th Lutteur was beaten a length in a 4,000 metre steeplechase at Auteuil and four days later he won the Prix Canot ridden by that fine French jockey George Parfrement, whose father was a Yorkshireman long connected with French racing.

Lutteur was certainly being kept busy, bearing in mind he was only a four-year-old, but there was no respite for him and he seemed to thrive on hard work. On November 15th, partnered by Parfrement, he won the Prix de Nice, a 5,000 metre steeplechase at Auteuil and on November 22nd, ridden by A. V. Chapman, he won the Prix Montgomery, a 5,500 metre steeplechase at Auteuil. He was twice placed during the first two days of December and then M. Hennessy and Batchelor decided to give him a breather and make the Liverpool Grand National his big spring objective. Between

October 24th and December 10th he had run in nine races; so much for M. Hennessy's "lightly raced".

Lutteur reappeared at Auteuil on February 18th and was beaten a short head by a very useful horse in a 3,100 metre hurdle race. He was then sent to Harry Escott at Lewes for the completion of his Grand National preparation. Escott found him very fit and well and decided to run him in the Champion Chase at Hurst Park. This race was run at level weights and Lutteur obtained no concession on account of his age from good horses such as Leinster, Mount Prospect's Fortune and Rustic Queen. Leinster had been given 11 st. 7 lb. in the Grand National, in which Lutteur's weight was 10 st. 11 lb. and Rustic Queen 12 st. Mount Prospect's Fortune had carried 11 st. 11 lb. in the National the year before.

Lutteur III did not greatly impress the paddock critics at Hurst Park and compared to the traditional massive "Aintree types" of that period, he seemed light and lacking in substance. In the race, though, he could not be faulted. He seemed thoroughly at ease round the Hurst Park bends and his jumping was swift and accurate. Beautifully handled by Parfrement, he won decisively by six lengths.

Clearly on that form Lutteur had a wonderful chance in the National at the weights and he was at once substantially backed. The confidence of his supporters, though, was badly shaken a few days before the big Aintree race when Lutteur was galloped over fences at Kempton Park with two horses belonging to King Edward VII. Parfrement was not available to ride Lutteur and for reasons now obscured by the mists of time, Lutteur was partnered by a Dutch amateur rider, Mr. Koster. The partnership was not a happy one. Lutteur made several mistakes and eventually a particularly bad blunder unseated the unfortunate Mr. Koster. As soon as the news of this Kempton fiasco leaked out, there were plenty of people to say that if Lutteur could not negotiate Kempton, he did not possess a hope of getting round Aintree.

Despite the Kempton incident, Lutteur started joint favourite for the Grand National with Mr. Paul Nelke's Shady Girl (10 st. 9 lb.). The weather was perfect and for once every fence on the course was clearly visible from the stands. The going was fast and good. Parfrement had walked the course carefully, studied the fences, and judged it expedient to let his leathers down a couple of holes. In those days the runners jumped a preliminary hurdle on the way down to the start. Lutteur did not please his backers by jumping it very big and slowly and spending a lot of time in the air.

After a false start in which Lutteur galloped quite a distance before Parfrement could pull him up, the field set off. It had been suggested that Lutteur had jumped off his forehand when he won at Hurst Park and that he did not use his hocks enough to cope with the formidable Aintree fences, but right from the start he jumped boldly and with machine-like accuracy. The fast pace evidently suited him and he never put a foot wrong throughout.

Rubio, the American-bred horse that had won the year before, fell at the water and Ascetic's Silver, winner in 1906, found his burden of 12 st. 6 lb. too much for him. With a mile to go Mr. B. W. Farr's Judas (10 st. 10 lb.) was in front and going strong, but Lutteur was nicely in touch and Parfrement was riding with the utmost confidence. At the last fence but one, Judas and Lutteur landed together but from that point Lutteur gained the mastery and ran on strongly in the long run-in to win decisively. Caubeen (11 st. 7 lb.) was third and Tom West (10 st. 9 lb.), who had made one very bad mistake, fourth. Of the thirty-two runners, seventeen (in some accounts nineteen) of the runners completed the course. Lutteur's time was 9 minutes $53\frac{1}{5}$ seconds. In the following year, on perfect going, the time taken by Jenkinstown (10 st. 5 lb.) was 10 minutes $44\frac{1}{5}$ seconds.

Lutteur was given a great reception and in particular there was outspoken admiration for the riding of Parfrement. Unfortunately M. Hennessy was not present to witness his horse's triumph. He had been obliged to leave Liverpool that morning to attend a funeral in France the following day. He heard that Lutteur had won on his arrival in Paris.

Possibly Lutteur, who had won the Grand National just over a year after his first appearance on a racecourse was never quite as good again. M. Hennessy in fact always declared that Lutteur's finest performance was his victory in the Champion Chase. Lutteur ran once more that season and was fourth in a hurdle race at Auteuil in April. He was then given a hard-earned rest.

Lutteur was by no means an easy horse to train and he did not run again till December 10th 1910 and it was not until March 2nd 1911 that he again struck winning form. On that day, ridden by Parfrement, he won a chase at Auteuil. He was again entered for the National and was given the stiff weight of 12 st. 3 lb. However hopes ran high when on March 18th he won the Open Chase at

Hurst Park in his very best style. On the strength of that performance he started a hot favourite for the National at 7–2. The going was terribly heavy at Aintree that year and Lutteur appeared to slip just as he was taking off at a fence. He made a tremendous effort to get over but he and Parfrement got stuck on top. The winner was the 20–1 Glenside, an unsound, one-eyed horse that had been far from well on the morning of the race, ridden by Jack Anthony who was then an amateur. Later that spring Lutteur was third in the Grand Steeplechase de Paris, but he then had leg trouble again and was unable to run before December 1913.

On his return to the racecourse Lutteur soon showed that he was no back-number and with Alec Carter up he won at Auteuil on December 2nd and again on December 14th. Once again the Grand National was made his objective and he went off to Harry Escott for the final stages of his preparation. On March 2nd he ran in the Champion Chase at Hurst Park but was defeated by another French horse, M. H. de Mumm's grey gelding Trianon III, ridden by Hawkins. Behind them was Sir Charles Assheton-Smith's Covert-coat, winner of the Grand National in 1913.

Covertcoat (12 st. 7 lb.), however, was favourite for the National. Lutteur III (12 st. 6 lb), ridden by Carter, was on offer at 10–1 and Trianon III at 100–9.

Lutteur III ran a magnificent race, particularly in view of the leg trouble from which he had suffered, but he could not quite bring it off and in the end he was third to Mr. T. Tyler's Sunloch (9 st. 7 lb.), who had made virtually all the running, and Trianon III. Lutteur was thus giving 41 lb. to the winner and Trianon III 30 lb. so the two French chasers had covered themselves with glory.

Lutteur remained in England with Escott. In the autumn he failed in the Grand Sefton at Aintree but in December, ridden by Hawkins, he won the Richmond Chase at Kempton. With the restrictions on National Hunt racing imposed by the war, he was taken out of training and hunted with the Garth by M. Hennessy's niece, Miss Dorothy Hennessy. Like many another good chaser, he was far from proving an ideal hunter and in fact was a singularly uncomfortable ride.

After the war Lutteur was an old horse but there was still plenty of zest in him and back he went into training. In November 1919, aged fifteen, he won the Richmond Chase at Kempton, but in January 1920 he fell in a race over the same course and it was decided to send him back to France. His final appearance was at Auteuil when in his eighteenth year. The old hero jumped magnificently, but not surprisingly he could not go the pace. It was twelve years after his Aintree triumph and very rightly the decision was taken to retire him.

Lutteur III ran thirty-five times, twenty-two times at Auteuil, ten times in England, twice at Enghien and once at Saint Ouen. He won fourteen races and was ten times placed. He lived in placid retirement till his death at M. Hennessy's stud near Beauvais in 1927.

Bayardo

Bayardo failed to finish in the first three in the Two Thousand Guineas or the Derby, and gained his only Classic victory in the St. Leger. Despite this unexceptional Classic record, most contemporary observers regarded him as one of the greatest thoroughbreds they had ever seen, and, viewed in the perspective of the years, Bayardo emerges as one of the horses of the century.

Among thoroughbreds Bayardo was a genuine eccentric, and in this respect he matched his owner Mr. A. W. Cox. Born in 1857, Alfred Cox was the second son of a wealthy Liverpool jute merchant. In those days it was the custom for eldest sons to go into the family business and for the remainder to go into the professions. The army was selected for Alfred Cox, but at Malvern he concentrated on cricket, football and boxing, at all of which he excelled, to the total neglect of his studies. As a result he failed, even with the aid of a crammer, to pass into the army, and at the age of twenty was despatched to Australia with £100 in his pocket to make his own way of life. He passed much of the time on the long voyage playing cards, and by the time he landed in Australia he was the possessor of a share in a derelict sheep farm in New South Wales, received in settlement of a poker debt. Not long afterwards, scuffing his feet in the dusty soil of his property, he noticed something glinting in the sunlight. He was standing on the site of what was to become famous as the Broken Hill silver mines.

Ten years later Cox was back in England, having sold his share in the Broken Hill property for a sum reputed to be in the region of half a million pounds sterling. With this comfortable fortune he settled down to live in style in St. James's Street, remaining a bachelor until his death, which was accelerated by a surfeit of whisky, just after the first world war. He went into racing on a substantial scale, and most of his attention during the thirty years after his return from Australia was directed to the successful development of his racing and breeding interests.

As befitted a self-made man, Alfred Cox scorned the social graces and refused to court popularity inside or outside the racing community. He chose to race under the name "Mr. Fairie", ownership under assumed names being permitted by the racing authorities in those days, though the reason why he should have selected that particular name remained a mystery even within his own family. He knew what he wanted in racing and pursued his aims with the combination of flair and the luck which had brought him a fortune in Australia. One of his shrewdest decisions was to send his horses to Alec Taylor, who was not only an exceptionally skilful and patient trainer but was unwavering in his respect for the patrons of his stable. Unlike some other great trainers, Taylor was always ready to defer to the wishes of his owners even when it meant subordinating his own better judgment.

The combination of flair and luck which marked Cox's activities on the Turf was exemplified by the breeding of Bayardo. He sent Bayardo's grandam Isolecta to Galopin when that distinguished Derby winner and sire of the mighty St. Simon was twenty-five years old and at the very end of his stud career, and as a result bred Galicia, who was to earn the reputation of one of the outstanding broodmares of all time by breeding the Derby winner Lemberg besides Bayardo. And he bred Bayardo, a finer specimen of the thoroughbred than Lemberg, by sending Galicia to Bay Ronald in the last stud season before that horse was exported to France.

As in other matters, Cox declined to follow fashion when arranging his matings. Bay Ronald, who stood at the Lordship Stud at Newmarket at a fee of 75 guineas, was not generally regarded as a potential Classic stallion. He had won only five of his twenty-six races and had gained his principal successes in the Hardwicke Stakes at Ascot as a four-year-old and in the City and Suburban Handicap, in which he carried 8 st., the next year. His owner Major Leonard Brassey admitted that Bay Ronald could not be described as quite a first class racehorse, and expressed the opinion that hard preparations for long distance races when he was none too robust as a young horse may have taken some of the steel out of him. But Cox discerned some valuable quality in Bay Ronald which others had missed, and his insight was richly rewarded.

Galicia had more racing merit than her performances indicated. She won the Biennial Stakes at Ascot as a two-year-old, but split a pastern in her next race and never really recovered her form, though she ran several times as a three-year-old and was going like a winner when she broke down on her final appearance in the Derby Cup. At stud she easily made up for disappointments on the racecourse. Indeed, Bayardo probably inherited a great deal of his speed and precocity from her, as Bay Ronald had failed to win as a two-year-old. Bayardo's speed and exceptional promise were evident to Taylor as soon as he went into training. Taylor got Otto Madden, then one of the leading jockeys, down to ride him in a trial about a fortnight before the Royal Ascot meeting when he was a two-year-old, and Bayardo revealed his prowess by beating the three-year-old Seedcake by six lengths at level weights, with six other two-year-olds trailing behind. Madden, perhaps not the most observant or intelligent of men, thought that he had been riding the three-year-old and concluded that the Manton two-year-olds must be no good Accordingly he engaged himself to ride another horse in the New Stakes, the race chosen for Bayardo's debut, and the mount was given to Bernard Dillon. How serious Madden's mistake had been became clear when Bayardo won easily and was promptly acclaimed the best two-year-old yet seen out. "Rapier" commented in the *Illustrated Sporting and Dramatic News:* "Mr. Fairie has had some horses of high class, and he tells me he thinks Bayardo undoubtedly the best he has ever owned."

After Royal Ascot Danny Maher began the successful if sometimes controversial partnership with Bayardo which was to continue until that horse's retirement two years later. Bayardo was not beaten as a two-year-old, going on to win the National Breeders Produce Stakes, the Richmond Stakes, the Buckenham Stakes, the Rous Memorial Stakes, the Middle Park Plate and the Dewhurst Plate. He was uncharacteristically lethargic when he ran in the Middle Park Plate and was at his least impressive in beating Vivid by a length, but was back at his sparkling best for the Dewhurst Plate, in which he beat the next year's Oaks winner Perola with the greatest of ease. Inevitably he was placed top of the two-year-old Free Handicap. The 1909 Classic races were considered to be at his mercy.

Spring was late in 1909. Bitterly cold north and east winds persisted throughout February and March. Like many another thoroughbred, Bayardo wanted some warmth in the air and some sun on his back, and he did not thrive. Moreover, the winds parched the ground and stopped the young grass coming through on the exposed gallops at Manton, on the Downs just above Marlborough, so that the going was unseasonably firm. The state of the going found out Bayardo's principal defect, which was his fleshy and sensitive feet. To make things still worse, he slipped up one frosty morning when fooling about at exercise and lamed himself temporarily. This combination of circumstances meant that Taylor was unable to give him a normal preparation or get him to his liking in time for the Guineas and advised that he should miss the first of the Classic races, but Cox insisted that he should run. Bayardo's reputation was such that he started at odds-on favourite, but his trainer's misgivings proved only too well founded when he ran without any dash and finished fourth behind Minoru, owned by King Edward VII, Phaleron and Louviers.

It was not until about two weeks before the Derby that Bayardo really began to pick up and please his trainer. The question was whether his recovery had come too late. Minoru's trainer Dick Marsh had a look at Bayardo at Epsom in the paddock and was duly impressed. "He looked a different horse and the sight of him really set my anxieties alight again", he wrote in his memoirs. The race was not entirely satisfactory. The American horse Sir Martin started favourite, but stumbled and fell at the descent to Tattenham Corner. Several of the other runners were hampered when Sir Martin fell, and Maher afterwards claimed that Bayardo lost half a dozen lengths, though few spectators seemed to notice his predicament in the excitement of the moment as Minoru battled out the finish with Louviers to gain a short head victory for the King. What is certain, because the impression of onlookers was confirmed by photographic evidence, is that Maher accepted inevitable defeat a long way from home and finished standing up in his stirrups. He was in fifth place.

Bayardo had failed in the Derby through no fault of his own, but that defeat marked the end of his troubles for more than a year. With a generosity none too common in his profession, Marsh admitted that Bayardo would probably have beaten Minoru if the Derby had been run a fortnight later: "When once Alec Taylor got Bayardo right as a three-year-old his excellence was undeniable. Fortunately for us that did not happen until after Minoru had won the Derby." Nor was concrete evidence lacking to support this opinion. Bayardo went to Royal Ascot, where he won the Prince of Wales's Stakes, and then to Sandown Park, where he not only won the Sandringham Foal Stakes but finished many lengths in front of Louviers, the Derby runner-up, at level weights. A few weeks later Bayardo was backed at Sandown to win the semi-Classic Eclipse Stakes, a race worth £8,870 even in those days of exiguous prize money, with the previous year's St. Leger winner Your Majesty behind him.

Bayardo had one more race before the St. Leger. This was the Duchess of York Plate over the Eclipse Stakes distance of 1¼ miles at Hurst Park, in which he had no difficulty in beating Valens, who had been showing much improved form since finishing unplaced in the Derby. The measure of the growth of Bayardo's reputation since the Derby is that he was preferred to Minoru in the betting on the St. Leger, for which he started at 11-10 on, with Minoru at 7-4 against. Minoru had been having some trouble with his feet, but Marsh was convinced that he would take a great deal of beating. In the event he met serious interference and was only fourth, though his trainer, realistic and broad-minded as ever, agreed that he would have had no chance with Bayardo even if he had had a clear run. For a time in the straight the outsiders Valens and Mirador seemed to have the race between them, but then Bayardo appeared on the scene, settled the issue in a few strides and won in the style of a colt a class above any of his rivals.

"Fairie" Cox did not believe in keeping his horses in cotton wool. The St. Leger had taken so little out of Bayardo that he was brought out again for the Doncaster Stakes, worth the paltry sum of £475, two days later, and he won in canter. He was kept busily employed during the autumn, and by the end of the season had victories in the Champion Stakes, the Lowther Stakes and the Limekiln Stakes at Newmarket, and the Sandown Park Foal Stakes and the Liverpool St. Leger to his credit.

During the final stages of his three-year-old career Bayardo's quirks of character became more pronounced. Although entirely free from vice, he always had a will of his own. Sometimes on returning from exercise he would stand stock-still in the middle of the stable yard, and nothing would induce him to move and enter his box until he felt so inclined. He took a rooted objection to cantering down to the start in front of the stands on the Rowley Mile course in his three races at Newmarket during the autumn of 1909. The moment he turned the corner after leaving the paddock gate and saw the straight 1¼ miles stretching away in front of him he dug his toes in and refused to budge. Maher was a beautiful horseman with perfect hands, but all his powers of persuasion were ineffective with Bayardo. The permission of the Stewards had to be obtained for Bayardo to go to the start round the back of the stands, and immediately he had his own way Bayardo behaved as quietly as a park hack.

No doubt his mulish behaviour at Newmarket was partly responsible for the fact that many critics, while acknowledging his brilliance, condemned Bayardo as ungenerous at the end of his three-year-old season. The unfavourable impression received by the critics was aggravated by the extreme waiting tactics adopted by Maher. Taylor tried to persuade Maher that these tactics were unnecessary and would lead to disaster one day, but the jockey could be as obstinate as Bayardo himself and insisted that Bayardo hated to be in front and must be kept covered up till the last possible moment.

Fortunately Bayardo took decisive action as a four-year-old to erase the false idea that his heart was not in racing. His first two races in 1910 were the Newmarket Biennial Stakes and the Chester Vase. He won both, though Maher nearly fell into the trap of giving him too much ground to make up on the sharp little Chester course and only got up in the last stride to beat William The Fourth, who had been third to Minoru in the Derby, by a head. The real test of his courage and ability came in the Ascot Gold Cup. The field of thirteen for the Gold Cup has never been exceeded in numbers in the history of the $2\frac{1}{2}$ miles race and included the French horse Sea Sick II, whose sire Elf II had won the race in 1898. Sea Sick II had won the French Derby the previous year, and his connections considered him unbeatable. Bayardo too was absolutely at his peak, and showed his high spirits by throwing Maher at the start. As usual Maher kept him well back in the early stages but at halfway, where Sea Sick had gone to the front galloping very strongly, he had moved closer to the leaders. With six furlongs still to be covered Bayardo suddenly took hold of his bit and, with a truly sensational burst of speed, shot past Sea Sick into the lead. He swept round the last bend clear of his pursuers, and, although Sea Sick never gave in, continued to increase his lead all the way up the straight to win by four lengths.

Bayardo had given incontrovertible proof of his will to win, and it is astonishing that Maher did not learn his lesson. He won his next race, the Dullingham Plate at Newmarket, without any bother, but then came his final outing in the Goodwood Cup. Although he had to give 36 lb. to the three-year-old Magic over the $2\frac{1}{2}$ miles of the

Goodwood race, no one thought that he would have any difficulty in doing so successfully, and odds of 20–1 were laid on him. Maher simply threw the race away by lying an unimaginable distance out of his ground. Bayardo came storming up in the last two furlongs, but he was too late and failed to catch Magic by a neck.

Various explanations of Bayardo's defeat were put forward. Some said that Magic had had a special preparation for the race and was a good horse on the day. But Alec Taylor, never a man to criticize a jockey unfairly, had no doubt where the blame lay. "Maher let Magic get a furlong in front and never attempted to close the tremendous gap until reaching the comparatively short straight— and he was giving away all that weight too," he said.

The sad aspect of the affair was that Bayardo had to retire from the Turf on a note of anticlimax. Yet the last doubters had been silenced by his brilliant performance in the Ascot Gold Cup and he went to stud with the deserved reputation of a racehorse of superlative merit, courage and character.

Bayardo was a bay or brown horse who stood a little under 16 hands when he was in training. He was not particularly handsome and stood over somewhat at the knees though, as far as soundness is concerned, this is a fault on the right side. He was a lengthy, well-proportioned horse, with nothing flashy about him. He had lop ears and could not bear to have any covering on them, probably because he had the odd habit of moving his ears backwards and in rhythm with his stride. Another idiosyncrasy of his was to knock noisily on the manger with his chin. The lads called it "Bayardo's drum".

Unfortunately Bayardo did not have a normal life span, as he contracted thrombosis, resulting in paralysis of his hind quarters, and died at the age of only eleven. Although his stud career was cut short so drastically, he was leading sire of winners twice and sired two war-time Triple Crown winners, Gay Crusader and Gainsborough. Through Gainsborough and Gainsborough's son Hyperion, he has had a profound influence on the modern thoroughbred. Granted a further half dozen seasons at stud he would probably have become as great a sire as he was a racehorse.

The Tetrarch

The Tetrarch made an indelible impression on all who saw him; first by his extraordinary appearance—Steve Donoghue described him as "a sort of elephant grey, with big blotches of lime colour, looking as though someone had splashed him all over"—and second by his phenomenal speed. No other horse who has raced only as a two-year-old has laid such an undeniable claim to greatness, and the leg injury which terminated his racing career during his preparation for the 1914 Derby must be accounted one of the tragedies of Turf history. "Could a horse who possessed such devastating speed have stayed $1\frac{1}{2}$ miles and won the Derby?" is the question that the critics of his own and later times have asked repeatedly, and The Tetrarch's trainer Atty Persse made his own attempt to give the authentic answer when he said: "I honestly don't think he would ever have been beaten, at any distance. He was a freak and there will never be another like him."

"Freak" was a well-chosen word. Everything about him was abnormal, from his breeding, through his racing prowess, to his own stud record. In the first place no one in his senses would have dared to predict that his sire Roi Herode, whose racing class was that of a good staying handicapper, was capable of getting a horse destined to become a synonym for brilliance in the thoroughbred. Roi Herode owed his chance to do so to the facts that he belonged to the male line of Herod and that Mr. Edward ("Cub") Kennedy, of the Straffan Station Stud in County Kildare, was determined to revive the fortunes of that line, which was on the verge of extinction in England and Ireland. For this purpose Kennedy bought first The Victory from Australia in 1904 and then, after The Victory had died four years later without siring anything of note, Roi Herode from France. That Herod stood ten generations back in the pedigrees of

The Victory and Roi Herode and so was genetically insignificant did not worry him in the least.

Roi Herode, a grey horse foaled in 1904, was superbly bred, for he was by the French St. Leger winner Le Samaritain out of the French Oaks winner Roxelane. He ran mostly in good company, but with little success. He was second in the Prix du President de la Republique (later called the Grand Prix de Saint-Cloud) as a three-year-old, and two years later won the Grand Prix de Vichy and was second in the Doncaster Cup. It was after he had run at Doncaster that Kennedy bought him for £2,000.

In 1910 providence took a decisive hand in shaping the success of Kennedy's experiment. The Irish breeder kept him in training, but Roi Herode broke down in the course of his preparation for the Chester Cup and there was no alternative to sending him to the stud immediately. It was far too late in the breeding season to get a proper complement of mares for him, and Kennedy had only two or three mares of his own who had not already been covered. One of these was Vahren, a thirteen-year-old mare by Bona Vista who had won three small races and been bought by Kennedy for stud for £200. Vahren was apt to be a shy breeder, but that year she was due to foal late to John o' Gaunt, and when she did so she was mated with Roi Herode. The result of this fortuitous mating was The Tetrarch.

When he was foaled The Tetrarch was chestnut with black splotches, some egg-shaped, some elongated and some merely spots. His colour and marking at an early age formed a striking example of the manner in which characteristics may lie dormant for long periods, for the same colour scheme was noted in the case of Pantaloon, who was seven generations back in the male line ancestry of The Tetrarch. By the time he was a yearling the chestnut had turned to iron grey and the splotches to white. He was a tall, gangling, ungainly colt. A fellow Irish breeder asked Kennedy what he was going to do with him, and when told that he was sending him to the Doncaster Sales commented that it would be better to geld him and put him away as a jumper. This opinion was not shared by Persse, who visited the Straffan Station Stud before the sales. He had trained one of the previous off-spring of Vahren, the good sprinter Nicola, and so paid close attention to her colt by Roi Herode. He liked what he saw. Curiously marked and ungainly Vahren's son might be, but he was a magnificent walker, printing with his hind feet far in front of his forefeet. Persse determined to have him, and bought him for 1,300 guineas. He might have had to pay a good deal more if Daniel Gant, who went to the sales with the intention of bidding, had not been dissuaded by his trainer, who told him that he would make a fool of himself if he bought a colt more likely to make a good hunter than a racehorse.

Those who did not see The Tetrarch until he appeared on the racecourse, and the thousands more in his own and later times who knew him only from his photographs, could scarcely credit that he had been so adversely criticized as a yearling. Nicknamed derisively "The Rocking Horse" when he arrived at Doncaster, he was dubbed "The Spotted Wonder" long before his triumphant return to Doncaster for the Champagne Stakes a year later. In training he developed into a magnificent specimen of the thoroughbred, with his lovely bloodlike head, exceptional length of rein, powerful but classically moulded quarters and remarkable hip to hock length which must have given him the spring for his bounding stride. Persse summed up his mechanical perfection when he said of him: "When he galloped his back seemed to get shorter and his legs longer. That was due to extraordinary hind leverage; his hind-legs seemed to project right out in front of his fore-legs."

A month after Persse had brought the colt to his stables at Chattis Hill his cousin Dermot McCalmont, then a captain in the 7th Hussars, returned from India and asked him whether he had bought anything at Doncaster. Persse replied that he had bought the grey colt by Roi Herode out of Vahren, and that if McCalmont liked he could have the colt for what he had paid for him, or else they would go shares. McCalmont, diminutive in stature but considerable in wealth, preferred to be the sole owner.

Persse, christened Henry Seymour but known throughout his life as Atty, was in his middle forties and had been training for a dozen years when The Tetrarch entered his yard. A first class amateur rider who was third on Aunt May in the 1906 Grand National, he had a sparkling wit and an irrepressible sense of fun. But behind the Irish charm lay one of the most ruthless brains in the training profession. Fundamentally his method consisted in "training" in the literal sense of the word—that is, in teaching a horse his job and getting him thoroughly fit before he ever got to the racecourse. He always maintained that there was no reason why a two-year-old should not show his best form first time out, and indeed many of his best betting coups for himself and his owners were landed with two-year-olds making their debuts. One of his greatest coups was when Sir Archibald, who was second in the Two Thousand Guineas the following year, won his first race at Newmarket at the remunerative odds of 90–1 in the spring of 1907. For this reason The Tetrarch was performing strictly in accordance with Chattis Hill tradition when he won the Maiden Two-Year-Old Plate at the Newmarket Craven meeting in 1913 on his first appearance in public, though even Persse's horses did not usually win in quite such spectacular fashion at the first time of asking. His twenty opponents included Mount William, who was made favourite on the strength of a recent easy victory at Newbury, but there was inspired support for The Tetrarch at 5–1 and 9–2. In the race there was only one horse in it for The Tetrarch, who was never out of a loping canter, pulverized the rest of the field to beat Mount William by 4 lengths.

The Tetrarch next ran in the Woodcote Stakes at Epsom on the day before the Derby. His surprisingly generous starting price of evens was due to support for Parhelion, owned by Mr. Jack Joel, whose two-year-olds were always much respected at Epsom. The Tetrarch streaked away from Parhelion in the straight, and as he passed the winning post Charles Morton, Joel's trainer, scratched his head, spat, and then uttered the admiring comment: "Well, I'm jiggered. He's a marvel and no mistake. He went past my horse as if he were going past a tree."

The Tetrarch made hacks of his rivals in the Coventry Stakes at Royal Ascot, which he won by ten lengths, but came close to disaster for the first and only time in his racing career in the National Breeders Produce Stakes at Sandown Park. He nearly collided with the tapes at the start and was backing away as they rose. He then leapt forward, struck the quarters of another runner, and was many lengths behind the leaders by the time Donoghue had him clear of interference and properly balanced. His cause looked hopeless at half-way, but he shot forward like a rocket in the last couple of furlongs to catch Calandria, to whom he was giving 17 lb., close to the finish and win by a neck. On returning to scale Donoghue calmly informed Persse that he had won quite easily in the end, though bad visibility had concealed the start and few of the spectators realized why his winning margin had been so slight.

The three remaining victories of The Tetrarch were gained in effortless fashion; he beat Princess Dorrie, the winner of the next year's One Thousand Guineas, by six lengths in the Rous Memorial Stakes at Goodwood, outclassed the highly thought of Stornoway in the Champion Breeders Foal Stakes at Derby, and cantered away with the Champagne Stakes at Doncaster to raise his score to seven wins worth £11,336.

The Champagne Stakes was The Tetrarch's last race. It was intended that he should run in the Imperial Produce Stakes at Kempton Park, but he rapped his off-fore fetlock joint in a gallop a few days before the race and could not take part. His performances had been so brilliant that he was allotted 9 st. 10 lb. in the Free Handicap, 10 lb. more than the next best Corcyra, the winner of the Middle Park Plate. This was one of the largest margins that have ever separated the first and second two-year-olds in the Free Handicap.

The affected joint was pin-fired as a precautionary measure that autumn. During the winter there was an unexpected willingness on the part of ante-post bookmakers to lay The Tetrarch for the 1914 Classic races. Apparently they were influenced partly by doubts whether a horse so generously endowed with speed could also stay, and partly by the not unreasonable thought that a horse who had rapped himself once could do so again. Persse considered that he was as sound as at any time in his life in the spring of 1914, but announced that he would miss the Two Thousand Guineas as he was rather backward and be specially trained for the Derby. Again not unreasonably, bookmakers and others thought it ominous that The Tetrarch should be missing the Guineas, a race which should have been at the mercy of such a brilliant colt. Rumours multiplied, and finally were substantiated when Persse issued the following statement on May 13th, during the Second Spring meeting at Newmarket: "Having received information from my head man at Stockbridge after racing yesterday that The Tetrarch's leg had filled subsequent to his gallop on Tuesday, and having ascertained later more fully the extent of the injury, I wired to Captain McCalmont, who is out training with his regiment in Ireland, advising him to scratch the horse for the Derby." A later veterinary bulletin gave the additional information that he had injured his fetlock joint and suspensory ligament, which rendered it impossible for him to go on with his Derby preparation.

With benefit of hindsight it is possible to deduce that the odds had always been against The Tetrarch standing up to a full-scale Classic preparation. Although he moved perfectly straight at the gallop, he tended to plait his fore-legs, crossing one in front of the other, in his slower paces, and this involved the ever-present danger that he would rap himself badly sooner or later. In a case of a horse like The Tetrarch whose racing career is curtailed by injury, form shown at home assumes more than usual importance as a means of assessing his true ability. Persse described the first serious work of The Tetrarch as "the most exciting trial I have seen". His account continued: "I had three in that gallop, a couple of two-year-olds I knew went a bit, and an old horse that was giving away 21 lb. As this was the first time that The Tetrarch had been really jumped off I told the boy who was riding him to lie beside the others, and, when he commenced to tire, to ease him up. Imagine my surprise to see, after three furlongs, the old horse and the speedy two-year-olds hard-ridden, but The Tetrarch two lengths ahead of the rest and still going at apparently half-speed. The boy on his back was sitting quite still and doing nothing to urge his mount forward, though the others were all out."

Fearing that the gallop must have been false, Persse arranged a formal trial for The Tetrarch on April 5th, two days later. The Tetrarch and the aged horse Captain Symons, who won a good handicap at Chester the following month, carried 8 st. each, and the two-year-old won in a canter. The trial was repeated a week later, but this time The Tetrarch gave a stone to Captain Symons and again beat him in a canter, while the two-year-old Land of Song, receiving 21 lb. from The Tetrarch, was third. Allowing for the scale of weight-for-age in April, The Tetrarch was really giving 61 lb. to the useful old handicapper, while the magnitude of his achievement in the trial was revealed even more clearly by the fact that Land of Song won the Windsor Castle Stakes, beating Princess Dorrie, at Royal Ascot on his first appearance on a racecourse. The Tetrarch must have been one of the finest betting propositions of all time when he ran in that maiden plate at the Craven meeting.

Not content with this accumulation of evidence of The Tetrarch's brilliance, Persse tried him again just before Ascot. On this occasion he was set to give 10 lb. each to the older horses Noromac, who won the Claremont Handicap over 5 furlongs at Sandown Park with 8 st. 10 lb. soon after, and Hallaton, who had won the Portland Handicap with 8 st. 6 lb. three years earlier. He beat Noromac pulling up by ten lengths, drawing from his trainer the terse comment: "It was no kind of a gallop at all." As The Tetrarch should have received 35 lb. from the older horses according to the scale, the result testified to his greatness perhaps even more strongly than his earlier trials.

Like so many other great horses The Tetrarch was a real character, a curious mixture of docility and sharp temper. He could be a devil on the rare occasions he was roused. Two things he hated; one was physic and the other was being shod in the presence of a stranger. The first time he was given a "ball" it broke in his mouth and he never forgot the taste of bitter aloes, so that ever after it was necessary to give a tasteless powder in his mash. He never gave any trouble when he was shod by Persse's own farrier; but the first time he ran at Newmarket the course farrier had a terrible battle to get him plated. Thereafter the Chattis Hill farrier accompanied him to all meetings.

Another peculiarity of The Tetrarch, which he shared with other great horses like Bayardo and Hyperion, was a habit of suddenly coming to a halt at exercise and gazing into the distance, refusing to move on until he felt inclined. He even did this in the parade ring before his race at Goodwood.

The same dreaminess infected The Tetrarch's behaviour at stud. He appeared to be totally uninterested in sex, and it took all the patience and perseverence of the staff at his owner's Ballylinch Stud in County Kildare to persuade him to cover any mares at all. He was an appalling foal-getter, became steadily worse and had been sterile for ten years before his death in 1935. He got only 130 foals altogether, compared with the 554 foals got by the wonderfully prolific St. Simon.

In the circumstances The Tetrarch did remarkably well as a sire of winners, heading the list in 1919 and being third twice. His success in siring the St. Leger winners Caligula, Polemarch and Salmon Trout lent support to the claim that he would have stayed if he had been able to race as a three-year-old. On the other hand his influence was transmitted to later generations mostly through his speedy sons Tetratema and Stefan the Great and daughter Mumtaz Mahal; and a quarter of a century or so after his death his descendants Pall Mall and Caergwrle, having heavy concentrations of his blood, displayed much of his brilliant speed combined with a strictly limited ration of stamina. And The Tetrarch enigma, like so many others in Turf history, remains insoluble.

Man o' War

There have been great racehorses in many different countries and many different periods; but the horses that really capture the imagination of not only the contemporary racing public but of posterity also, the horses that become legends, have a quality over and above mere speed and stamina and all the other factors that make up an efficient racing machine. They have a presence and a personality that makes them glow in the memory. By this standard Man o' War was one of the greatest of the greats, for his character was overwhelming and Will Harburt, the stallion man who used to look after him during his stud career, used to refer to him as "de mostest hoss dat ever was".

That transcendent quality was the unanswerable retort to the critics of "Big Red", as Man o' War was universally called. For he had critics, despite his majestic victories in twenty of his twenty-one races and his numerous triumphs on the watch. They said that he seldom met another really good horse, that he was allowed to have matters all his own way in many of his races, that he was not kept in training as a four-year-old to meet the Classic performers of a younger age group. They pointed out that his sire Fair Play became so savage that he was practically useless as a four-year-old, and that his owner Samuel D. Riddle declined to keep him in training to meet "Old Bones" Exterminator, the tenacious gelding who was champion handicap horse four years in succession, in a special 50,000 dollar race or to accept an invitation to race in England. That these criticisms were invalid will emerge as the story of his racing life unfolds, but the truth is that they never had much force in view of the feelings of admiration, amounting almost to hero-worship, which he inspired.

Man o' War was bred by Major August Belmont II, chairman of

the New York Jockey Club and a dominant personality in American racing, at his Nursery Stud near Lexington, Kentucky. Foaled on March 29th, 1917, Man o' War was by Fair Play, a son of the ferocious Hastings and himself a horse of dubious temper, out of Mahubah, by the English Triple Crown winner Rock Sand. Fair Play had shown high class form as a three-year-old, when he won the Dwyer Stakes and the Lawrence Realisation, but Mahubah had been of little account on the racecourse and won only one small race. Although Belmont was sixty-five years old when the United States entered the First World War, he volunteered immediately, was commissioned with the rank of Major and given the job of buying mules for the army. In normal times he raced all the produce of his own stud, but he decided to sell his entire 1917 crop of twenty-one foals as yearlings, so that he could concentrate on his war work. His original intention was to exclude the Mahubah colt alone from the sale, and Belmont's wife, the former actress Eleanor Robson, gave the colt the extravagantly sentimental name of "My Man o' War". Later when Belmont decided that this colt must be sold with the rest, the "my" was dropped and he was sold simply as Man o' War.

Evidently Belmont must have discerned special promise in Man o' War, otherwise he would not have been so hesitant about selling him, but the colt's virtues were not obvious at a first glance. Louis Feustel, formerly employed by Belmont and then trainer to Samuel D. Riddle, went to have a look at him and reported that he was very tall and gangling and so on the leg as to give the same ungainly impression as a week-old foal. Riddle, a Pennsylvania textile manufacturer who had been prominent in Maryland hunting and steeplechase circles, thought that he might develop into a good type of hunter. Nevertheless Feustel and Riddle agreed that Man o' War was worth having and bought him for 5,000 dollars, the third highest price realized by any of the Belmont yearlings, in spite of the fact that the underbidder Robert Gerry had wanted him simply as a potential hunter. Bloodstock prices were depressed by war-time restrictions, but at that price Man o' War proved one of the greatest bargains of racing history.

Man o' War was taken back to his new owner's Glen Riddle Farm in Maryland, where Riddle was rapidly expanding his racing interests. The colt was a rich, glowing chestnut colour, and was promptly nick-named "Big Red" by the stable lads. This name clung to him in public and private throughout his life, and his registered name was used purely for formal purposes. In a very short time "Big Red" showed that he was colourful in character besides appearance. He gave a rodeo display round the paddock the first time the tackle and saddle were tried on him, and it took the combined strength of several men to catch and control him. The first man to mount him was bucked off the moment he threw a leg across his back. But once Man o' War had got this protest against human domination out of his system he gave no further trouble. He was always perfectly docile in the stable, though he was a veritable equine dynamo, bursting with energy and impatience, as soon as he got on the track to work or to race. Once when Johnny Loftus, the stable jockey in his two-year-old days, rode him at work he stood practically erect on his hind legs as soon as he stepped onto the track, gave three enormous bounds and then seized hold of his bit and galloped half a mile in 47 seconds dead. Loftus, one of the most experienced jockeys then riding, was white and shaking when he got back to the stable.

That Man o' War became so strong that he was virtually impossible to restrain and that he was so healthy that he never had a day's sickness the whole time he was in training was due in no small part to his apparently inexhaustible appetite. He was such a good "doer" that he had to be bitted at feed times to prevent him bolting his generous rations of oats. He was given his first feed at 3.30 a.m. and his last at 5.15 p.m., and he got through 12 quarts of oats a day.

When Man o' War went into serious training in the spring of 1919 he lost no time in showing that he was exceptional in speed as well as character and appetite. His first track work-out at Pimlico was impressive enough. Several other fast two-year-olds were in the gallop but Man o' War, after losing a length or two at the start, easily overtook the others and was in front after a couple of furlongs. Loftus was impressed with the way he galloped, but less than satisfied with his sluggish start. Thereafter he made deliberate efforts to get the colt hotted up at the start, with the result that Man o' War became so excitable that he often delayed his races by displays of over-eagerness.

Man o' War's first race was at Belmont on June 6th. It was only a small race and his trial form had been so impressive that he started at 5–3 on, odds that he landed without effort by six lengths. Three days later he came out again for the more important Keene Memorial, and again streaked ahead from the start to win unchallenged. By August 2nd he had added further successes at Jamaica, Aqueduct (twice) and Saratoga to his tally, capturing the important United States Hotel Stakes at the last-named track.

Some people were already hailing Man o' War as invincible, but this opinion was not universally held. Harry Payne Whitney, who had several fast two-year-olds, was confident that he could beat him with Upset, and Riddle's niece Mrs. Walter Jeffords had not lost faith in Golden Broom, a more mature colt who had outpaced Man o' War in a gallop over a quarter of a mile when they were both still yearlings. These three colts met in the Sanford Memorial over six furlongs at Saratoga on August 13th, a race which was to produce a sensational finish and give rise to endless controversy. The trouble began at the start. The regular starter Mars Cassidy was off duty, and his substitute C. H. Pettingill was, to say the least, unfortunate in his efforts. Man o' War, impatient to be off, had to be pulled back repeatedly, and, in those stall-less days, was turned half round when Pettingill released the barrier. He lost several lengths in a generally straggling start, and then got badly boxed in on the inside rail. There was barely a furlong to go when Loftus made up his mind that he was not going to get through and switched to the outside. By that time Golden Broom, who had been disputing the lead, was beginning to lose ground, but Upset was still going strong. Although Man o' War produced a terrific turn of speed and was catching the aptly named Upset hand over fist, he was just too late and failed by half a length.

This was not a bad performance by Man o' War even if it was accepted at its face value, because Upset was highly thought of and Man o' War was trying to concede him 15 lb. Ten days later Man o' War and Upset met again in the Grand Union Hotel Stakes over the same course and distance, and this time Man o' War gave 5 lb. to his rival and beat him by a length pulling up. "Big Red" had two more outings that year, in the Hopeful Stakes at Saratoga and the Belmont Futurity, two of the most important two-year-old races, and won them both easily, though he was at his most impetuous before the former race and delayed the start by twelve minutes.

Loftus had ridden Man o' War in all his races as a two-year-old, but when he applied for a renewal of his jockey's licence for 1920 it was not granted. The assumption was that the authorities had frowned on his riding in the Sanford Memorial, but no specific charge was ever preferred and no official enquiry was held. If this

4

was justice it was certainly rough, and the English Jockey Club at its most dictatorial can seldom have meted out such high handed treatment as this by its American counterpart. Loftus sank into obscurity and when, in 1960, he was elected to the National Jockeys Hall of Fame at Pimlico he could not be traced. Clarence Kummer succeeded him as Man o' War's regular jockey, though Earl Sande and Andy Schuttinger had one mount each on him as a three-year-old. Kummer received 1,000 dollars for each of his first eight mounts on Man o' War, and 5,000 dollars for the last.

Inexplicably Man o' War was not entered for the Kentucky Derby, but he did win the other two races of the American Triple Crown, the Preakness Stakes over 1⅛ miles at Pimlico, and the Belmont Stakes over 1⅜ miles at Belmont Park. The Preakness on May 18th was his first outing of the year, and at that stage there were still a few owners who were not convinced that he was unbeatable, or else believed in a recurrence of the kind of miracle that had aided Upset in the Sanford Memorial. Eight horses opposed him in the Pimlico Classic race, but optimism about the prospect of ever beating him died a sudden death after he had galloped his early pursuers into the ground and then held off the late challenge of the Whitney colts Upset and Wildair without the slightest difficulty. After that three was the greatest number of runners that ever took him on, and in six of his eleven races as a three-year-old he had but one rival.

Eleven days after the Preakness he won the Withers Stakes over a mile at Belmont Park in the new American record time of 1 minute 34.8 seconds, and on June 12th beat his solitary opponent Donnacona by twenty lengths in the Belmont Stakes in the new world record time of 2 minutes 14.2 seconds. Altogether he broke seven track, American or world records during his three-year-old career. Perhaps his most astonishing record-breaking effort was in the Lawrence Realisation at Belmont Park in September. Other owners were so unwilling to run against him by that stage of the season that he looked like having a walk-over until Mrs. Jeffords agreed to start Hoodwink to help make a spectacle. Kummer was instructed to hold Man o' War back as much as possible, but there was little he could do. Although he was standing up in his stirrups pulling at Man o' War the whole way, he still won by one hundred lengths, or nearly a quarter of a mile and, almost incredibly, "Big Red" returned the new world record time of 2 minutes 40.8 seconds.

Times apart, Man o' War probably gave his finest performances in the Dwyer Stakes at Aqueduct in July and the Potomac Handicap at Havre de Grace two months later. In the nine furlongs Dwyer had to give 18 lb. to his only rival John P. Grier, a high-class horse who went on to win four races, all hotly contested, in a row. Man o' War and John P. Grier jumped off together and battled neck and neck until a furlong from home, where John P. Grier gained a slight advantage. There was a roar from the crowd as they thought Man o' War was beaten. Kummer had to draw his whip and give his horse a tap. The response was immediate. Man o' War bounded forward, quickly mastered his gallant opponent, and went away to win by $1\frac{1}{2}$ lengths.

In the Potomac Handicap he had three excellent opponents— Wildair, Blazes and the Kentucky Derby winner Paul Jones—and was set to give at least 24 lb. to each of them. He put himself at a further disadvantage by swerving to the right as the barrier rose and losing three lengths. But none of his opponents was able to exploit the situation, and Man o' War was an easy winner, beating Wildair going away by $1\frac{1}{2}$ lengths. Needless to say, Man o' War beat the record in both the Dwyer and the Potomac Handicap.

Man o' War's last race was a special match for 80,000 dollars against the four-year-old Sir Barton, the leading handicap horse of the year, over $1\frac{1}{4}$ miles at Kenilworth Park in Canada. It was really no race at all, as Man o' War beat his hapless opponent by seven lengths and, just for good measure, lowered the track record by a full six seconds in the process.

One of the charms of racing is that few owners regard their good horses purely as profitable investments, but are genuinely fond of them. Perhaps Samuel Riddle, a horseman and horse-lover himself, carried this admirable trait to excess, for his adulation was such that he would permit only the most fulsome praise of Man o' War to be expressed in his presence. He had a special stud, Faraway Farm, built for the horse a few miles north of Lexington, with a small house for himself so that he could be close to his idol for a few weeks every year. He limited him to twenty-five mares, mostly his own, each year, and sold the spare nominations to favoured friends at 5,000 dollars each, an unheard of fee in those days. This restrictive practice may not have given Man o' War the best possible chance to distinguish himself as a stallion, and he headed the list of American sires only once. On the other hand, he was very far from being a failure. He got an outstanding horse, American Flag, in his first crop of foals, and a winner of the American Triple Crown, War Admiral, much later in his life; his son Battleship was one of the gamest, if one of the smallest, winners of the Grand National.

The influence of Man o' War could be detected in the pedigrees of brilliant racehorses long after his death at Faraway Farm at the ripe age of thirty. War Admiral was the maternal grandsire of Never Say Die, winner of the Derby and St. Leger; War Relic, another son of Man o' War, was the grandsire of Relance, the famous mare who bred the Classic winners, Match III, Relko and Reliance; and Man o' War's daughter Salaminia was the third dam of Sir Ivor, that amazingly tough and resilient horse who won the Two Thousand Guineas and the Derby, the Champion Stakes and the Washington International.

Of all the other great horses of racing history Man o' War may have resembled the Australian champion Phar Lap most closely. They had the same "red" chestnut colour and were renowned for their great size, splendid limbs and rugged strength—though Man o' War, at 16 hands 2¼ inches and ten hundredweight in hard training, was nearly two inches shorter and 1½ hundredweight lighter than Phar Lap. They were both wonderful athletes with a stride of more than twenty-five feet.

How great a racehorse was Man o' War? The least gracious answer to this fascinating question was given by Frank Gray Griswold, who wrote: "He was hailed the champion racehorse of all times, yet he had not met a really good horse in his two years racing career, for John P. Grier, though a fast horse, could not stay, and when he met Sir Barton the latter was no longer the champion he had been in 1919." Adverse criticism, to stick, must be found in fact. Griswold failed this elementary test, because John P. Grier afterwards won the Annapolis Handicap over 1½ miles, and Sir Barton had won four races off the reel before meeting Man o' War.

Riddle was said to have asked the American Jockey Club Handicapper Walter Vosburgh how much weight Man o' War would have to carry if he remained in training as a four-year-old. Vosburgh replied that he could not answer that question exactly, since the weight would depend on the class of his opponents, but he would certainly assign Man o' War more weight than he had ever set a horse to carry before. That expert view surely confirms "Big Red's" place among the best horses of any age and any country.

Oleander

Oleander was one of the most famous of German thoroughbreds. Moreover he achieved greatness despite a very severe accident as a two-year-old when he fractured his pelvis, an injury that would certainly have terminated the racing career of the vast majority of horses.

Bred by Baron Alfred Oppenheim at the Schlenderhan Stud about ten miles from Cologne, Oleander was by Prunus out of Orchidee II, by the English Triple Crown winner Galtee More. Prunus, also bred at Schlenderhan, was by the English-bred Dark Ronald, winner of the Royal Hunt Cup and Princess of Wales's Stakes and sire of that fine stayer Son-in-Law, out of Pomegranate, by the Derby winner Persimmon. The victories of Prunus included the German Two Thousand Guineas and the German St. Leger. He was leading sire in Germany in 1927, 1928, 1933 and 1934.

Oleander's origin was substantially British as Orchidee II was out of Orseis, by St. Serf out of Orsova, by Bend Or. Galtee More, sire of Orchidee II, had been exported in 1898 to Russia and he proved immensely successful there. After standing there for some years he was sold again and sent to Germany, where on the whole his record was disappointing. Orseis was bred in England by Mr. J. S. Harrison and sold as a yearling in 1898 for 710 guineas. She never saw a racecourse and at the Newmarket December Sales six years later she was sold for 40 guineas and despatched to Germany. It is perhaps worth mentioning that Orsova, grandam of Orchidee II, was a half-sister of Douranee, grandam of Gondolette, one of the Stanley House Stud's foundation mares and in fact one of the most famous mares in the Stud Book. Moreover Orsova's dam Fenella was a half-sister of La Francaise, ancestress of Tenerani, the sire of Ribot.

Orchidee II was no beauty and has been described as having "a long, light neck, high withers, soft loins and a pointed croup. Altogether she was very light and rather tucked up." Nor was her appearance improved by her colour, which was a distinctly un- attractive yellowish chestnut. She never ran as a two-year-old, but at three years of age she was very good indeed and won nine of her eleven races. She won the German Oaks in a canter and the German St. Leger by five lengths in what was then a record time. One of her defeats was curious as despite her outstanding merit, she was required to act as pacemaker for her stable-companion Dolomit who in fact won the race. Like many another filly with a fine record at three years of age, she trained off at four and was unplaced in both her outings.

Orchidee II was not an immediate success as a brood mare but her owner was patient. Furthermore, he had immense confidence in the blood, based on the remarkable success of Austria, a half- sister of Orseis. The Austria family proved extremely successful in Germany, and Austria herself was regarded as the foundation mare of the Schlenderhan Stud. At thirteen years of age Orchidee II had her first success at the stud when she bred Odaliske who won five races herself and was subsequently the dam of Orgelton, winner of both the German Two Thousand Guineas and the German Derby in 1938. Odaliske also produced Octavianus, winner of the German St. Leger in 1939, and Osterblume, dam of the 1948 German Two Thousand Guineas winner, Ostermorgen.

Orchidee II next produced Oleander, foaled in 1924. A good deal more handsome than his dam, Oleander, a bay, showed high pro- mise from his earliest days. As a two-year-old he won his first two races, the Adresse Stakes and the Sierstorpff Stakes, both valuable events at that time, in a canter. He then met with his accident and was thereupon scratched from all his Classic engagements. The 1927 German Derby was in fact won by his stable-companion Mah Jong, another son of Prunus. The going for that event was hock deep and took place during a torrential downpour. The time in conse- quence was the astonishing one of 3 minutes 30 seconds, nearly a full minute over the record.

Veterinary surgeons asserted that Oleander would never be fit to carry out stud duties, let alone to continue his racing career, and they advised that he ought to be put down forthwith. However Oleander's trainer, Arnull, persevered day and night to save Oleander's life, firmly believing that the colt was a potential champion. Thanks almost entirely to Arnull's devotion, Oleander duly recovered. He began by winning a couple of minor events as a three-year-old, but against sterner opposition in the Grosser Preis von Hamburg he could only finish third. However, after winning the Rhein Stakes of a mile, he gave irrefutable proof of his merit by winning the important Fürstenberg-Rennen by the decisive margin of ten lengths. He then won the Grosser Preis von Baden, beating a couple of very useful French horses, and the fourteen furlong Gladiatoren-Rennen.

Oleander started his four-year-old career with a surprise defeat in the Chamant-Rennen but he then won in succession the Jubilee Stakes in Berlin; the mile and three quarter Grosser Preis von Berlin; the St. Simon Stakes; the Grosser Preis von Osterreich; the Grosser Preis von Baden; and the Gladiatoren-Rennen. He finished the season by running fifth behind Kantar in the Prix de l'Arc de Triomphe at Longchamp, the only time in his life that he was unplaced.

At five years of age Oleander was better than ever. He won successively the Chamant-Rennen; the Grosser Preis von Berlin; the St. Simon Stakes; the Grosser Preis von Osterreich (by ten lengths from a strong field of German, Austrian, Hungarian and French horses); and the Grosser Preis von Baden. In winning this last event three times running, he equalled the record of the famous Hungarian mare Kincsem. In the Prix de l'Arc de Triomphe he was third to the good Italian horse Ortello and Kantar. He had no luck in running and his rider Joe Childs was emphatic that he ought to have won, as indeed were most of those who watched the race. Behind Oleander were Palais Royal II, winner of the Cambridgeshire; Vatout, winner of the French Two Thousand Guineas; Ukrania, winner of the French Oaks; Calandria, winner of the French St. Leger; Charlemagne, winner of the Grand Prix de Deauville; and Guy Fawkes, winner of the Prix d'Harcourt. This was Oleander's final race. In twenty-three starts he had won nineteen races and the equivalent of £30,000 in stakes.

Right from the start Oleander did well at the stud. His very first crop included Schwarzliesel, winner of the German One Thousand Guineas and dam of Schwarzgold, one of the greatest of German horses who won the German Derby by no less than ten lengths and the Grosser Preis von Berlin by a distance. Ebro, who won eighteen races, was also in Oleander's first crop.

In Oleander's second crop was Schwarzliesel's brother Sturm-vogel, destined to be killed in an air-raid. He won the German Two Thousand Guineas, the German Derby and twice the Grosser Preis von Berlin. In his first victory in the Grosser Preis he defeated Admiral Drake, winner of the Grand Prix du Paris. Also in this second crop were Dornrose, winner of the German One Thousand Guineas and the German Oaks, and another good filly, Contessina. Thanks to these three brilliant performers, Oleander was champion sire in 1935.

In 1936 Oleander was second on the list. His main winner was Nereide, a splendid filly that won the German One Thousand Guineas, German Oaks, German Derby and the German Brown Ribbon in which she beat M. M. Boussac's famous filly Corrida, by Coronach. Corrida, incidentally, was confiscated by the Germans during the war and was never recovered. In 1937 Oleander headed the list again and remained at the top for eight years, beating the record of the 1877 Two Thousand Guineas winner Chamant, champion sire in Germany in 1885–86–87–90–91–92–97.

Right up to his death, which took place in 1947, Oleander con-tinued to sire good winners, among them Marschall Vorwärts (German St. Leger); Samurai (German St. Leger and Grosser Preis von Baden); Scilla (German Oaks); Orsenigo (Italian Derby and Gran Premio di Milano); Nordlicht (German Derby and Austrian Derby); Espace Vital (Prix du Conseil Municipal, Prix Jean Prat and Prix du Cadran); and Asterios (German Two Thousand Guineas and German St. Leger).

Oleander is best remembered in England as sire of Pink Flower. In 1939 Lord Astor sent the twenty-one-year-old mare Plymstock, dam of the Oaks winner Pennycomequick, to Germany to be covered by Oleander. Plymstock's matings with the French sires Belfonds and Chateau Bouscaut had proved fruitless, but to Oleander she produced a colt foal that was named Pink Flower. Unfortunately Pink Flower was small and weedy, so much so that Lord Astor gave him away to his stud groom, who in due course passed him on to Mr. W. Halford, a Newmarket farmer. Pink Flower persistently refused to grow and Mr. Halford seriously considered sending him to the knacker's yard. However he relented and in January 1942 sent him to the Newmarket Sales where he was sold for a paltry 18 guineas to Mr. J. Russell, who promptly re-sold him to Sir Alec Black. Sir Alec died a few months later and in September there was a dispersal sale of his bloodstock. Pink Flower, who had displayed a certain promise on the racecourse, was bought for 1,050 guineas by Harvey Leader on behalf of his friend Captain Gillson. Before the season was over Pink Flower won three races for Captain Gillson.

The following year Pink Flower nearly provided a superb climax to his remarkable story, as he was only beaten by inches by Kingsway in the Two Thousand Guineas. He was probably unlucky to lose as he was racing alone on the far side of the course and was only headed in the last few strides. Early in 1944 Captain Gillson was killed in action and Pink Flower was bequeathed to Harvey Leader, who retired him to the Brickfields Stud, Newmarket. The best horse Pink Flower sired was Wilwyn who won twenty races for his breeder, Mr. R. C. Boucher, among them the Washington International at Laurel Park. Wilwyn is the only English-trained horse that has won that race so far.

It only remains to add in conclusion that on racial grounds the Schlenderhan Stud was confiscated during the Hitler regime by the S.S. and the Oppenheim family did not manage to get their horses back until 1947.

Phar Lap

Contemporary writers referred to Phar Lap as a "phenomenal racing machine", and this seems an entirely fair description of the towering, inelegant and immensely powerful chestnut gelding who dominated Australian racing for three seasons in 1929 and the early nineteen-thirties and finally earned an international reputation by winning in America. If he was not one of the most beautiful specimens of the thoroughbred, he was certainly one of the most efficient, and his magnificent performances raised him to the status of an Australian national hero. When he died of poisoning at Menlo Park in California shortly after his record-breaking victory in the Agua Caliente Handicap at Tanforan his death was mourned as an Australian national calamity only partially relieved by pride in his achievement. His total stakes earnings, including his American prize money at the existing rate of exchange, amounted to more than £66,000 and made him, at the time, the highest stakes earner ever bred in the British Empire, eclipsing the long-standing record of £57,450 held by Isinglass.

Like many outstanding horses who have raced in Australia, Phar Lap was New Zealand bred. He was raised at Timaru, in the northern part of the South Island, where the soil is rich in limestone and must have helped to build the wonderful bone, soundness and constitution needed to see such a big, heavy horse through an arduous programme. His name, the Sinhalese for lightning, was prophetic, though his pedigree was suggestive of out-and-out stamina rather than the combination of speed and staying power that Phar Lap possessed to a remarkable degree. He was by Night Raid, a horse of the most modest class in both England and Australia but a son of the high-class stayer Radium, winner of the Goodwood and Doncaster Cups. Entreaty, the dam of Phar Lap, was by Winkie, a horse by the Ascot Gold Cup winner William The Third out of Lord Astor's celebrated foundation mare Conjure. Although Winkie achieved no distinction on the racecourse, he was a brother of Winkipop, winner of the One Thousand Guineas, and Pilliwinkie, winner of the King Edward VII Stakes at Royal Ascot. Night Raid was not highly esteemed when he went to stud, but became one of the most fashionable sires in New Zealand after he had sired Night March in his first crop and Phar Lap in his second.

H. R. Telford, who trained in New Zealand and at Melbourne and Sydney at various times, noticed Phar Lap in the catalogue of the New Zealand yearling sales, liked his breeding, and persuaded Mr. D. Davis to buy him for 160 guineas. He then secured a three-year lease of the horse, with the arrangement that he should pay all the training expenses and retain a third of any money Phar Lap won. Telford was what was known as a "battling trainer", a term which was not defamatory but denoted a trainer who had to struggle against adversity with a small string of second-class horses and slender financial resources. In the case of Telford, the marvellous and sustained success of Phar Lap alleviated the severity of the struggle in dramatic fashion.

As was to be expected with such a big horse, Phar Lap was backward in his early days and took some time to reveal any real ability. He was unplaced in his first four races and it was only on his final appearance as a two-year-old on April 27th, 1929, that he came to the fore with a victory in the Rosehill Maiden Juvenile Handicap over six furlongs. Nor did he exactly carry all before him in the early part of his three-year-old season, and again he was unplaced in his first four races. The first indication that he was developing into something out of the ordinary was his performance in the Chelmsford Stakes at the Sydney course of Randwick in mid-September. The distance of $1\frac{1}{4}$ miles was the longest that Phar Lap had yet run, but even so the poor early pace was all in favour of the four-year-old Mollison, a horse of great speed who had accumulated a record sum in stakes as a two-year-old. Mollison looked like winning easily soon after entering the straight, but then Phar Lap came on the scene, making rapid progress with his long stride on the outside of the field, and Mollison had to be hard ridden to hold him off by half a length.

Phar Lap had been gelded because he was so big and had looked likely to take a long time to mature. Fortunately geldings were eligible for the Australian Classic races in those days, and, after his promising display against Mollison, Phar Lap lost no time in snapping up the Rosehill Guineas and the A.J.C. Derby, a double which had proved elusive to many good horses in the past. He was set a searching test in the Derby, as Queen Nassau went off at a tremendous gallop and was fifteen lengths in front at half way. In the second half Jim Pike, known as "The Master", steadily reduced the gap on Phar Lap, and took the lead more than a quarter of a mile from the finish to win easily.

Telford had caused some consternation before the Derby by announcing that Phar Lap would in no circumstances run in the Melbourne Cup as he was still too immature to be subjected to such a severe race. Many people, including the horse's owner, had backed Phar Lap before the announcement, and doubtless they regretted in the end that Telford did not abide by his decision. When it came to the point the lure of the Cup's £10,000 prize was too strong, and in the meantime Phar Lap had given two more superb performances. Four days after the A.J.C. Derby he decisively turned the tables on his former conqueror Mollison in the Craven Plate, a weight-for-age race over 1¼ miles, and then travelled to Melbourne to land the odds of 9–2 laid on him in the Victoria Derby. He had won his two Derbys in the identical time of 2 minutes 31¼ seconds, setting up a new world record in each case.

Phar Lap started at evens in the Melbourne Cup, but events conspired against him. The field of fourteen was the smallest for sixty years, and none of the jockeys wanted to make the running. Pike could not do the weight and Lewis, who deputised on Phar Lap, was unable to prevent the hard pulling gelding taking the lead. Accepting the inevitable, Lewis tried to ride a waiting race in front. He kicked on and tried to make the best of his way home three-quarters of a mile from the finish, but he could not get away from his field. Night March went past him in the straight to win easily, and in the closing stages Phar Lap had to yield second place to Paquito.

Phar Lap was temporarily dismissed as a non-stayer, but his performances in the autumn completely falsified that impression. This was the period in which he established his greatness beyond the possibility of doubt. He won his last nine races of the season. They included the Victoria and A.J.C. St. Legers, but his most overwhelming victory of all was in the A.J.C. Plate over 2¼ miles at

Randwick on April 26th. This race was the occasion of his second encounter with Night March, and he turned his four lengths defeat by that horse in the Melbourne Cup into a ten lengths victory. Some onlookers thought that the official verdict underestimated Phar Lap's superiority, and claimed that his true winning margin was more like a furlong. Other aspects of his performance provide the most eloquent testimony to his supreme merit. He made all the running and galloped his rivals practically to a standstill, covering the first six furlongs in 1 minute 12¾ seconds, a good time for a sprinter, and the first 1½ miles in 2 minutes 29¼ seconds, which was faster than any race time recorded for that distance in Australia up to that date. His time of 3 minutes 49½ seconds for the whole race has less significance because he was so far in front with a quarter of a mile still to go that Pike began to pull him up and he merely cantered past the post.

Although his performance in the A.J.C. Plate was his most spectacular, Phar Lap slammed his opponents in such uncompromising fashion in race after race in the second half of his three-year-old season that he was nicknamed "The Red Terror". With his bright chestnut colour, tremendous size and strength and exceptionally long stride he was a formidable sight in action. He always wore bandages on his forelegs, but these were purely precautionary, and he never had a moment's unsoundness in his life.

Phar Lap lived up to his reputation as a four-year-old. His only defeats in sixteen races were on his first and last appearances, when he was second, beaten by a short head and a neck respectively. There was a scare before the Melbourne Stakes on November 1st, when he was alleged to have been shot at from the window of a car as he returned from morning exercise. The car then drove off at speed. Miraculously, as the shot was said to have been fired at point blank range, the horse was not hit by a single pellet. Some time later the incident was exposed as a hoax devised by a group of enterprising if unscrupulous journalists bent on fabricating a news story. The unharmed Phar Lap duly won the Melbourne Stakes as a preliminary to his major engagement in the two miles Melbourne Cup three days later. Phar Lap had been allotted 9 st. 12 lb. in the big race, admittedly 7 lb. less than the mighty Carbine had carried to victory forty years earlier, but all the same a heavy burden indeed to carry in Australia's most coveted race. Yet such was the confidence in Phar Lap's supreme ability that he started at 11-8 on and was the hottest favourite in the history of the race. Nor was this confidence misplaced. Although Phar Lap pulled hard for his head when the pace was poor again in the early stages, Pike soon got him settled in a good position just behind the leaders. In the straight he asserted himself without difficulty and drew away to win with complete authority.

Telford had turned down several offers for the remainder of the lease during the last few weeks before the Melbourne Cup. Shortly before the lease expired three months later, in February 1931, he was able to buy a share in the horse, and Phar Lap raced as the joint property of Davis and Telford for the rest of 1930–31 and during the following season. He continued to pile up success upon success after the new season opened in August 1931, and had eight more victories to his credit by the time he went out to try and win his second Melbourne Cup on November 3rd. The handicapper had taken few chances by setting him to carry 10 st. 10 lb. and he would have had to be a horse and a half to have won under such a weight. White Nose, receiving only 2 lb. less than 4 st. from Phar Lap, was in the first two the whole way, and shook off one opponent after another in the closing stages to win by two lengths from Shadow King, who had been third to Phar Lap the previous year. Phar Lap finished no nearer than eighth. Nevertheless he was certainly not disgraced. He had been close to the leaders and going well at the turn into the straight, but soon after the turn the weight began to tell and it became obvious that he would not win. Wisely Pike did not persevere or give him a hard race when he was beaten.

Davis had been on a visit to America before the Melbourne Cup, and while there had made arrangements for Phar Lap to run in the Agua Caliente Handicap the following March. Accordingly Phar Lap was shipped to California in January to complete his preparation. As there was restrictive betting legislation in the state of California, the race was run at Tanforan just over the Mexican border. Although he was carrying 9 st. 3 lb. and giving from 9 to 39 lb., to his opponents, Phar Lap was made a 3–2 favourite. Ridden by Urn Elliott, he opened up a lead of several lengths soon after the start, but took things easily coming round the final bend with the result that Reveille Boy crept up to his head. With a furlong to run Elliott shook him up and he strode away to win the ten furlongs race decisively in 2 minutes 2$\frac{4}{5}$ seconds, a course record.

Phar Lap got an enthusiastic reception. There were tentative plans that he should go on to run in Chicago and other parts of the United States, and in the meantime he retired to Menlo Park for a rest. Then came the news that shocked the racing publics of Australia and the United States. Phar Lap was dead. He had been turned out in a field and, it is supposed, ate some plants that had been sprayed with poison.

Phar Lap's heart was sent back to Sydney University Medical School for examination. Dr. Stewart McKay, who performed the autopsy with two other professors of the University, found that the valves of the heart were sound, but on opening the pericardium discovered the whole of the left side of the heart covered with blood. McKay wrote, in his book *The Staying Power of the Racehorse*, that he had read of some instances where similar conditions were found on the hearts of human beings who had died of arsenical poisoning. The mystery of Phar Lap's death was never solved.

McKay recorded that Phar Lap's heart weighed 14½ lb. and that the walls of the left ventricle were 4.3 centimetres thick, whereas the corresponding figures for another good racehorse examined were 10 lb. and 2.5 centimetres. He concluded: "Phar Lap's heart during his racing life had possessed the power to pump blood in a way that made him a horse that could practically execute any task with such consummate ease, and at such a high rate of speed, and over any distance, that he demonstrated time after time that he had reached the very highest degree of staying power ever likely to be reached by any racer."

Perhaps the unbeaten Hurry On was the English horse that resembled Phar Lap most closely. Like Phar Lap, Hurry On was a great stayer, winning the substitute St. Leger, the Newmarket St. Leger and the Jockey Club Cup in 1916. Like Phar Lap, Hurry On was a chestnut horse of tremendous size and power, if somewhat ungainly appearance. They were both seventeen hands tall, and Hurry On measured 82½ inches and Phar Lap about 79 inches at the girth. But in one respect there was a world of difference between them. Hurry On ran only at three years of age and took part in no more than six races; Phar Lap ran in fifty races from two to five years of age and won thirty-six of them. The soundness and constitution of Phar Lap were as admirable as his racing class.

Phar Lap had one other great asset, and that was his charming temperament. There has never been a kinder horse. He used to stick his tongue out of the side of his mouth for his trainer to pull in a manner that was also characteristic of another fine stayer of a quarter of a century later, the French horse Vieux Manoir. Phar Lap was indeed a horse of whom Australia and New Zealand could be proud.

Plate 9   Sceptre

Plate 10   Pretty Polly

Plate 11 Lutteur III

Plate 12 Bayardo

Plate 13   The Tetrarch

Plate 14   Man o' War

Plate 15   Oleander

Plate 16   Phar Lap

Golden Miller

Comparisons between steeplechasers of today and those of thirty years ago are not rendered any easier by the fact that National Hunt racing has undergone a considerable change. In 1930 there were only five steeplechases during the entire season worth as much as £1,000 to the winner. These were the Grand National, the Champion Chase and the Grand Sefton Chase, all run at Aintree; the Lancashire Chase at Manchester and the National Hunt Steeplechase at Cheltenham. The Cheltenham Gold Cup earned the winner less than £700. Sponsored races were unknown and with the general level of prize money so low, the best chasers usually took their chance at Aintree, a far stiffer course then than it is now.

Nowadays thousand pound races are a commonplace and £5,000 chases by no means unusual. The Gold Cup in 1967 was worth £7,999 to Woodland Venture and only three events at the big Cheltenham meeting were less than £1,000 to the winner. Arkle has won a fortune in stakes for his owner without the necessity of racing at Aintree, a course still regarded as the supreme test of a chaser. Golden Miller, the great chaser of the nineteen thirties, was defeated far more often than Arkle, the champion of the nineteen sixties, but his career was beyond argument a more exacting one.

Officially, the credit for breeding Golden Miller goes to Mr. Julius Solomon, a Dublin businessman. In 1914 Mr. Solomon decided he would like to buy a mare and for £100 bought Miller's Pride from Mr. James Nugent. Miller's Pride was actually selected by Mr. Solomon's chauffeur. Mr. Solomon, who knew nothing about bloodstock, remained snugly inside his limousine, while the chauffeur picked the mare out in a field.

Mr. Solomon sent Miller's Pride to board with Mr. Laurence

Geraghty in Co. Meath. Mr. Geraghty arranged for her to be covered but she proved barren. The intensification of the war reduced the demand for bloodstock and Mr. Solomon lost interest in his mare. However Mr. Geraghty treated her as if she was his own and bred several foals from her, one of which, May Crescent, was mildly fancied for the 1930 Grand National. In 1926 Miller's Pride was covered by Goldcourt, a five guinea sire owned by Mr. P. Byrne of Maynooth. The resultant foal, subsequently named Golden Miller, was a good one and when sold the following year to Mr. P. Quinn of Tipperary, realized 100 guineas, a good price at that time for a "store" yearling. Mr. Geraghty appeared in the Ballsbridge catalogue as the vendor of Golden Miller and Mr. Solomon seemed to have vanished from the scene completely. However, when Golden Miller began to win races, Mr. Solomon decided he might at least secure a share in the prestige, and with some difficulty he succeeded in getting himself recognized in the General Stud Book as Golden Miller's breeder. The true credit of course remained with Mr. Geraghty.

Golden Miller's half-brother, May Crescent, had been bought in Ireland early in his career by a certain Captain Farmer acting on behalf of a young man called Basil Briscoe. Briscoe hunted May Crescent, won races on him and only sold him because of a suspicion that the horse had developed a weak heart. A highly-strung man of considerable charm and immense generosity, Briscoe loved hunting and racing and thoroughly enjoyed a tilt at the bookmakers. After education at Eton and Cambridge he worked for two years in an estate office, but his heart had always been in racing, so at the end of that period he took out a trainer's licence and set up a stable at Maddingley, near Cambridge. He soon showed he had a flair for his new profession and as the number of horses under his care began to increase, he moved his stable to the family home of Longstowe in Cambridgeshire.

In March 1930 Briscoe received a telegram from Captain Farmer offering him Golden Miller, then an unbroken three-year-old, for £500. Remembering how well May Crescent had served him, Briscoe took up the offer and bought Golden Miller "blind".

Briscoe and his head lad were both singularly unimpressed with Golden Miller when he arrived at Longstowe. His condition was poor and he seemed listless and lacking in spirit. He gave no trouble at all when he was broken but when put into training he worked so badly that it looked long odds against him winning a race of even the humblest description.

His first racecourse appearance was on September 1st, 1930 in a hurdle race at Southwell. He finished well down the course and never for a single stride displayed a hint of promise. Briscoe then thought a few days' hunting might improve what seemed likely to turn out an expensive purchase, so he took Golden Miller out with the Fitzwilliam. This experiment was not a success. Golden Miller rooted his fences and did not appear to have sufficient speed to keep in touch with hounds. To make matters worse, he lamed himself and a vet diagnosed a sprung tendon.

The picture was indeed a gloomy one but at least Golden Miller was improving in appearance and developing a livelier disposition. One of Briscoe's patrons, Mr. Philip Carr, father of the England cricket captain, Mr. A. W. Carr, took a liking to the horse and decided to buy him. Briscoe made no secret of his modest opinion of Golden Miller's capabilities nor of the veterinary diagnosis, but Mr. Carr was not to be put off and the sale took place, the price being £1,000.

The tendon trouble cleared up much sooner than had been anticipated and on November 29th Golden Miller was one of twenty-one competitors for the Moderate Handicap Hurdle at Newbury. Ridden by Bob Lyall and starting at 100–6, he ran a most promising race to finish third behind Black Armstrong, the mount of Mr. "Ginger" Whitfield, an extremely good amateur rider who was killed by a bad fall not long afterwards. Lyall was enthusiastic about the way Golden Miller had run and for the first time it really looked as if Golden Miller was going to make a very useful horse.

In January Golden Miller won two modest events over hurdles, one at Leicester, the other at Nottingham. After these successes Briscoe schooled him over fences and the four-year-old showed himself to be beyond doubt a brilliant natural jumper. On February 21st Golden Miller lined up for the two mile Spring Chase at Newbury, ridden for the first time by Gerry Wilson who was subsequently to be his partner both in triumph and disaster. In the straight Golden Miller and the favourite, Rolie, a ten-year-old ridden by the lionhearted Billy Stott, drew clear of the remainder and in a terrific struggle from the last fence Rolie just mastered his far younger rival, who was receiving 16 lb., to win by a head. It was generally agreed that Golden Miller had put up a fine performance and had a big future ahead of him. He did not run again that season.

Not long afterwards Mr. Carr became gravely ill and gave instructions for his horse to be sold. At this period Miss Dorothy Paget, with immense financial resources upon which she could call, was just becoming one of the leading personalities in National Hunt racing. She bought Golden Miller for £6,000 and she also bought another of Mr. Carr's horses, Insurance, who was destined to win the Champion Hurdle twice. Both Golden Miller and Insurance remained with Briscoe.

The second daughter of Lord Queensborough, Miss Dorothy Paget was a self-willed and eccentric individual, her eccentricity being supposedly due to the fact that she was morbidly shy and determined to avoid all human contact whenever possible with the exception of her small, devoted and exclusively female entourage. Her appearance was both distinctive and unprepossessing. Stout and ungainly, she had a large, round, pallid, rather sullen face framed in dark, straight hair that owed nothing to the art of the coiffeur. Her habitual uniform on the racecourse consisted of a blue felt hat that made no concession to current fashion, and a long shapeless grey coat. Her memory was retentive, at times disconcertingly so, and her knowledge of bloodstock breeding sound. Though not in the slightest need of money, she got a kick out of punting in very large sums indeed. The few people who knew her at all well tended to like her, but she was notoriously tricky to work for and her career on the Turf was punctuated by sudden, and occasionally painful, breaches with those who served her. Firmness, combined with tact, was needed to keep her sweet. She soon became a legend in the racing world which circulated a stream of stories about her curious life as a recluse in her house at Chalfont St. Giles; her voracious appetite and the fantastic amount she was alleged to consume in the Pullman Car on the return journey, for example, from Lingfield; the unconventional hours that she kept and her interminable conferences with her trainer and her team of secretaries, often held in a racecourse restaurant long after all other racegoers had left for home. Though frequently the subject of censure and disparagement, she was in the end regarded with something approaching affection and she was certainly very much missed when she died in 1960 at the comparatively early age of fifty-four.

Golden Miller was not hurried into the top class the following season and when he reappeared in October it was in the Witham

Hurdle, worth £63 to the winner, at Chelmsford, a curious little track, the perimeter of which enclosed a church. Ridden by Stott, he started at 11–4 on and won by ten lengths. He was then third in a handicap hurdle at Sandown and third in an amateur riders' hurdle at Manchester, his partner on this second occasion being Mr. Robin Mount, a good horseman and also a poet. His first outing of the winter over fences was in a two mile novices chase at Newbury early in December. Starting at 11–10 and ridden by Ted Leader, he duly won but unfortunately Briscoe had misread the conditions and Golden Miller carried the wrong weight. He was disqualified and the race was awarded to Forbra who won the Grand National the following year. At the next Newbury meeting Golden Miller won the two mile Reading Chase, again ridden by Leader and beating some good young chasers including Kellsboro' Jack who won the 1933 Grand National and was never defeated at Aintree.

In the two mile Sefton Chase at Newbury in January, Golden Miller was a hot favourite but failed by two lengths to concede 5 lb. to a very useful eight-year-old, Parsons Well. Later in the month he met Parsons Well again, this time over three miles of the stiff Gatwick course. Golden Miller won by a distance from Parsons Well who fell and was then re-mounted.

Although Golden Miller was only five years of age and just emerging from the novice class, it was decided to let him take his chance in the Gold Cup at Cheltenham. As a matter of fact Briscoe was not keen to run him as the going was very firm and Golden Miller was at his best when there was plenty of give in the ground. That year the Cheltenham fences were extremely severe. Just before the meeting began, they were viewed by the Inspector of Courses, and as a result of his critical observations, six inches was taken off the top of each obstacle with the obvious result that the tops were much stiffer than was usually the case. During the meeting no fewer than fifty-six horses fell in the steeplechases and one rider was killed.

There were six runners for the Cup. Grakle, ridden by Jack Fawcus, at that time an amateur, was favourite at 11–10 on. Second favourite was the hard-pulling Kingsford at 3–1 and Golden Miller, ridden by Leader, was on offer at 13–2. Luck on this occasion was clearly on Golden Miller's side. At the fence after the water Aruntius made a horrible mistake. The impetuous Kingsford was unsighted, fell heavily and received fatal injuries. Grakle swerved sharply on landing to avoid Kingsford and in so doing unseated

Fawcus. Golden Miller from that point only had to stand up to win, and although he made a couple of minor errors he never looked like coming down, winning comfortably from Inverse and Aruntius. In the whole of his career Golden Miller never fell on a park course.

Golden Miller's only other outing that season was in the Lancashire Chase at Manchester on Easter Monday. Ridden by Leader and carrying 11 st. 10 lb., he started favourite, but never looked like catching Huic Holloa who won with the utmost ease by twenty lengths. Golden Miller finished fifth of the eight runners to complete the course.

The following season it was planned to bring off with Golden Miller the double, never previously achieved, of the Gold Cup and the Grand National. He had been given a long summer rest, during which time Briscoe moved his stable from Longstowe to Beechwood, near Newmarket, and he did not appear on a racecourse till December when he won over two and a half miles at Kempton. He then won three races in succession over three miles. He was impressive when carrying 12 st. 7 lb. to victory in the Mitre Chase at Hurst Park, even more so when winning the Troytown Chase at Lingfield, a race of considerable significance in those days and worth £600 to the winner. Carrying 12 st. 10 lb. on yielding ground, he gave Stott a wonderful ride to win by a length from Buck Willow who was receiving 31 lb. This was a magnificent performance and silenced those critics who had reckoned him an overrated horse, whose Gold Cup victory had frankly been a hollow one. From then onwards Golden Miller was a tremendous favourite with the racing public, and despite the subsequent vicissitudes of his career, retained that popularity till the day of his retirement.

The going was soft at Cheltenham on Gold Cup day. Golden Miller, partnered by Stott, was a hot favourite at 7–4 on, the only horse seriously backed to beat him being Mr. J. H. Whitney's gallant little chestnut Thomond II. Thomond II held a slight advantage at the last open ditch but soon afterwards he was headed by the favourite who drew clear up the hill to win as he pleased by ten lengths, an impressive and popular victory. Delaneige, a fine Aintree horse, was third, five lengths behind Thomond II, while among the unplaced contingent was Kellsboro' Jack, who later that month won the Grand National.

A big, powerfully-built, beautifully-proportioned bay with a bold, intelligent head, Golden Miller was ideally suited to Cheltenham with its stiff uphill finish. He really did stay, and though his rider often had to niggle at him in the early stages of a race, Golden Miller's long, raking stride was always liable to crush his opponents in the final mile. He was an economic jumper who skimmed over his fences with the minimum of fuss and if he did make a mistake, he was too strong and too well-balanced to come down. He jumped, in fact, off his forehand and though this practice was perfectly in order on park courses, it was hardly suitable for Aintree. He never really liked those big drop fences at Aintree, where it was his class and his courage that saw him through when he triumphed in the Grand National.

As a six-year-old carrying 12 st. 2 lb., Golden Miller had a formidable task in the National, but public faith in him was such that he started favourite at 9–1. Coming to Becher's second time round he was ideally placed but made a bad mistake there. Although he recovered cleverly, his confidence was shaken and he fell heavily at the Canal Turn. Kellsboro' Jack, carrying 11 st. 9 lb., jumped brilliantly and won in what was then the record time of 9 minutes 28 seconds. He was only a seven-year-old and might well have won the race more than once, but his owner, Mrs. F. Ambrose Clark, firmly declined to run him in it again.

Stott, a tough, brave and accomplished rider, was replaced on Golden Miller in the Grand National by Ted Leader, the excuse given for this rather shabby treatment being that Stott was too short in the leg to be suited to Aintree. The public resented the change and both Miss Paget and her trainer were severely criticized. Stott rode the gigantic Pelorus Jack who was level with Kellsboro' Jack when he crashed at the very last fence.

The following season Gerry Wilson, a fine horseman well schooled in the hunting-field and a most determined rider on any horse, good or indifferent, was Golden Miller's partner. Golden Miller started off by winning at Lingfield, but over two and a half miles on the rather sharp Kempton course he was beaten by Thomond II, who was receiving 7 lb. In the Star and Garter Chase at Hurst Park in January Golden Miller finished behind the nine-year-old Southern Hero, but it was no disgrace to fail to give 28 lb. to this admirable park-course chaser who won the Scottish Grand National for the third time when in his fifteenth year and carrying 12 st. 3 lb.

In the Gold Cup, in which Thomond II did not run, Golden

Miller started favourite at 6–5 on, the second favourite being Mr. E. Robson's El Hadjar, recently imported from France. The crucial point in the race came when El Hadjar moved up to challenge three fences from home. Unfortunately he met that fence all wrong and came down. Kellsboro' Jack headed Golden Miller for a few strides afterwards, but Golden Miller soon mastered him up the hill and went on to win by six lengths from a very good five-year-old, Avenger, destined to be killed in the National the following year. Kellsboro' Jack was a further six lengths away third.

Really True, ridden by Mr. Frank Furlong who won the race the following year on Reynoldstown, was favourite for the Grand National at 7–1, Golden Miller being second favourite at 8–1. Carrying the stiff burden of 12 st. 2 lb., Golden Miller put up what was undoubtedly the finest performance of his career to win by five lengths, beating the record time established the previous year by Kellsboro' Jack by nearly eight seconds. Two high-class chasers, Delaneige (11st. 6 lb.) and Thomond II (12 st. 4 lb.) were second and third, while the 1932 winner Forbra (11 st. 7 lb.) was fourth. Really True was up with the leaders and going remarkably well when he came down on the second circuit at the fence after Valentine's.

Delaneige, jumping superbly, made most of the running and at the last open ditch he held a slight lead of Golden Miller, Forbra and Thomond II. Delaneige landed first over the last but in the long run-in, Golden Miller's great stride soon settled the issue and he drew clear to win with ease. It is arguable that this particular performance on the part of Golden Miller was superior to any single performance on the part of Arkle. No horse has succeeded in bringing off the Gold Cup–Grand National double since.

The following season it was decided to try and bring off the double again. Golden Miller did not appear till December when, ridden by Baxter, who was attached to Briscoe's stable, he won at Wolverhampton. He then won three more races and was seen at his brilliant best in the Prince of Wales's Chase run over three miles and five furlongs at Sandown. Carrying 12 st. 7 lb. he stormed up the hill to victory, giving 18 lb. to Really True and 14 lb. to Delaneige, who had both been second in the National.

It looked as if Golden Miller's task in his fourth Gold Cup was going to be comparatively simple as Thomond II was scheduled to run in the two mile Coventry Cup. At the eleventh hour, though, Mr.

Whitney changed his mind and decided to take on Golden Miller. Briscoe was naturally perturbed as he did not want Golden Miller to have a hard race so close to Aintree. He did his utmost to get Mr. Whitney to change his mind but his pleas were of no avail.

It is generally conceded that the 1935 Gold Cup was one of the finest steeplechases ever run. Golden Miller, ridden by Wilson, was favourite at 2–1 on, while Thomond, ridden by Speck, was on offer at 5–2. The pace was a cracker from the start and as the field turned for home Golden Miller and Thomond were the only two left with a chance. Wilson was riding Golden Miller for all he was worth, and coming down the hill, Thomond was undoubtedly going the easier of the two. As soon as they met the rising ground, though, Golden Miller's tremendous stride began to tell and approaching the last he led by half a length.

Speck was a very short man, but broad-shouldered and strong. He sat down and rode Thomond into the last for all he was worth and Thomond, responding bravely, landed level. Amids roars of encouragement from the partisans of these two good and gallant horses, a gruelling battle ensued in the uphill run-in. Gradually Golden Miller wore down his smaller opponent and passed the post three parts of a length to the good. Kellsboro' Jack was five lengths away third. It was the hardest race Golden Miller had ever had. The going was firmer than he liked and Briscoe, thinking Golden Miller's task would be an easy one, had left a little bit to work on before the National. There is no doubt that the race left its mark on Golden Miller and his star never shone quite so brightly again.

Golden Miller had 12 st. 7 lb. to carry in the Grand National, but despite that the public backed him as if defeat was out of the question and he started at the ludicrous price of 2–1. Alas, the public had a poor run for their money. At the fence after Valentine's Golden Miller screwed badly to the left as he took off. He landed awkwardly and unseated Wilson. Only those with good binoculars and hawk-like vision could pick out this incident from the stands, and when the field streamed on to the racecourse proper without Golden Miller, ninety per cent of those present—there was of course no commentary in those days—had no idea what had happened to the favourite. The race was won by Reynoldstown from Blue Prince and the stouthearted Thomond II.

After the race Golden Miller was examined by a veterinary surgeon who found nothing amiss. It was thereupon decided to start him in the Champion Chase the following day. It proved an unfortunate decision as Golden Miller made a nonsense of the very first fence, and though he did not actually fall, he parted company with Wilson. As the horse was led back to the paddock, a storm of ugly booing arose from the stands.

The following week the racing world was flooded with rumours, mostly scandalous, nearly all improbable, about Golden Miller, his owner, his trainer, and above all about his rider. Undeniably Miss Paget and Wilson were at loggerheads with Briscoe. The upshot was that Golden Miller and six other jumpers belonging to Miss Paget left Briscoe's stable for that of Donald Snow at Briscoe's insistence. The following August Golden Miller was sent to be trained by Owen Anthony, who looked after him for the rest of his racing career.

The bookmakers stood to lose a fortune if Golden Miller won the Grand National, but there has never been a shred of evidence that anything illegal took place. Probably Golden Miller had not fully recovered from his very hard race at Cheltenham when not one hundred per cent at his best. Certainly, despite his victory the year before, he never relished those big black Aintree fences.

The row over Golden Miller, coupled with the death of his young wife, hit Briscoe very hard indeed. He moved his stable to Royston where he trained the Cambridgeshire winner Commander III but he gave up completely soon after the outbreak of war. His racing friends had not set eyes on him for years when he died in 1951.

Golden Miller began the next season by running third in one of those dreary and now fortunately defunct events, a National Hunt flat-race. This one took place at Sandown in December and Golden Miller was ridden by Mr. Hector Gordon. Later that month Golden Miller put up one of his most scintillating performances in winning a two mile handicap chase at Newbury with 12 st. 10 lb. It looked as if he had forgotten his troubles at Aintree, but in a three mile chase at Newbury in February he was never going kindly and ran out five fences from home. After the race Wilson made it quite clear that he wished to be relieved of the responsibility of riding Golden Miller in the future and Evan Williams was chosen to ride Golden Miller in the Gold Cup. A young Welshman whose father acted as starter at various meetings, Williams had ridden with success as an amateur before turning professional. It is interesting to compare the long partnership between Arkle and Pat Taaffe with the fact that Golden

Miller was ridden under National Hunt rules by G. Wilson, W. Stott, T. Leader, R. Lyall, J. Baxter, T. James, E. Williams, D. Morgan, H. Nicholson, F. Walwyn, A. Scratchley, G. Archibald, Mr. R. Mount and Mr. J. H. Gordon.

With Thomond II an absentee, Golden Miller's task in the Gold Cup looked easier than in the previous years, but after his antics at Aintree and Newbury public faith in him had declined and he started at 21–20 on. He looked superb in the paddock and he ran one of his most masterful races, winning unchallenged by twelve lengths from Royal Mail, who won the Grand National the following year, with his old rival Kellsboro' Jack two lengths away third. It was his fifth successive Gold Cup victory, a record that may never be equalled, and the huge crowd gave him a hero's welcome when he walked into the unsaddling enclosure.

Most unwisely, Golden Miller was sent up to Aintree again for the Grand National. He was knocked over at the very first fence. Williams remounted him but Golden Miller was hopelessly tailed off and stuck his toes in at the fence after Valentine's.

There was no Gold Cup in 1937 because of the weather or Golden Miller might well have won it six years running. In the Grand National he was ridden by Danny Morgan, one of the best riders that failed to win the big Aintree event. Golden Miller jumped the early fences impeccably, but approaching that fatal fence after Valentine's, Morgan sensed he was in for trouble. He was right, too. Golden Miller ducked out to the left and when put to the fence again, he refused. That was his final appearance at Aintree.

The 1937–38 season ws Golden Miller's last. He was in his twelfth year and perceptibly slipping downhill. He won two of his four races before Cheltenham, but he was twice beaten by a good young horse called Macaulay, the second time at level weights. In the Gold Cup he was ridden by "Frenchy" Nicholson, a very strong and extremely determined rider. Favourite at 7–4 with Macaulay second favourite at 3–1, Golden Miller gave everything he had, but it was not quite enough and he was beaten two lengths by the younger and speedier Morse Code. At the last fence Golden Miller landed half a length behind Morse Code, but the old horse would not give in and under extreme pressure he managed to draw level. Morse Code, though, still had something in reserve and in the final hundred yards was able to shake off his gallant opponent. A little sentiment is not out of place in racing and it is pleasant to record that when Golden Miller was being unsaddled, the crowd cheered him again and again, just as if he had won.

That was Golden Miller's final race. He had run fifty-five times, three times under Jockey Club rules, and had won twenty-nine races. He earned £15,000 in prize money, a meagre total by modern standards, but the Gold Cup today is worth more than Golden Miller's five victories put together. He had captured the imagination and affection of the public and there is no doubt that he and his brilliant predecessor, Easter Hero, who won two Gold Cups by twenty lengths and was second in the Grand National in a field of sixty-six under 12 st. 7 lb., did much to raise the status of National Hunt racing and to increase public interest in the sport.

Reynoldstown

So far only six horses have won the Grand National twice. These are Abd-el-Kader (1850 and 1851); The Lamb (1868 and 1871); The Colonel (1869 and 1870); Manifesto (1897 and 1899); Poethlyn (1918 and 1919); and Reynoldstown (1935 and 1936). Poethlyn hardly comes into the same category as the others as his first victory was in a war-substitute Grand National run at Gatwick.

Reynoldstown was bred by Mr. Richard Ball at Reynoldstown, Naul, Co. Dublin. There were in fact at the time two Richard Balls, father and son, living at Reynoldstown and acting in unison with regard to farming and bloodstock. Reynoldstown's dam actually belonged to Mr. Ball senior, but neither father nor son ever claimed to the exclusion of the other the honour of having bred Reynoldstown. Mr. Ball junior subsequently bred the great Irish horse Ballymoss, whose many victories included the St. Leger and the Prix de l'Arc de Triomphe.

Foaled in 1927, Reynoldstown was by My Prince, by Marcovil, out of Fromage, by Frontino whose sire St. Frusquin had won the Two Thousand Guineas. My Prince was an outstanding sire of jumpers and his winners included Easter Hero, twice winner of the Cheltenham Gold Cup by twenty lengths; Gregalach who beat Easter Hero in the Grand National of 1929; and Royal Mail, winner of the Grand National in 1937. In 1915 Lord St. Davids, who then owned My Prince, sent all his bloodstock up to Newmarket to be sold. No one seemed to want My Prince, a handsome four-year-old with quite a good racing record, and he was withdrawn at 95 guineas. His reserve had been only 100 guineas and for that price the British Bloodstock Agency purchased him before he left the sale paddocks. Six weeks later he was bought for £200 by the Irish Board of Agriculture and sent to stand at Lusk, not far from Dublin.

Homage, dam of Fromage, was by a horse called Hominy that won the Irish Grand Military Steeplechase as a four-year-old. Homage won a point-to-point and was placed in a farmers' race at Fairyhouse. At the stud she produced seven foals of which Fromage was the sixth. Fromage herself never raced. Her first four foals were all fillies. Three of them won point-to-points and one of the three, Kate Brandon, was winning the National Hunt Chase at Cheltenham when she broke down close to home. Her fifth foal was Reynoldstown.

Reynoldstown was broken in the spring when he was three years of age and a year later he was shown hounds for the first time. Mr. Ball junior then hunted him for a season in Meath before schooling him over made-up fences. The Balls had always held a high opinion of Reynoldstown and with a view to finding a buyer, Mr. Ball junior had shown him to Mr. Sidney Galtrey, "Hotspur" of the *Daily Telegraph*. Galtrey tried to interest Sir Frederick Eley in Reynoldstown but to no purpose. Mr. J. H. Whitney was informed of the horse but could not find time to come and look at him during his visit to Ireland. This left the way clear for Major Noel Furlong, who was then running a small family stable in Leicestershire. A good judge of a horse, Major Furlong had originally lived in Co. Cork, emigrating to England during the Troubles. As soon as he saw Reynoldstown he was determined to buy him. "He's the best-looking horse in Ireland," he declared, "and I've seen over a hundred." To which Mr. Ball junior replied: "He's not half ready yet. It will take you two years to make anything of him."

Reynoldstown's first outing was in a novices chase at Leicester in December 1932. He finished unplaced. Soon afterwards he fell in a similar type of event at Cheltenham, but nevertheless Major Furlong was pleased with the way he was coming on and ran him in the Broadway Novices Chase at the National Hunt Meeting at Cheltenham in March. Reynoldstown was quite well backed at 8–1 and was going very well indeed when he came down in the straight. To restore his confidence he ran in a maiden hurdle at Wolverhampton the following week and ridden by his owner's son, Mr. Frank Furlong, he won by a short head at 100–8. Frank Furlong was educated at Harrow and the R.M.C. and then joined the 9th Lancers, in which, however, he only served for a brief period. A good horseman, he had won "The Saddle" at the R.M.C. and he soon became a strong and effective race-rider. Besides winning the Grand National on Reynoldstown, he was second in that race on

Really True. He also won the National Hunt Chase on Robin-a-Tiptoe. Increasing weight cut short his riding career. He was killed flying on active service in World War II.

Reynoldstown began the following season by running fourth over hurdles at Stratford and second at Newbury. He then struck form and won three hurdle races in quick succession. In the second and third of these successes he carried 12 st. 7 lb. and he was particularly impressive when beating twenty-two opponents by fifteen lengths over three miles at Cheltenham. There was not much money in jumping in those days and Reynoldstown's three wins earned a total of £223 for Major Furlong.

Reynoldstown then reverted to fences but though he ran well in three races, he was slightly disappointing in that he failed to win any of them, finishing third in the Sefton Chase at Newbury, fourth in the New Century Chase at Hurst Park, and third in the Newbury Handicap Chase. After these defeats he had another go at hurdling but was unplaced over two miles and five furlongs at the Grand Military meeting at Sandown. Although still a maiden over fences he ran in the then important Lancashire Chase at Manchester at Easter and put up a very useful performance in finishing second to the brilliant Avenger who was conceding him 8 lb. On the whole it was rather a disappointing season for Reynoldstown who failed to win over fences although more than once he ran really well against quite formidable opposition. The probability is that he still had not grown to his full strength.

The following December Reynoldstown at long last won his first steeplechase. It was not a very gaudy success as the race, the Belvoir Chase at Leicester, was worth only £83 to the winner and the opposition was anything but imposing. Later that month he finished in front of Avenger, who was giving him 15 lb., at Derby, but was himself beaten by Huic Holloa a useful horse to whom he was conceding 18 lb. In a third race that month he registered his best performance to date when winning the three mile Lambourn Handicap Chase at Newbury. He carried the appreciable weight of 11 st. 12 lb. and among those he beat was the 1933 Grand National winner Kellsboro' Jack, who was conceding him 9 lb.

In January he finished second over three miles at Leicester and then the following month he put himself right into the Grand National picture by winning the three and a half mile Nottingham Handicap Chase at Nottingham carrying 12 st. 2 lb. He was conceding weight to twelve of his fourteen opponents and his jumping, which combined boldness with accuracy, was most impressive. Good judges who saw him that day reckoned that Major Furlong would surely win the National if, as many supposed, he had an even stronger candidate in Really True, second to Kellsboro' Jack at Aintree in 1933. In fact there was a phase when Major Furlong thought of leaving the National to Really True and letting Reynolds-town have a cut at Golden Miller in the Gold Cup, but in the end it was decided to let Reynoldstown take his chance at Aintree, too.

Reynoldstown's final outing before Aintree was in the National Trial Chase run over the stiff Gatwick course. Quite early in the race Frank Furlong broke a leather. He negotiated the next four fences successfully but then he and Reynoldstown parted company. The general public remained unaware of what had happened. They reckoned that Reynoldstown had fallen or alternatively that Furlong had fallen off and lost interest in the pair as a Grand National proposition.

Reynoldstown had the appreciable weight of 11 st. 4 lb. in the National. He always went more kindly for Frank Furlong than any-one else and Furlong rode him at Aintree though Really True, partnered by Danny Morgan, was preferred in the betting, 100–7 as against 22–1. Public faith in the brilliant Golden Miller was such that he started at the absurd price of 2–1. Second favourite was Thomond II (11 st. 13 lb.). The weather was fine, the going good, the crowd enormous.

The early leaders were Theras, Thomond II, Alexena, Golden Miller, Brienz, who had been third in the Derby, and Reynoldstown. Really True was one of several fallers at the fourth fence. At the fence after Valentine's, Golden Miller, whose victory would have dealt the bookmakers a fearful blow, screwed to the left on taking off, landed awkwardly and got rid of Gerry Wilson. Brienz fell at the first fence on the racecourse proper and Castle Irwell made a horrible mistake shortly afterwards but recovered brilliantly. At the water jump the plodding grey Uncle Batt led from Castle Irwell, Theras, Alexena, Royal Ransom, Blue Prince and Reynoldstown. It was noticeable at this point how smoothly Reynoldstown was travelling and early on the second circuit he moved up closer to the leaders.

Uncle Batt soon began to find the pace too hot and Castle Irwell went ahead with Thomond II hard on his heels. Just before the Canal Turn Thomond II passed Castle Irwell who jumped the

Canal Turn fence so sharply to the left that he parted company with that very good American amateur Mr. G. Bostwick. This left Reynoldstown second in front of Alexena, a former hunter ridden by Mr. Peter Payne-Gallwey, and Blue Prince, ridden by Billy Parvin. Alexena was very tired though and refused not long afterwards, at which point the issue seemed to lie solely between Thomond II and Reynoldstown.

Reynoldstown seemed to be going just the better of the two but Thomond II had the heart of a lion and he and Billy Speck refused to give in. At the last fence but one, though, Reynoldstown appeared at last to have mastered Thomond II. Blue Prince, however, had been making ground up steadily and to such good effect that he was now barely a length behind Reynoldstown and looking very dangerous indeed. At this highly critical juncture, fortunately perhaps for Reynoldstown, Blue Prince's saddle started to slip, placing the unfortunate Parvin at a serious disadvantage. Reynoldstown, however, was not home and dried yet. Thomond II rallied in the bravest style possible and jumped the last level with Reynoldstown. He was desperately tired, though, and he did not land quite straight over that final fence. He collided with Reynoldstown, and being the smaller and the more exhausted, he came off second best. Reynoldstown drew clear to win by three lengths from Blue Prince who passed the gallant Thomond II in the long run-in.

Frank Furlong said afterwards that Reynoldstown, despite lack of previous Aintree experience, had jumped superbly throughout and the only uneasy moments he himself experienced were when Thomond II cannoned into him on two occasions through jumping to the right.

Only six horses completed the course that year. Reynoldstown's time was the fast one of 9 minutes 21 seconds, $\frac{2}{5}$ths of a second outside the record established the year before by Golden Miller.

Reynoldstown did not run again that season. He had proved himself a really good horse but the following winter he reached the zenith of his powers and proved an even better one. Possibly he would never have beaten Golden Miller in the Gold Cup, but he was undoubtedly superior in merit to a number of horses that have won the big race at Cheltenham. Because of increasing weight Frank Furlong had retired from race-riding and Reynoldstown was partnered by Fulke Walwyn. Walwyn had been in the same company as Furlong at the R.M.C. and they had joined the 9th Lancers together.

5

Without belittling Furlong as a race-rider, Walwyn was undoubtedly his superior in that respect; in due course he turned professional and would have reached the top of the tree had he been less unlucky in the matter of injuries. He is one of the few men both to ride and train a Grand National winner.

The National was again Reynoldstown's target and he did not in fact run until January 6th when he won a three mile chase at Leicester. On February 25th he carried 12 st. 7 lb. in the Stayers Handicap Chase run over three miles and three furlongs at Birmingham, starting favourite at 6–4 in a strong field of nineteen. Considering Major Furlong's home gallops had been frozen up and Reynoldstown was not quite at his best, he put up a splendid performance to finish second to Avenger, a high-class chaser to whom he was conceding 4 lb. On March 7th he won the Shaun Spadah Chase at Lingfield, giving his rider what Walwyn described as the best ride he had ever had.

By Grand National day Major Furlong had Reynoldstown in tip-top condition and the big, rangey black gelding had never looked better. Despite his substantial weight of 12 st. 2 lb. Reynoldstown was heavily backed at 10–1. Avenger was favourite at 100–30 and Golden Miller, forgiven his failure of the previous year, had no lack of supporters at 5–1. It was a wonderful day for spring racing with perfect visibility and excellent going. The crowd, as was customary in pre-war, pre-television days, was enormous.

The field soon began to thin out. Golden Miller was down at the very first fence. Delaneige, a great Aintree horse, fell at the Canal Turn and Blue Prince, runner-up the year before, came down at Valentine's. Right from the start the leader had been a 100–1 outsider, Davy Jones, a tubed chestnut ridden by Mr. Anthony Mildmay and owned by Lord Mildmay of Flete. At the water jump Davy Jones, whose jumping had been faultless, led from Avenger, Inversible, Emancipator, Kiltoi, Reynoldstown and Keen Blade. At the first fence on the second circuit Avenger hit the top of the jump hard and fell on his head, breaking his neck. It was a tragic end to a brief and brilliant career. Happily his owner Mrs. Mundy, who was devoted to him, had not come to Liverpool to watch the race.

In the meantime Reynoldstown was going extremely well and to the satisfaction of his backers had moved up to join Davy Jones, the pair being a long way ahead of the third horse, Lord Rosebery's Keen Blade. From then on it was a desperate duel between the two leaders and on that clear sunny afternoon every detail could be observed from the stands. At Valentine's Davy Jones, showing no sign of distress, was leading by a length. At the last open ditch which has a nasty drop on the landing side Keen Blade fell and Reynoldstown made a horrible mistake. Walwyn lost an iron but he recovered brilliantly and set off in dogged pursuit. He now, though, had a dozen lengths to make up on the leader, whose gallant but somewhat inexperienced rider was by then having visions of achieving the one great ambition of his life.

Reynoldstown was by now a tired horse but he was also an extremely game one and by the second last fence he had drawn appreciably closer to Davy Jones. At that jump Davy Jones pecked slightly on landing and to give him every chance to recover Mildmay let slip his reins to the buckle. At this point Mildmay became the victim of cruel and totally unmerited misfortune. The prong of the buckle slipped through the hasp and all of a sudden the reins were flapping loosely round Davy Jones's neck. With no means of steering him, Davy Jones ran out at the final fence. Reynoldstown was thus left to win comfortably from Ego, ridden by Mr. Harry Llewellyn, and Bachelor Prince. It was a tame conclusion to what had looked like being a thrilling finish. It is interesting to speculate on the feelings of the late Mr. J. V. Rank, owner of Bachelor Prince; he had wanted to buy Reynoldstown as a young horse but had been put off by a friend who assured him that Reynoldstown would never be any good.

Some people reckoned that Reynoldstown would still have won even if Davy Jones had not run out. Walwyn afterwards said that Reynoldstown had been winded by his mistake but had got his second wind coming to the last fence, by which time he was hard on Davy Jones's heels. On the other hand Davy Jones looked less weary than Reynoldstown when the disaster occurred. If it had come to a battle in the long run-in, Walwyn would have been able to give his mount far more assistance than Mildmay, who at this early stage of his career was still a somewhat weak finisher.

However, leaving aside questions that can never be answered, Reynoldstown had won his second Grand National and no horse has been victorious with a weight as big as his since. In fact he is the last Grand National winner to have carried 12 st. or over. Admittedly he had good fortune on his side on both occasions, but he was good enough to take advantage of the luck that came his way and in any case many Grand National winners are substantially assisted by the misfortunes that overtake dangerous opponents.

Although great horses like Arkle tend nowadays to give Aintree a miss, Aintree is in fact nothing like as formidable as it used to be. The fences are notably weaker and horses make huge gaps in them with apparent impunity. Moreover the fences now have a nice friendly slope on the take-off side so that horses are compelled to stand back and cannot get underneath them as so often used to happen in the old days. The old heroic element has vanished for ever from the Grand National. No longer is it rated a notable achievement merely to complete the course; the race is really little more than a very long steeplechase on the shabbiest racecourse in England. Reynoldstown's victories were achieved when conditions were still really tough and when the Grand National was at the peak of its fame and popularity. To win such an exacting race twice, Reynoldstown had to be a great stayer, a magnificent jumper, and above all to possess a superb degree of courage.

That Grand National was virtually the end of Reynoldstown's career. Because of bad weather there was no Gold Cup the following year. Furthermore Major Furlong declined to enter his horse for the Grand National. "There is such a thing," he said, "as taking the pitcher to the well too often. As he has won in successive years, I think he has done enough. Apart from that, and it is a fact that has influenced me considerably, it is my opinion that the alteration in the conditions of the race is not fair to the best horses. One does not want to see high-class horses beaten by selling platers receiving a lot of weight." The alteration in the conditions referred to was permitting the handicapper to make the lowest weight 10 st. instead of 10 st. 7 lb.

Hyperion

One of the most familiar of racing maxims runs: "A good big 'un will always beat a good little 'un." It is generally true, but it would be wise to add the conditional clause "—unless the good little 'un happens to be Hyperion." For few horses ever foaled would have beaten that wonderful midget on the sunny last day of May in 1933 when he gained his runaway Derby victory in record time.

Hyperion stood well under 15 hands when he went into training, and was only 15 hands 1½ inches when he ran in the Derby; he was the smallest Derby winner since Little Wonder, who was suspected of being a four-year-old, ninety-three years earlier. Hyperion's small stature threw a revealing beam of light on the devious working of heredity. Many students of the thoroughbred have concentrated, quite erroneously, on the direct male and female lines of a horse's pedigree, while ignoring, or allowing only secondary importance, to the rest. But in the case of Hyperion the serpentine route by which he received the undersized characteristic can be traced clearly through his tabulated pedigree. His dam Selene was tiny, and Selene inherited her smallness from her sire Chaucer, who was described by his trainer George Lambton as "a little pony"; and Chaucer owed his lack of inches to the influence of his dam Canterbury Pilgrim, who was small when she went into training as a yearling and did not grow much afterwards. Significantly, this smallness was linked with marked racing ability in each generation. Canterbury Pilgrim won the Oaks; Chaucer, though retarded by a serious illness as a three-year-old, became a first-class performer during the next three seasons; and Selene was probably the best three-year-old of either sex in England in the autumn of 1922. There is no room for doubt that Selene, and her small but gifted ancestor, were as potent a factor in the inherited make-up of Hyperion as his sire, the war-time Triple Crown and substitute Gold Cup winner Gainsborough.

It was singularly appropriate that Canterbury Pilgrim should, at a remove of three generations, have transmitted valuable qualities to Hyperion, as she was one of the first animals purchased by Lord Stanley, afterwards the 17th Earl of Derby, when the Stanley family stud and stable were being restocked in the eighteen nineties. The 12th Earl of Derby had given his name to the principal Classic race, and won the Derby with Sir Peter Teazle in 1787. After the death of the 12th Earl the family interest in racing waned, and it was not until George Lambton was engaged as trainer during the Royal Ascot meeting of 1893 that it revived. The 17th Earl, whose rotund figure, ruddy complexion and unfailing sportsmanship made him one of the most popular owner-breeders ever to tread the Turf, was determined to build up his stud to the point at which it could provide him with a Derby winner. He achieved his ambition when Sansovino galloped through the mud to victory at Epsom in 1924, but good horse though Sansovino was in the appalling ground he did not bear comparison with Hyperion, who gave him his second victory in the race nine years later.

George Lambton, who had charge of Lord Derby's horses from Canterbury Pilgrim to Hyperion, was a trainer of immense skill and understanding who believed in making his horses work at home and on the racecourse. Although his love of a bet landed him in financial difficulties of varying degrees of intensity from time to time, the knowledge gained from experience with generation after generation of the same bloodlines, combined with his professional expertise, enabled him to render wonderful service to Lord Derby's racing interests. It would not be easy to exaggerate the value of continuity in the training of successive generations of products of a great stud, and this value has seldom been more evident than in the case of Hyperion. Selene was so small when she went into training that Lambton struck her out of her Classic engagements at the first forfeit stage, but she was so active and full of spirit that she never stopped improving from the time she began to race. As a two-year-old she won eight races, including a dead-heat, and had the Cheveley Park Stakes, regarded as the championship race for fillies of that age, among her successes. She won the same number of races the next season. There is little doubt that she could have won the St. Leger, which went to the second class Royal Lancer, but had to be content with a victory in the Park Hill Stakes, the "Fillies' St. Leger", instead. On her final appearance she cantered away from a strong field composed of both sexes in the Hampton Court Great Three-Year-Old Stakes at Hurst Park in the middle of November.

After seeing that lack of inches did not prevent Selene becoming a top-class filly, Lambton did not repeat the mistake of striking Hyperion out of his Classic engagements. As far as the Classic races are concerned, the only omission which has to be regretted in the case of Hyperion is that he was not entered in the Two Thousand Guineas. The fact that both his sire and his dam possessed abundant stamina had suggested that the mile of the first of the Classic races might be too short for him, but he was endowed with brilliant speed and was so superior to his contemporaries that he would surely have beaten the French horse Rodosto, who profited from his absence to win the Guineas.

The little chesnut Hyperion, with his sweet manners and his perfect conformation in miniature, became a favourite of his trainer from the moment that Lambton first set eyes on him. However the colt had not showed any very marked ability when he was put into serious work on the gallops at Newmarket as a two-year-old, and it was evident that he was either very lazy or rather slow. Lambton did not even bother to go and see him run when he had his first outing in the Zetland Maiden Plate over five furlongs at Doncaster in May. The race was of minimal importance and the other members of the field have long been forgotten, but the atmosphere of the racecourse did serve the purpose of waking Hyperion up, and in finishing fourth he conveyed the clear idea that he was capable of much better things in future. His next race was the New Stakes at Royal Ascot in which he had to meet the exceptionally fast filly Nun's Veil, who had won her two previous races with a lot in hand. Nun's Veil came from the powerful Beckhampton stable of Fred Darling, which had already won the Coventry Stakes with Manitoba and the Queen Mary Stakes with Supervisor at the meeting. Darling thought that Nun's Veil was unbeatable after those earlier two-year-old victories and Nun's Veil started a hot favourite at 6–4. Hyperion was second favourite at 6–1, and he upset expectations completely when he came out of the starting gate like a flash and blazed up the course to beat Nun's Veil easily by three lengths. By one of the strange coincidences of racing history it was a mating of Hyperion with Nun's Veil's daughter Clarence that produced Sun Chariot, winner of three Classic races in 1942.

Although he was meeting Nun's Veil on 7 lb. better terms than weight-for-sex, Hyperion gave one of the finest performances of his career in the New Stakes. Indeed it was an astonishing performance by a colt bred to stay, as he covered the stiff five furlongs course in 61 seconds dead, ⅘ths of a second less than the top-class three-year-old sprinter Gold Bridge had taken to cover the same five furlongs earlier in the afternoon. Observers of the race could hardly believe their eyes, for Hyperion in action was hardly recognizable as the tiny horse who had paraded beforehand. The explanation was that he was abnormally lengthy in relation to his height, and this enabled him to cover so much ground with every stride that he gave the impression of not being a small horse at all.

The scintillating victory of Hyperion was difficult to reconcile with his moderate displays in his next two races. He was an odds-on favourite for the Prince of Wales's Stakes at Goodwood and only avoided the ignominy of defeat by forcing a dead-heat with the Nancy Stair Filly, afterwards named Stairway. Worse followed in the Boscawen Stakes at Newmarket in September, when Hyperion finished a poor third of four, eight lengths behind the winner Manitoba.

It is surmised that Hyperion, deprived of the exhilaration of Royal Ascot, had relapsed into his former lethargy. This supposition gains colour from the fact that he worked appallingly before his final outing of the season in the Dewhurst Stakes over seven furlongs at Newmarket in October, and was running sluggishly in the race until Tommy Weston gave him a cut with the whip going up Bushes Hill. Directly he got this reminder he fairly shot forward and went ahead up the hill to beat Jesmond Dene by two lengths with the odds-on favourite Felicitation, whom he was to meet so often in the future, in fourth place. This was a performance more in keeping with the reputation he had enjoyed after Ascot, and justified the hope that he would be good enough for the Derby the following year.

As Hyperion was not in the Guineas his first appearance as a three-year-old was delayed until the Chester Vase over the full Derby distance of 1½ miles in May. Although the sharp Chester course is less than a mile in circumference, it is dead flat and non-stayers do not win there. The going was heavy on the day of the Vase, and by winning decisively by two lengths Hyperion gave a satisfactory answer to the question whether her stamina was equal to Derby requirements. His work at home was less satisfactory, because he had become lazier than ever and Lambton had the greatest difficulty in making him exert himself at all. His final gallop before Epsom was particularly unimpressive, and at one time his Derby odds were extended to 10–1. Shortly before the race however, the market was convulsed in a most extraordinary manner. Manitoba, who had been favourite, drifted and was replaced as favourite by Hyperion, who started at 6–1. Meanwhile an inexplicable furore developed for Miss Dorothy Paget's Tuppence, who had been unplaced in the Two Thousand Guineas and the Chester Vase and had been on offer at 125–1 a few days earlier. Unfounded rumours of a coup circulated, and support for Tuppence snow-balled to such an extent that he started fourth favourite at 10–1. The folly of this market move was revealed when Tuppence finished nineteenth of the field of twenty-four, and the only success of this moderate colt was when he earned £53 by dead-heating in a maiden plate at Hamilton Park three months later.

Lazy though he might be at home, Hyperion was on his toes when it came to the great occasion. Thrapston, with Steve Donoghue riding, had been put in to make the pace for Hyperion. The riding of a pacemaker requires almost as much skill as the riding of the fancied candidate and Donoghue, who had won four Epsom Derbys and was probably the greatest exponent of riding the course that has ever lived, did the job to perfection. Donoghue set a fast but not mad pace, and left Hyperion room to come up on his inside at the approach to Tattenham Corner. The stable companions came round the bend together, and immediately after Weston and Hyperion set sail for the winning post. Weston gave the long-striding little chesnut just one tap with the whip so that he would not think he had done enough when he was in front, and the race was virtually over. Increasing his lead with every stride, Hyperion beat King Salmon pulling up by a distance officially described as four lengths, but which photographs showed was six lengths at least.

In that golden age of Derby winners Hyperion's record time of 2 minutes 34 seconds did not last long. It was equalled by Windsor Lad the next year and beaten by ½th of a second by Mahmoud in 1936. Nevertheless it was a brilliant performance by any standard, and especially so in view of the ease of his victory. Lord Derby, who loved his racing and was at no pains to conceal his delight at the moment of victory, was fully entitled to his beaming smile and ponderous jig of triumph as Weston trotted Hyperion back, after pulling up, to be led into the winner's enclosure.

Hyperion did not have much trouble in winning the Prince of Wales's Stakes over one mile five furlongs at Royal Ascot, and then his supremacy in his own age group was so assured that it seemed only an accident could prevent him winning the St. Leger. And an accident nearly did do just that. In July he was found to be lame in his hind quarters, and a slight dislocation of the stifle joint, probably caused by getting up awkwardly in his box, was diagnosed. He had to miss the race named in his honour at Hurst Park in August, and the ante-post market had such an attack of jitters that his St. Leger price was pushed out to 20–1 at one time. Happily the injury soon mended, and in the weeks before the Doncaster meeting Lambton's chief worry was to ensure that the incorrigibly idle Hyperion was fit enough to do himself justice.

No doubt the scare about Hyperion's soundness was responsible for as many as thirteen horses taking him on in the St. Leger. They included the Derby second and fourth, King Salmon and Scarlet Tiger, besides Felicitation and the French Derby winner Thor II. In the race Hyperion again threw off his lethargy and won in impeccable style. He had to make his own running, because the ground was too hard for his intended pacemaker Highlander to be started and none of the other jockeys was willing to go in front, and was perfectly happy to do so. At no stage of the race was he fully extended and Weston was pulling him up and patting his neck as they passed the winning post three lengths in front of Felicitation. The superiority of the English Classic form was demonstrated by Thor's final position of thirteenth.

Hyperion's four-year-old season, which should have set the seal on his fame with a victory in the Ascot Gold Cup, ended unhappily, clouded by disagreement and recrimination. The seed of the trouble had been sown the previous May, when Lambton had a fall at home, sprained his Achilles tendon severely and was unable to travel to Epsom to saddle Hyperion for the Derby. Lord Derby came to the conclusion that Lambton had reached retiring age and terminated his contract as private trainer from the end of the season. Colledge Leader was appointed as his successor and Leader, though unquestionably a fine horsemaster, may not have understood the peculiarities of Hyperion as well as Lambton.

In a physical sense Hyperion thrived during the winter, growing nearly an inch and putting on a lot of muscle. Moreover his four-year-old campaign began auspiciously with victories at Newmarket in the March Stakes, in which he again beat Felicitation, and the Burwell Stakes, in which he confirmed his Derby superiority over King Salmon. Unfortunately the spring and early summer of 1934 were abnormally dry and hot. The training grounds at Newmarket became as hard as a road and Leader, whose methods were anyhow less rigorous than those of his predecessor, found increasing difficulty in giving the lazy Hyperion a thorough Gold Cup preparation. The ground was so hard for the Epsom meeting that Leader did not dare risk Hyperion in his planned engagement in the Coronation Cup, and, having missed that race, the colt worked deplorably in his final gallop before Ascot. In spite of these ominous signs, the public retained confidence in Hyperion for the $2\frac{1}{2}$ miles test of stamina, for which the international field included the American Mate, the French Thor II and the Italian Crapom besides Hyperion's old rival Felicitation, who had earned his place by winning the Churchill Stakes in a canter the previous day. The result of the race was a bitter disappointment for the thousands who revered Hyperion as a champion of champions. Felicitation was in front practically the whole way; in the Swinley Bottom he was ten lengths clear, and kept up the gallop relentlessly to pass the winning post with eight lengths to spare from Thor, with a desperately weary Hyperion a further $1\frac{1}{2}$ lengths behind in third place.

The inevitable post-mortems followed. Had Hyperion been found wanting in stamina? Had Leader erred on the side of leniency in his training? Had hard ground on the gallops been an insuperable natural disadvantage? The correct answer may have been that a combination of these three causes was responsible for the defeat. Leader and Weston were at loggerheads, and Hyperion's short-head defeat by the three-year-old Caithness in the Dullingham Stakes at the Newmarket July meeting did nothing to mend the breach. After the Dullingham Stakes reverse Hyperion retired from the Turf with his glory a little tarnished, though no defeat could rob him of the greatness of his performances in the New Stakes and the Derby.

If Hyperion was a great racehorse, he was as certainly a great character and a great sire. A lovable horse who revelled in the adulation of his many visitors, he yet had a mind of his own. Some-times at exercise, in the manner of his paternal grandsire Bayardo, he would suddenly stand stock-still and refuse to move until he felt inclined to do so; and at Ascot before the Gold Cup, having caught sight of George Lambton in a wheel chair beside the parade ring, he stopped to greet his old friend and was persuaded only with difficulty to continue on his way. Like another great horse, The Tetrarch, he loathed physic and generally refused to take it.

Except for a period of war-time exile in Yorkshire, Hyperion spent his stud career at Lord Derby's Woodland Stud at Newmarket where his statue by John Skeaping now stands. His success was as steady as it was spectacular. He was leading sire of winners six times, three times fewer than St. Simon but still a marvellous achievement. In spite of this degree of success, for a time his male line seemed insecure in England until Aureole, the last of his top-class sons on the racecourse, stepped in to give it a firm base at home. Elsewhere, in almost every country in which racing flourishes and especially the United States, the Hyperion line became a cornerstone of Classic breeding. For generations to come the presence of Hyperion in scores of high-class pedigrees will serve as a perpetual reminder of the greatest of little horses.

Windsor Lad

Foaled in 1931, Windsor Lad was beyond doubt one of the outstanding Derby winners of the inter-war period. Quite ordinary as a two-year-old, he was very good at three and magnificent at four. Unfortunately his stud career was dogged by ill-health and he died at the early age of twelve.

He was bred in Ireland by Mr. Dan Sullivan, a sound judge of a pedigree and of conformation, and was by the great stallion Blandford, sire of four Derby winners, out of Resplendent, by By George! out of Sunbridge, by Bridge of Earn. Resplendent was a high-class mare, finishing second in the Oaks and winning the Irish Oaks and the Irish One Thousand Guineas. Besides Windsor Lad, she was dam of Radiant, second in the Oaks, and Lady Gabrial, winner of the Cheveley Park Stakes at Newmarket. By George!, by Lally, was a good two-year-old, winning the Imperial Produce Stakes at Kempton. Later he became difficult to train and retired to the stud in Ireland at the rock-bottom fee of nine guineas. Most of the mares he served before he was exported to Canada were third-raters. Sunbridge only won a couple of small races herself, but at the stud she produced, besides Resplendent, Soldumeno (Irish Two Thousand Guineas); Sol Speranza (Irish One Thousand Guineas and Irish Oaks); Ferrybridge (third in the One Thousand Guineas); and Queen Scotia, ancestress of King of the Tudors (Eclipse Stakes) and Our Babu (Two Thousand Guineas). Bridge of Earn was a moderate racehorse but did quite well as a sire and his name appears in the pedigrees of Donatello II and of Foxbridge, champion sire in New Zealand for eleven successive seasons.

As a yearling Windsor Lad was angular and unfurnished and when he came up for sale at Doncaster Mr. Sullivan, a realist in such matters, reckoned a reserve of 1,000 guineas would be quite sufficient. However "Atty" Persse, who trained for Mr. Sullivan in England, persuaded him to boost the reserve to 2,000 guineas. Later on Mr. Sullivan reverted to his original valuation but omitted to inform Persse, who had intended to bid for the colt. Persse was surprised, to put it mildly, when Windsor Lad was knocked down for 1,300 guineas to young Marcus Marsh, acting on behalf of the Maharajah of Rajpipla. Marsh, twenty-eight years of age at the time, is the son of the famous Richard Marsh who won the Derby with Persimmon, Jeddah, Diamond Jubilee and Minoru.

Windsor Lad was noticeably backward as a two-year-old and wisely Marsh gave him plenty of time to develop his strength. The colt's first appearance was in the Two-Year-Old Sale Stakes at the Newmarket Second July Meeting. The class was moderate but nevertheless Windsor Lad was unable to finish in the first eight out of fourteen runners. At Goodwood, in the Prince of Wales's Stakes, his task was more formidable as he came up against Lord Glanely's Colombo, a brilliant Manna colt that was beyond question the best of his age. Windsor Lad in fact ran reasonably well to finish fourth of eight. He was then rested till the autumn when he won the six furlong Criterion Stakes at Newmarket by inches from Lord Astor's Bright Bird. In the Free Handicap he was given 8 st. 3 lb., 18 lb. less than Colombo. He had made steady improvement throughout the season and from his manner of racing, he looked like making a stayer. There was no obvious reason to presume, though, that he was ever likely to reach true classic standard.

Windsor Lad thrived during the winter and filled out in the right places. Marsh made no attempt to hurry him and his first appearance was in the mile and a half Chester Vase at Chester. His appearance made a very favourable impression on the paddock critics and he started favourite at 3–1. He won more easily than a margin of half a length might suggest from Zelina, who was conceding him 3 lb. Zelina was a very useful filly that had won the Greenham Plate at Newbury and later finished second in the Oaks. A week later Windsor Lad completed his Derby preparation by running in the ten furlong Newmarket Stakes, at that time a Derby trial of no little significance. Ridden by Smirke, who was to ride him in the Derby, he started favourite and won by a length from Flamenco who had been fourth in the Two Thousand Guineas.

Clearly Windsor Lad possessed a sound chance in the Derby but the general public refused to look beyond Colombo who had

followed up his brilliant two-year-old career by winning the Craven
Stakes and the Two Thousand Guineas. In a strong Derby field
Colombo started a hot favourite at 11–8. Second favourite at 7–1
was the Aga Khan's Umidwar, who later in the season won the
Jockey Club Stakes and the Champion Stakes. Windsor Lad was a
popular each way chance at 15–2 and Easton, a French-bred colt
that had been second in the Two Thousand Guineas, was on offer
at 100–9. Other runners were Admiral Drake, who shortly afterwards carried off the Grand Prix; Tiberius, winner of the Ascot
Gold Cup and the Goodwood Cup as a four-year-old; and Bonds-
man, destined to become General Eisenhower's hack and to win
under National Hunt Rules when he was sixteen years of age. The
going was hard.

There was an unpleasant background of ill-feeling in connection
with the race. Colombo was ridden by W. R. Johnstone, an Australian
who had ridden with success in India and France, but had little
experience in England. The year before, Colombo had been ridden
more than once by the great Steve Donoghue who made no secret
of the fact that he thought that he ought to have been riding Lord
Glanely's colt rather than the Beckhampton second string, Medieval
Knight. As things turned out, this ill-feeling proved a very important
factor in the race.

From the start Colombo was prominent on the rails. Coming
down the hill towards Tattenham Corner, though, Johnstone found
himself shut in behind Medieval Knight, whose rider, not surprisingly under the circumstances, declined to let him through although
Medieval Knight was clearly weakening at this stage. In fact
Medieval Knight stopped so quickly that Colombo had to be
checked, losing his downhill impetus and becoming unbalanced in
the process. In addition Colombo lost more ground by coming
distinctly wide on the final bend.

Windsor Lad, on the other hand, skilfully piloted by Smirke,
had a trouble-free run and entered the straight well ahead of
Colombo. Soon after Tattenham Corner, Fleetfoot was deprived of
the lead by Tiberius who remained in front till a quarter of a mile
from home when he was challenged and headed by Windsor Lad.
Running on like the true stayer that he was, Windsor Lad held off
a dangerous and determined late challenge by Easton, ridden by
Gordon Richards, to win by a length. A neck away third was the
unfortunate Colombo who had made valiant efforts to retrieve the

situation and get on terms. At one point indeed he had looked like pulling it off, but he could not quite sustain the effort and weakened inside the final hundred yards. Thus the Maharajah of Rajpipla won the "Blue Riband" of English racing with his very first runner in the Derby. The race was a triumph, too, for the irrepressible Smirke, who had been banned by the Jockey Club from 1928 until October 1933 following an incident at the start of a race at Gatwick.

The general view after the Derby was that Johnstone had ridden a poor race and had managed to get himself into every sort of trouble. Donoghue, whose views could hardly be described as unbiased, subsequently wrote: "Had I ridden Colombo, he would have won on the bit by many lengths. Had any other jockey, who knew the course, ridden him, he would have won comfortably." It was no great surprise when Johnstone, retained for the season by Lord Glanely, ceased to ride for him soon afterwards. Windsor Lad and Colombo never met again. At Ascot Colombo, who had not fully recovered from his gruelling battle at Epsom, was defeated in a sensational race for the St. James's Palace Stakes by Flamenco and that was the end of his racing career.

Windsor Lad next ran in the ten furlong Eclipse Stakes at Sandown, a race that proved almost as productive of controversy and gossip as the Derby had been. Windsor Lad was favourite at 5–2, second favourite being Umidwar, who was receiving 10 lb. Unfortunately Smirke, usually at his best on important occasions, took a leaf out of Johnstone's notebook and rode one of his less successful races. Windsor Lad got hopelessly boxed in and was undeservedly beaten half a length and the same by the four-year-old King Salmon, who was giving him 9 lb., and Umidwar. Windsor Lad should never have lost that race and he was never beaten again. After the Derby the Maharajah could have obtained £60,000 for Windsor Lad. Following the Eclipse, some rather complicated negotiations took place and Windsor Lad passed into the possession of Mr. M. H. Benson, a bookmaker, who is said to have written out a cheque for £50,000. In Mr. Benson's colours, Windsor Lad won the Great Yorkshire Stakes at York carrying 9 st. 9 lb. and then the St. Leger, in which he started at 9–4 on and won by two lengths and the same from Tiberius and Lo Zingaro. That race concluded Windsor Lad's three-year-old career.

As a four-year-old Windsor Lad was a magnificent specimen of

Plate 17   Golden Miller

Plate 18   Reynoldstown

Plate 19   Hyperion

Plate 20   Windsor Lad

Plate 21   Nearco

Plate 22 Pharis

Plate 23 National Spirit

Plate 24 Alycidon

Plate 25 Native Dancer

the thoroughbred and looked powerful enough to carry a fifteen stone man to hounds across Leicestershire. He was as good as he looked, too, but unfortunately Mr. Benson decided that prudence would be more profitable than valour. "My object now is to see he is not beaten before he retires to the stud," was his uninspiring summing-up of the situation. Windsor Lad was in fact entered for the Ascot Gold Cup but was subsequently taken out of that race, much to the disappointment of those who hoped he would be England's most formidable representative in the Cup against the great French horse Brantôme. Mr. Bob Lyle, the lively racing correspondent of *The Times* newspaper, who was never averse to making highly controversial statements, supported Mr. Benson and wrote in *The Times* as follows: "Hardly a winner of that great and severe race has made a successful sire. . . . No doubt Mr. Benson would dearly love to win the race, but owners of potentially great sires owe a duty to the thoroughbred industry, a duty which Mr. Benson is not forgetting."

This effusion drew a broadside in *The Times* from Lord Hamilton of Dalzell: "The comments made by your Racing Correspondent last Monday regarding the decision of the owner of Windsor Lad to withdraw his horse from the Gold Cup at Ascot were so damaging to the horses that have run or will run for that race and to the reputation for stoutness of our breed of thoroughbred horses that I feel compelled to answer what was said.

"Your Correspondent says that owners of potentially great sires owe a duty to the thoroughbred industry, a duty which Mr. Benson is not forgetting. The assumption underlying this statement is that the effort of galloping this $2\frac{1}{2}$ mile course is so great that it will impair the constitution of horses which are subjected to it to an extent that will prevent their success at the stud. Certain instances of winners of the Gold Cup that have not been conspicuously successful as sires are quoted in support of this theory. Against that it is only necessary to recall the names of a few of the great sires that have won the race. Touchstone, Doncaster, Isonomy, St. Simon, Santoi, Isinglass, Love Wisely, Persimmon, Cyllene, William the Third, Bayardo and Solario are a dozen that occur to me at the moment. St. Simon, the greatest sire of modern times, won the Gold Cup as a three-year-old.

"I would be the last to question the right of an owner to decide on the races for which his horses shall run. Mr. Benson need not have entered his horse for the race. He did so, and it is not unreasonable to suppose that this was done with the idea of running if the race seemed an easy one to win; nor is it unreasonable to suppose that the presence of Brantôme, Felicitation and Tai-Yang in the entry—to name three only of the probable opposition—may have had some influence on the decision to strike him out. To say that it was done for the reason given by your Correspondent is equivalent to saying that a man who has accepted an invitation to dinner and has subsequently declined to attend has done so because the host's wine is so bad that it always gives his guests a headache."

Windsor Lad's first race as a four-year-old was the mile and a half Burwell Stakes at Newmarket and this he won as he pleased by five lengths. His next target was the Coronation Cup run over the Derby course and in this race he came up against Easton who had finished second to him in the Derby the year before. Easton, a big, handsome colt by Dark Legend standing well over sixteen hands, was confidently expected to reverse the Derby form. He had begun the season by giving 24 lb. and a beating at Lingfield to Sea Bequest who was subsequently third in the Two Thousand Guineas. Easton then took on Umidwar in the March Stakes at Newmarket and trounced him.

The meeting between these two very good four-year-olds aroused immense interest. The betting public could not decide between them and the pair went down to the post joint-favourites at evens after slight odds had been laid on each in turn. Beresfell, acting as pacemaker for Windsor Lad, set a good gallop and there was never any question of the race being a dawdle followed by a sprint. With six furlongs to go Smirke sent Windsor Lad into the lead and Richards had to niggle a bit at Easton to keep in touch. At Tattenham Corner Windsor Lad led by a length and soon afterwards, following a single tap with the whip, he increased his advantage. From that point he was never in the slightest danger of defeat and won by a length and a half from Easton with Caymanas four lengths away third in the good time of 2 minutes 33⅕th seconds. No longer could it be inferred, as it had often been in the past, that Windsor Lad was an out-and-out stayer but deficient in top-class speed.

At Ascot Windsor Lad gave further proof of his turn of foot by winning the Rous Memorial Stakes over a distance just short of a mile. His final race was the Eclipse Stakes at Sandown Park, the event in which he had been so unlucky the year before. The pace was a slow one which did not suit him, particularly as he had to make his own running. He came into the straight in front with those two fast horses Fair Trial and Theft waiting to pounce. With two furlongs to go Fair Trial accelerated and there was a roar of encouragement from his supporters as the Beckhampton chestnut got his head in front. Windsor Lad, though, rallied like a champion, and fighting back gamely he regained the lead just as it seemed that Fair Trial was going to win. Fair Trial could find no more, but then came Theft with a powerful late run. Windsor Lad, however, withstood this challenge, too, and amid terrific cheering passed the post three parts of a length ahead of Theft, who was the same distance in front of Fair Trial. In a race that was certainly not run to suit him Windsor Lad had given irrefutable proof both of his speed and his courage. Altogether he had won ten races worth £36,257. It is undeniable that he ought never to have been beaten after his two-year-old career.

Unfortunately at the stud Windsor Lad developed a very bad sinus. The best brains in the veterinary world, augmented by a Harley Street doctor, were unable to bring about a cure. He suffered a lot and his owner wished, on humane grounds, to have him destroyed but the underwriters refused to agree to this. In the end the underwriters paid out a certain sum and took over the horse. Eventually, at the age of twelve, he was put down. For his first three seasons at the stud he had a good fertility return; he then had to be withdrawn from stud duties for a season and on resumption he turned out to be a poor foal-getter. The best of his stock was Windsor Slipper, winner of the Irish "Triple Crown".

Nearco

It is arguable that the two most influential European breeders of
bloodstock this century have been the 17th Earl of Derby and
Signor Federico Tesio. At Dormello, Signor Tesio's home on the
shores of Lake Maggiore, there is a private stud-book that contains
in detail the family histories of the many famous horses bred at the
Dormello Stud. This type of stud-book, the pages of which are
twenty by twenty-four inches, was designed by Prince Lubomirski,
owner of the Kruszyna Stud in Poland, and he presented a copy to
Signora Lydia Tesio when her husband started to breed bloodstock
in 1899. The two most famous horses so far bred at Dormello have
been Nearco and Ribot. Nearco is summed up in the Dormello stud-
book as follows: "Beautifully balanced, of perfect size and great
quality. Won all his 14 races as soon as he was asked. Not a true
stayer though he won up to 3,000 metres (Gran Premio di Milano
and the Grand Prix de Paris). He won these longer races by his
superb class and brilliant speed."

Nearco, foaled in 1935, was brown in colour and was by Pharos
out of Nogara, by Havresac II out of Catnip. Pharos was bred by
Lord Derby whose colours he carried. A full brother to the St.
Leger winner Fairway, he won fourteen races in four strenuous
seasons, and although ten furlongs was his best distance, he was
only just beaten by Papyrus in the Derby. He proved an outstanding
stud success and was champion sire once in England and twice in
France. His best winners were Cameronian (Two Thousand Guineas
and the Derby); Firdaussi (St. Leger); Nearco (Grand Prix); and
Pharis II (Prix du Jockey Club and Grand Prix).

Catnip, grandam of Nearco, was bred by Major Eustace Loder
and was by his Derby winner Spearmint out of Sibola, by the
Cambridgeshire winner Sailor Prince. Sibola was bred in America

and brought to England where she won the One Thousand Guineas and was second in the Oaks. She gained admission to the General Stud Book when, from 1901 to 1909, the qualifications for entry were relaxed in favour of certain horses and mares from America and Australia.

Catnip herself was a weedy little filly when in training and possessed scant racing merit, her solitary success being in a £100 nursery at Newcastle. In December 1915 she came up for sale at Newmarket in foal to Pretty Polly's very moderate brother Cock-a-Hoop. At this stage of the war the bloodstock market was in a depressed condition and furthermore most English breeders were prejudiced at that time against American blood. Signor Tesio, therefore, was able to buy Catnip for 75 guineas. She proved a marvellous bargain as apart from producing Nearco's dam Nogara she bred Nesiotes, by Hurry On, who won fifteen races and did well as a sire in Italy; Neri di Bicci, by Tracery, who won eight races and was ancestress of some very good horses; and Nomellina, by St. Amant, winner of eight races. It seems a bit hard on Nomellina that the only comment she caused in the Dormello stud-book was "No Use"!

Nogara was foaled in 1928. Her sire Havresac II was bred in France and exported to Italy, where he won nine races and was leading sire on ten occasions. He was by the English-bred Rabelais, who was by St. Simon and won the Goodwood Cup. Rabelais in fact was closely inbred to St. Simon. Nogara herself won the Criterium Nazionale as a two-year-old and the following year both the Italian One Thousand and Two Thousand Guineas. The Dormello stud-book describes her as "small, rather lightly-made but well-balanced with magnificent action. A first class racer from 1200 to 1600 metres".

Besides Nearco, Nogara bred five winners. These were Niccolo dell' Arca, by Coronach, whose victories included the Italian Derby by twenty lengths, the Gran Premio di Milano, and the Grosser Preis des Reichhauptstadt in Berlin; Nicolaus, by Solario, who won from five furlongs to a mile and a half and sired the Grand National winner Nicolaus Silver; Nakamuro, by Cameronian, second in the Italian Derby; Nervesa, by Ortello, who won the Italian Oaks; and Naucide, by Bellini, who was unbeaten as a two-year-old and was third in the Italian Derby. In 1951 Nogara broke a leg and had to be put down. At the time five of her sons were standing at stud in England or Ireland.

Nearco ran seven times as a two-year-old and won all his races, the total value of which was 220,800 lire. On each occasion he triumphed by a decisive margin and his superiority was such that his presence was liable to scare away other horses engaged in the race. His fourth race was the six furlong Criterium Nazionale at Milan. He started at 5–1 on and beat the only two other competitors as he pleased. In the seven and a half furlong Gran Criterium at Milan he again started at 5–1 on and won easily from his stable companion Gaddo Gaddi. In the Italian Free Handicap he was given 10 st. 3 lb., 3 lb more than his stable companion Domenico Ghirlandaio, a full brother to Donatello II.

As a three-year-old Nearco was better than ever and just as versatile. During his first season he had won from five furlongs to seven and a half-furlongs; as a three-year-old he won from seven to fifteen furlongs. He started off with a three lengths victory in the seven furlong Premio del Ministere del l'Agricoltura e delle Foreste at Pisa. He then won the Italian Two Thousand Guineas by half a dozen lengths. Over a mile and a quarter he won the Premio Principe Emanuele Filiberto at Milan by three lengths. The Italian Derby he brought to the fringe of farce in winning by a distance. After that he won the Gran Premio dell' Impero at Milan by six lengths and on June 20th the fifteen furlong Gran Premio di Milano by three lengths. That concluded his racing career in Italy. He had won thirteen races worth 1,005,500 lire and had never been extended. In appearance he was hard indeed to fault and superior in that respect both to his sire Pharos and to Pharos's other great son, Pharis, being perfectly proportioned and combining power and quality in a remarkable degree. He stood just over 16 hands and, unlike Pharis, he was not back at the knee, a trait that Pharos possessed and transmitted to many of his stock.

Although the Grand Prix de Paris came only six days after the Gran Premio di Milano, Signor Tesio determined to see if Nearco could succeed where Donatello II had so narrowly and unluckily failed the year before. Nearco's task was a stiff one as the field for the fifteen furlong Grand Prix included Bois Roussel and Cillas, winners respectively of the English Derby and the French Derby; Castel Fusano, winner of the Prix Lupin; and Féerie, winner of the French One Thousand Guineas and the French Oaks. Ridden by the Italian jockey Gubellini, Nearco started a firm favourite at 29–10, Bois Roussel's price being the liberal one of 29–4. It was always Signor

Tesio's contention that Nearco, like his sire, was not a true stayer and that in his two races over a mile and seven furlongs it was his speed and his class that saw him through. Be that as it may, Nearco was always going well within himself throughout the Grand Prix. In the straight he accelerated smoothly to take the lead and once in front he showed admirable resolution in holding off determined challenges from the fast-finishing Canot and from Bois Roussel whom he beat by a length and a half and a length. It was the first Italian victory in the Grand Prix and the jubilation of the many Italians present was unrestrained, doubtless to the chagrin of most French racegoers since at this dark and threatening period in world affairs, Frenchmen and Italians tended to view each other with unconcealed resentment and hostility. Moreover the brash Mussolini régime was apt to make a certain type of Italian unbearably truculent in moments of success.

Nearco's appearance and indisputable racing ability made a great impression on all who saw him at Longchamp. Before that race there had been no question of selling him, but afterwards it soon became known that a realistic offer would receive serious consideration. Mr. "Jock" Crawford of the British Bloodstock Agency had been particularly impressed by Nearco and he advised Mr. Martin Benson, bookmaker and bloodstock breeder, that he ought to make a bid for such an outstanding horse. Four days after the Grand Prix Mr. Benson bought Nearco for the then record sum of £60,000. Apart from the essential veterinary examination which took place two days later, the transaction was not a lengthy one and in fact was carried through in a brief conversation over the telephone. Within a few hours of Nearco's purchase, he was booked full for the next three years. Mr. Benson retired Nearco from racing forthwith. He also purchased at the same time Nearco's stable companion Bistolfi who had completed a Longchamp double for Signor Tesio by winning the Prix d'Ispahan. In England Bistolfi won the City and Suburban at Epsom.

Nearco was sent to the Beech House Stud, Newmarket, and there he remained till his death on June 27th, 1957. To begin with his fee was 400 guineas. In the middle of 1942, though, Mr. Benson decided to syndicate him at £1,550 a share. As early as September that same year the *Racing Calendar* carried an advertisement requesting two shares at £2,200 each. A few years later almost the same sum had to be paid for a single nomination to Nearco.

As a sire Nearco proved an outstanding success and by importing him into this country Mr. Benson performed a service of the utmost benefit to the racing industry. At the time of Nearco's death, his stock had won 571½ races worth £427,662 and it has to be borne in mind that prize money, particularly during the war years, was on a considerably lower scale than today. He was leading sire in 1947 and 1948; second in 1949 and 1951; third in 1945 and 1950; fourth in 1942, 1943, 1944 and 1956. For fifteen years running he figured among the ten leading sires, a wonderful record of consistency. He was leading sire of winning brood mares in 1952, 1955, and 1956; second in 1951, 1958, 1960 and 1961; third in 1953, 1954, 1957 and 1959. His daughters bred two Derby winners, Tulyar and Arctic Prince, and Rose Royale winner of the One Thousand Guineas. Other good winners out of Nearco mares were Aggressor (£36,203), Miralgo (£28,277), Palariva (£16,093), Tamerlane (£12,955), Ark Royal (£12,400) and Sarcelle (£10,555).

Nearco himself sired the following English classic winners: Dante (Derby); Nimbus (Two Thousand Guineas and Derby); Sayajirao (St. Leger); Masaka (Oaks); and Neasham Belle (Oaks). Other good winners were Hafiz II (Prix Greffulhe, Queen Elizabeth II Stakes and Champion Stakes); Infatuation (£9,994); By Thunder (£9,197); Noory (£7,803); Krakatao (£7,697); Neolight (£6,911); Norooz (£6,686); and Narrator (£6,451).

Three of Nearco's most influential sons, Nasrullah, Mossborough and Royal Charger, were not among his major stake-winners. Nasrullah, bred by the Aga Khan, was a potentially brilliant but decidedly temperamental horse whose victories included the Coventry Stakes and the Champion Stakes. He was also third in the Derby. His activities on the racecourse were restricted by war conditions and he never ran except at Newmarket, a course for which his affection appeared to be of a somewhat limited nature. Whatever his shortcomings on the racecourse, he was one of the greatest sires of this century even though he was inclined to transmit his temperament to some of his offspring. He was top sire in 1951 and got the classic winners Never Say Die (Derby and St. Leger); Nearula (Two Thousand Guineas); Musidora (One Thousand Guineas and Oaks); and Belle of All (One Thousand Guineas). He also sired the somewhat unreliable sprinter Grey Sovereign, who in fact proved a far greater success as a sire than his three-parts brother, the dual classic winner Nimbus.

Exported to the United States, Nasrullah maintained to the full his excellent record and became champion sire there as well. Among his American stock were Nashua who won £450,000 and was sold for £446,850; and the brilliant Bold Ruler who is doing so well as a sire.

Mossborough, bred by the late Lord Derby, won five races worth £4,606 and was really hardly better than a top-class handicapper. However, he sired the great horse Ballymoss, winner of the Irish Derby, the St. Leger, the Eclipse Stakes, the King George VI and Queen Elizabeth Stakes and the Prix de l'Arc de Triomphe; and that fine English-bred, Irish-trained filly Noblesse, winner of the Timeform Gold Cup and the Oaks. Ballymoss sired the 1967 Derby winner Royal Palace.

Royal Charger, bred by Sir John Jarvis, won six races worth £3,426 and was third in the Two Thousand Guineas. Six furlongs was probably his best distance and he won the Ayr Gold Cup under 9 st. 7 lb. Over here he sired Gilles de Retz (Two Thousand Guineas); Happy Laughter (One Thousand Guineas); and Sea Charger (Irish Two Thousand Guineas and Irish St. Leger). Exported to America he sired Turn To, the best American two-year-old of 1954 and later a successful sire.

Many of Nearco's sons were exported overseas for stud purposes and when he died no fewer than eighty of them were standing in various parts of the world.

In conclusion it is pertinent to mention that Nearco's sire Pharos was inbred to St. Simon, while Nearco's maternal grandsire, Havresac II, was also inbred to St. Simon. There is no doubt that Nearco possessed something of the same "electricity" that was such a feature of St. Simon, and as a racehorse he exercised at all distances an identical supremacy over his opponents. Like St. Simon, too, he was a prepotent sire. In fact he can be said to have resembled St. Simon more than any of St. Simon's own sons.

Pharis

The career of Pharis, like that of his famous English contemporary, Blue Peter, was curtailed by the outbreak of the second world war. In fact he only ran three times in his life. Nevertheless he gave clear proof that he was a great racehorse, and during that fateful summer of 1939 he captured the imagination and the affection of the French racing public in a remarkable way.

Pharis, foaled in 1936, was bred by the French industrialist M. M. Boussac, for years a leading patron of European racing, and was by Lord Derby's English-bred sire Pharos, out of Carissima, by the English-bred Clarissimus, who won the Two Thousand Guineas for Lord Falmouth. Pharos, by Phalaris out of the famous mare Scapa Flow, was a top-class racehorse whose best distance was probably ten furlongs even though he was only just beaten by Papyrus in the Derby. He certainly did not possess the stamina of his full-brother Fairway who won the St. Leger. Beginning his stud duties at the age of six, Pharos stood for two years at Newmarket and was then transferred to France where he died in 1937. Among his best winners, besides Pharis, were Cameronian (Two Thousand Guineas and Derby), Firdaussi (St. Leger), Rhodes Scholar (Eclipse Stakes) and Nearco (Grand Prix). Like Phalaris, he was noticeably back at the knee and had rather long pasterns, traits which he passed on to many of his offspring. Carissima, whose sire Clarissimus did particularly well as a sire of brood mares, won three races herself and was placed in the French Oaks. Altogether she bred eight winners, one of whom was Caprifolia, dam of The Solicitor, a useful winner himself and sire of that fast horse The Pie King. Carissima was also dam of the non-winning Libération, who bred the Gold Cup winner Elpenor.

Pharis was a tall, rangey brown colt that measured 16.2 hands as a three-year-old. He had plenty of scope and stood over a lot of ground, but he lacked the substance of Pharos and of Pharos's brilliant Italian-bred son Nearco. His forelegs were not his best point and like his sire, he was back at the knee. He took a long time to come to hand and A. Swann, who at that time was training for M. Boussac, very sensibly did not run him at all as a two-year-old. In fact Pharis's first racecourse appearance was in the mile and a half Prix Noailles at Longchamp on May the 17th. As might perhaps have been anticipated from his conformation, he did not negotiate the hill any too well, but once in the straight he lengthened his stride in impressive fashion to win with considerable ease. Not a few shrewd judges who saw him that day were convinced they had been watching a future champion.

On June 11th, again ridden by that fine English jockey Charlie Elliott, Pharis took the field at Chantilly in the Prix du Jockey Club, run over a mile and a half and the French equivalent of the Derby. M. Boussac also ran Horatius to act as pacemaker and the two were coupled favourite at 13–10. Pharis always took a bit of time to get warmed up and on the downhill run he was only lying 13th. Nor had he improved his place to any marked extent at the turn for home. His prospects at this stage looked poor indeed and to render the situation even more discouraging, Pharis was badly interfered with so that Elliott had to snatch him up.

By now Pharis's backers had resigned themselves to losing their money. Suddenly, though, a great shout went up as the field, led by Galérien, approached the stands. Pharis, in the centre of the course, was coming with a great run and passing horse after horse. For a few seconds it seemed as if his effort had come too late and that he would never get up, but such was his speed that he swept past Galérien and in the end won almost comfortably by two lengths and a half. It was a breathtaking performance that for a few seconds rendered even the most exuberant French spectators speechless and it was generally agreed that only a great horse could have overcome the difficulties he was faced with and have won as Pharis did. That victory made him the hero of the French racing world.

Pharis's third and last race was the Grand Prix de Paris run over a mile and seven furlongs at Longchamp on June 25th. This race is a very stern test for three-year-olds and not infrequently the winner is never quite as good again afterwards. On this occasion conditions were even severer than usual since the going was extremely heavy.

There were seventeen runners and Pharis and his pacemaker Horatius were coupled favourite at 11–10. Second in the betting came Baron E. de Rothschild's trio, Tricameron, Bacchus and Transtévère. Hypnotist, trained at Newmarket by Captain Cecil Boyd-Rochfort, stood at 24–1. Earlier that month he had won the King Edward VII Stakes at Ascot.

Horatius set a very fast pace and in view of the state of the ground it was hardly surprising that he was beginning to drop back at the top of the hill. At the turn for home Tricameron led with both Galérien and Birikil hard on his heels and looking dangerous. What of Pharis? Once again he was taking years off the lives of his supporters. Slow to get thoroughly warmed up, he was very nearly last coming down the hill into the straight. That was bad enough but in the straight opposite "Le Pavilion" he got hopelessly boxed in behind a number of beaten horses. At that point even his most fervent admirers must have given up hope. Suddenly, though, Elliott spotted a gap and in a trice Pharis was through it. The favourite's long stride and fabulous acceleration began to tell and well inside the final furlong Elliott drove him between Tricameron and Galérien to take the lead. Amid scenes of uninhibited enthusiasm, he went on to win by two lengths and a half from Tricameron with Etalon d'Or, who came with a late run, a similar distance away third. For the second time Pharis had won by a decisive margin when two furlongs from home after it had appeared inconceivable that he could win at all. The time of 3 minutes 21 seconds was a slow one, but it is essential to remember the state of the ground. Under the conditions that existed it was amazing that Pharis could accelerate as he did. A furlong from home Tricameron had apparently mastered Galérien and looked sure to win. His rider Bouillon said afterwards: "I heard a horse coming up behind me and looked round, but he had unfortunately already gone past."

M. Boussac at once made it known that Pharis would tackle Lord Rosebery's Blue Peter, who had won the Two Thousand Guineas and the Derby and was shortly to win the Eclipse Stakes, in the St. Leger. Towards the end of August Pharis was transferred to Steve Donoghue's stable at Blewbury and he was there when war was declared on September 3rd. The Doncaster meeting was abandoned and in view of the uncertainty existing over the future of racing both Pharis and Blue Peter were retired.

Blue Peter had accomplished a truly remarkable gallop before the

St. Leger and till his death Sir Jack Jarvis refused to believe that Blue Peter could possibly have been beaten. Unquestionably Blue Peter was the handsomer horse and possessed the better conformation; he would almost certainly have acted better on firm ground. There were in fact rumours circulating at the time that Pharis would not run if the going at Doncaster was firm. On soft going, though, it is at least conceivable that Pharis's tremendous acceleration would have proved the decisive factor.

Pharis proved a great success as a sire. His first crop of runners set him at the head of the list of sires of winning two-year-olds. It was all the more regrettable, therefore, that the Germans confiscated him in August 1940. He was installed at the Army Stud, Altenfeld, near Hesse, but like all the confiscated French sires bar Téléférique he was not a success in Germany, possibly because French blood-stock did not readily acclimatize themselves there. His best German winner was Asterblüte, winner of the German One Thousand Guineas. He did not return to France till May 1945 and of course covered very few mares in France that year. At the request of M. Boussac, the progeny of Pharis conceived during his sojourn in Germany were not admitted to the French Stud Book.

Back in France Pharis soon got back into his stride again and when he died in 1957 he had been Champion Sire in France on four occasions. He got four French Derby winners—Ardan, Scratch, Auriban and Philius. Ardan in due course sired Hard Sauce, sire of the Derby winner Hard Ridden. Two of Pharis's sons, Scratch and Talma, won the Doncaster St. Leger. Stymphale won the Prix Royal Oaks, the French St. Leger. Corejada and Palencia both won the French One Thousand Guineas and Corejada in addition won the Irish Oaks. Dynamiter won the Champion Stakes two years running, and Pardal, besides winning some £15,000 in stakes by his victories in France and in England, sired the Derby winner Psidium.

National Spirit

National Spirit belonged to the golden age of hurdlers—the period soon after the second world war when there were only three champions over a period of eight years. He was the first of that marvellous trio, winning the Champion Hurdle in 1947 and 1948. He was followed first by Hatton's Grace and then by Sir Ken, who held the championship for three years each. And such was the durability of National Spirit, an invaluable quality that fully matched his talent, that he was still running in the Champion Hurdle when Sir Ken gained the first of his victories in 1952.

Which was the greatest of those hurdlers of the golden age? Any attempt to give an answer to that question cannot help but be invidious, but there is no denying that it would be difficult to make a convincing claim for the superiority of National Spirit over Hatton's Grace or Sir Ken. Nor is there any certainty that National Spirit was a better hurdler than Wrack and Trespasser, the leading hurdlers respectively of the periods just before and just after the first world war when no proper championship test existed; and if the identity of the greatest hurdler of all time were to be decided, it would also be necessary to consider Insurance, winner of the Champion Hurdle twice in the early nineteen thirties, and Brown Jack, who won the Champion Hurdle as a four-year-old in 1928 before his attention was diverted to the more lucrative profession of winning important long distance races on the flat.

The reason for singling out National Spirit is not the supposition that he would come out best if all the champions, restored miraculously to their prime, could be assembled to do battle for some super title. Rather is it that National Spirit, more than any other champion, succeeded in capturing the imagination, and indeed the affection, of the racing public. His presence in a minor hurdle race was sufficient to attract the crowds, however feeble the opposition, and many onlookers made a habit of deserting the stands and taking post near one of the flights of hurdles the better to admire the sheer virtuosity of his jumping. In this respect, he was the only hurdler who has been able to hold a candle to Arkle, the most popular chaser there has ever been or is ever likely to be.

If steeplechasing is the poor relation of the flat, then hurdling is the poor relation of steeplechasing. In the early days hurdling was regarded with good-humoured contempt. "The chief merit of hurdle-racing is that it does not pretend to have any raison d'être except the encouragement of gambling, and it answers this purpose admirably," observed an eminent authority in the eighteen eighties. Right up to the second world war hurdle-racing was looked down on, if not frowned upon, and was starved of its fair share of the meagre prize money available under National Hunt Rules. The peculiar qualities of National Spirit were required to change the traditional balance and raise hurdling to a position more nearly of parity with the other branch of jumping. The fact that hurdling has become a highly specialized art, admirable and worth cultivating for its own sake and not merely as a gambling medium or a transitional stage on the way from the flat to fences, is due in no small measure to the education of public taste effected by National Spirit.

The irony is that National Spirit, the educator and the supreme artist in hurdling, was intended for a career exclusively as a chaser when he first went into training. There were the elements of romance in his origins and background which seem to be appropriate for an outstanding racehorse. His dam Cocktail had been bred by the Aga Khan, but had proved useless on the racecourse, finishing unplaced in the four races in which she took part. Mr. Len Abelson, a Birmingham businessman, was able to buy her for a song at the beginning of the war, when she was barren after being covered by the Triple Crown winner Bahram. Mr. Abelson took her to his farm in Warwickshire and had her covered by Scottish Union, who had won the St. Leger in 1938. The result of this mating was a chestnut colt, later gelded, who was to achieve fame under the name of National Spirit. Mr. Abelson then sold Cocktail, and events proved that he had disposed of her at exactly the right moment, because she was barren for the next three years, and only produced one more foal. National Spirit, foaled in 1941, was the only winner she bred.

National Spirit ran out on the farm, and had never even had shoes on his feet when he was sent into training with Vic Smyth at Epsom as a four-year-old. Smyth, a member of one of the best known families of trainers and jockeys, had been a leading jockey on the flat, winning the Oaks on Brownhylda and the Ascot Gold Cup on Happy Man, and became a successful trainer under both codes of rules after retiring from the saddle in 1925. He took a half-share in Mr. Abelson's chesnut gelding when the horse arrived at his stables in Burgh Heath Road, and this had one immediate good result. The gelding had been registered in the stud book as Avago, a totally inadmissible name for a good horse, but was changed to National Spirit, a name as euphonious as it was apt to his breeding, when he went to Vic Smyth.

Thus National Spirit began his racing career with a name having the ring of greatness. He also had a fine pedigree despite his dam's lack of racing ability. Cocktail was by the Derby winner Coronach, and from Coronach received the blood of Marco, so potent in the best jumping pedigrees. Scottish Union, a Classic winner on his own account, was to acquire an enviable reputation as a sire of jumpers. Looking at National Spirit's powerful frame, Smyth decided that he was cut out to be a chaser and should be introduced to fences with the least possible delay. For this purpose he had a couple of outings over hurdles at Fontwell Park and Windsor in November 1945, when he was a few weeks short of his official fifth birthday. Then, having shown that he could jump fences like a stag at home, he was despatched to Nottingham the following February to have his first outing over fences in a novices chase. Vic's nephew Ron Smyth, one of the leading jump jockeys at the time, was given the mount, but the outcome was far from auspicious. National Spirit seemed to have no liking for jumping fences in public, and soon took the opportunity to run out. His behaviour was considered too bad to be true, and he was taken to Windsor to run in another novices chase a week later. This time he got no further than the first fence, where he fell heavily. The lesson was unmistakable. "He tipped up properly at Windsor, and it seemed pointless to persevere," Smyth remarked as he meditated on National Spirit's career years later. National Spirit was to be a hurdler; not for the last time, he had got his own way.

A little more than a month after his Windsor fall National Spirit ran unplaced in a novices hurdle race at Wincanton, and a month later again he was placed for the first time when he was beaten by half a length by Home From Home in a similar race at Plumpton. May brought him his first successes in novices races at Fontwell Park and Plumpton, and on June 10th, at the very end of the season, John Hislop rode him to victory in an amateur riders' handicap hurdle at Fontwell Park.

That final success of the 1945–46 season nearly brought about a change in National Spirit's circumstances which would also have had far-reaching effects on the future of hurdling in England. Shortly after the race John Hislop conveyed to his owners an offer to buy the horse for export to the United States, where there was a strong demand for jumpers at the time, but fortunately the offer was refused.

In the meantime National Spirit was beginning a career on the flat which was to prove almost as rewarding as his hurdling ventures. He ran for the first time at Nottingham exactly a fortnight after his last Fontwell Park victory and, after an outing at Newmarket, returned to Nottingham to win a little race over one mile three furlongs. By a strange coincidence the name of the race, the Elvaston Stakes, was the same as that of the steeplechase in which he had run out five months earlier. Before the end of the season he had won long distance handicaps at Doncaster and Thirsk.

Less than three weeks after he had won at Thirsk in November National Spirit was running over hurdles at Wolverhampton, and his victory under 11 st. 10 lb. in a handicap showed that he had progressed far beyond the novice stage. Indeed he was getting stronger and more proficient almost day by day, and in December he proved that he was already on the verge of the top class when, with Fred Rickaby riding, he carried 12 st. 5 lb. to victory by five lengths over Legend of Rank in a field of experienced hurdlers for the Princess Elizabeth Handicap Hurdle at Doncaster.

There was a long spell of hard weather in February and March 1947. One of the casualties was the National Hunt meeting scheduled for the second week of March, and with it the Champion Hurdle. Luckily it proved possible to run some of the most important races, including the Cheltenham Gold Cup and the Champion Hurdle, in April. This was the occasion of National Spirit's first Champion Hurdle appearance, and Fred Rimell, then the most stylish rider over fences and hurdles, had been engaged to ride him. But in the previous race, the Gold Cup, Fred had a bad fall on Coloured School Boy and Danny Morgan, a most skilful and experienced rider with

6

a victory on Chenango in the 1934 Champion Hurdle to his credit, was brought in as substitute at the last minute. The French five-year-old Le Paillon was made favourite, and it is no disparagement of National Spirit or any of his other opponents to state that he ought to have won. Le Paillon was a top-class horse at the height of his powers, and later the same year brought off the astonishing and unprecedented double of victories in the French Champion Hurdle and the Prix de L'Arc de Triomphe. National Spirit, though a year older, had been in training for two seasons less and was relatively immature. But for a jockey Cheltenham takes as much knowing as does Newmarket on the flat, and has as many pitfalls for the unwary and the inexperienced. Alec Head, on Le Paillon, was riding at Cheltenham for the first time, and erred fatally by trying to keep out of trouble by staying on the outside of the field the whole way. Meanwhile Danny Morgan, who could have found his way round Cheltenham blindfold, was bringing National Spirit the shortest way home and, by letting the big horse really run along from the top of the hill six furlongs from home, completed the out-generalling of Head and gained the day by a length.

As a result of the postponement of the Champion Hurdle, National Spirit had already made his reappearance on the flat and won the King George VI Handicap at Liverpool on March 27th. For the rest of his active racing life his flat racing and hurdling careers alternated and sometimes overlapped. Much of his form on the flat was excellent. He won the King George VI Handicap at Liverpool a second time, and he had a predilection for the two miles course at Lingfield, over which he won five times. But his best performance was when he gained a head victory over Woodburn in the Melbourne Stakes over the last two miles of the Cesarewitch course in September 1948. A fortnight later Woodburn proved himself a high-class young stayer by winning the Cesarewitch, and the following year won the Yorkshire Cup.

Nevertheless National Spirit would not have left his name indelibly in the annals of the Turf by his flat racing performances alone. He remained primarily a hurdler, and in March 1948, when he won his second Champion Hurdle, there was not the slightest suggestion that he needed any luck to assist him. But down the field in fifth place that day was a somewhat unprepossessing but athletic Irish horse called Hatton's Grace, and by the time the Champion Hurdle came round again a year later Hatton's Grace, a first class and versatile horse on the flat, had developed his hurdling to a fine art. All the same, Vic Smyth was confident that National Spirit could win again. The horse was absolutely in his prime, his hurdling technique had attained perfection and his physical condition was tuned to the minute. He started a hot favourite at 5–4 in a field of fourteen, and when he could finish only fourth behind Hatton's Grace, Vatelys and Captain Fox, there was a crushing sense of disappointment in the huge crowd. Seldom has the defeat of a public idol been more exhaustively debated or a larger number of sensational theories been bandied about. The true explanation was probably the most obvious. Bryan Marshall, who rode him, was an accomplished and sometimes brilliant jockey. But on that occasion he made an error of judgment in trying to hold National Spirit up for a late challenge and not letting him run along from the top of the hill in the manner he liked and to which he was accustomed. Instead of being clear at the bend before the last hurdle National Spirit was badly hampered, and that meant the end of his chance.

That Smyth's confidence had not been misplaced was proved when National Spirit ran in the Cheltenham Hurdle, a consolation race over the same course, a month later. He then met Vatelys on 7 lb. worse terms, but turned a deficit of about four lengths into a comfortable winning margin of three lengths. If he had produced that form in the Champion Hurdle he must have won.

National Spirit still had three Champion Hurdles to go, and only in the last of them, when he had reached the age of eleven and his powers were definitely on the wane, did he fail to make his presence felt. In 1950 he might well have gained revenge for his luckless defeat the previous year if he had not been the victim of a dastardly attack by nobblers in his box on the Sunday night before the race, which left him with a badly swollen knee. The injury could, of course, have been caused innocently by an accidental knock, but much later the racecourse grapevine conveyed to Smyth the information that National Spirit had indeed been got at. The knee was so bad that it was touch-and-go whether he could run, and on arrival at the course he had to be kept continuously on the move to stop the knee stiffening up. In the circumstances, it was a marvellous effort on his part to lead to the last hurdle, where he blundered and dropped back to finish fourth again.

Dennis Dillon, who was his partner in most of his hurdle races in the latter part of his career, rode him on that occasion and again in 1951. Once more National Spirit was in front approaching the last hurdle, where he was joined by Hatton's Grace and, probably because he was tiring, shocked his host of admirers by falling.

National Spirit ran his last race in March 1953 when he was third in a little race at Wye. He had run his last race on the flat at Lincoln six months earlier when, ridden by his faithful friend Teddy Underdown, who often rode him in his work at Epsom, he was a bad last of three in an amateurs' race. His overall racing record speaks for itself. Under National Hunt Rules he ran in forty-four races and won nineteen of an aggregate value of £8,802; on the flat he ran in forty-one races and won thirteen of an aggregate value of £6,900. If the financial rewards seem derisory by the standards of a later period, no one in his own time was deceived by their inadequacy into estimating him as anything less than a horse great in ability and character.

Brilliance alone will not bring a racehorse popularity. Only if it is accompanied by the capacity for consistently honest endeavour, by personality or that indefinable something called "presence", and by the soundness of limb and constitution that makes frequent appearances possible, will the public take a horse to their hearts. National Spirit had these assets in abundance, together with spectacular jumping powers. His legs never had a mark or blemish in eight years in training except when viciously assaulted. Whereas most hurdlers, even champions, start to descend as soon as they have crossed the top of the hurdle, National Spirit continued to rise, and many a spectator, having stationed himself well beyond the hurdle on the landing side, was astounded to see National Spirit soaring past him in the air. Once he caught Frenchie Nicholson, one of the best horsemen of his generation, unawares by taking off outside the wing at Plumpton and jumped him off.

National Spirit was no oil-painting. His withers were so low that he was difficult to saddle, and his colour was washy. Yet his appearance was striking and unmistakable. He was a horse of character, suspicious of anything strange, immensely strong and brave. He had his peculiar sense of humour and loved to "drop" his rider at exercise by whipping round without warning, but used then to stand perfectly still to be remounted. One man he never tried to drop, and that was Bill Magee, the elderly Irish "lad" who looked after him. "There's National Spirit taking Bill Magee out for exercise," people used to say as they emerged into Burgh Heath Road in the morning.

National Spirit had not made his last public appearance when he had run at Wye in the Spring of 1953. A race was founded in his honour at Fontwell Park, the sharp little left-handed track which had suited him so well and where he had won five races, including the Rank Cup three times. He paraded on the course before the race the first time the "National Spirit" Hurdle was run, and his jaunty stride and gay, characteristic swish of his tail showed how he appreciated the rapturous applause that greeted him.

Alycidon

Alycidon marked the end of a racing era, for he was the last of the great stayers. Two years after his resounding victories in the "Cup" races of 1949 the King George VI and Queen Elizabeth Stakes was inaugurated as the racing industry's contribution to the Festival of Britain celebrations; and the £20,000 prize for the new race, run over 1½ miles at Ascot in July, was the death sentence for the ancient prestige of the Ascot Gold Cup, run over an additional mile but worth only half as much, at the Royal meeting a month earlier. Traditionally the Gold Cup had been the objective of overriding importance for any top class four-year-old, but with the advent of the King George VI and Queen Elizabeth Stakes it was set aside and the shorter race, with other middle distance races like the Eclipse Stakes and the Champion Stakes in England and the Grand Prix de Saint-Cloud and the Prix de l'Arc de Triomphe in France, superseded it and consigned it to a backwater.

The *Bloodstock Breeders Review*, the authoritative annual publication devoted to the British Thoroughbred, began its account of the Royal Ascot meeting of 1949 with the sentence: "Perhaps no other race has so stirred the imagination in recent years as did the meeting this year between Black Tarquin and Alycidon in the Ascot Gold Cup." Yet the status of the Gold Cup declined so much after that epic contest that within a few years it became necessary for a Gold Cup winner to follow up with a victory in one of the top-ranking middle distance races in order to refute the assumption that he was a one-paced stayer and to establish himself as an attractive stud proposition. Thus Sheshoon, after winning the 1960 Gold Cup, was instantly switched to a middle distance to prove his worth in the Grand Prix de Saint-Cloud.

Alycidon won the "Cup" Triple Crown of important middle

distance races comprising the Goodwood Cup (2 miles 5 furlongs) and the Doncaster Cup ($2\frac{1}{4}$ miles) besides the Ascot Gold Cup, in contrast to the Classic Triple Crown comprising the Two Thousand Guineas (1 mile), the Derby ($1\frac{1}{2}$ miles) and the St. Leger (1 mile 6 furlongs and 132 yards). There had been no "Cup" Triple Crown winner since the pony-sized Isonomy in 1870. And lest it be supposed that the Cup races lacked prestige in the intervening period let it be said that the Ascot Gold Cup had been won by a line of outstanding horses whose reputation depended not only on racecourse performance but on achievement at stud. They included, to name only the most influential, St. Simon, Isinglass, Persimmon, Cyllene, Bayardo, Prince Palatine, Solario and Precipitation – makers of the modern thoroughbred. Alycidon, like Isonomy, bears comparison with any of these. For if Isonomy sired two Triple Crown winners, Isinglass and Common, Alycidon sired a female winner of three Classic races in Meld besides Alcide, who won the St. Leger and proceeded to adjust Alycidon's image to the post-"Cup" era by winning the King George VI and Queen Elizabeth Stakes.

Alycidon, a chesnut horse, was bred by the 17th Earl of Derby by the Italian-bred Donatello II out of Aurora whose sire Hyperion, also bred by the 17th Earl, had been hailed as one of the best Derby winners of the twentieth century when he won at Epsom in 1933. Aurora, though modest in her racecourse earnings, had been one of the first to indicate her sire's excellence as a stallion when she was second to Galatea II in the One Thousand Guineas of 1939. She became a wonderful brood mare, for her offspring included Borealis, second in the St. Leger, and Acropolis, third in the Derby, and six other winners besides Alycidon. Donatello II, unbeaten in his native Italy and second to Clairvoyant in the Grand Prix de Paris, had already sired the One Thousand Guineas winner Picture Play and was to set the seal on his fame later by siring the Derby winner Crepello.

The pedigree of Alycidon thus was as illustrious as could be; nor was it lacking in first-class speed and precocity, for Donatello II had won in the best company over five, six and seven and a half furlongs as a two-year-old, and Hyperion won over five furlongs in fast time at Royal Ascot in his first season. Surprisingly therefore, Alycidon was very slow to mature. He was never a tall horse, and when fully grown stood no more than 16 hands and $\frac{1}{2}$ an inch.

But in his youth his frame, which was unusually long in relation to his height, and his limbs were so loosely knit that it was obvious that a lot of time must elapse if he were to become an effective racing unit. So many horses of his kind of physique never do mature, and when he went into training with Walter Earl at Lord Derby's private stable, Stanley House at Newmarket, plenty of reservations were made about his ability to make the grade. There could be no question of giving him anything more than a couple of educative outings in the autumn of his two-year-old season, and when he did make his first appearance in the Chesterton Maiden Stakes over seven furlongs at Newmarket in mid-October it was apparent that he was as backward mentally as physically. He ducked his head as he passed under the six and five furlongs barrier starting gates as if fearful of hitting them, and finished far down the field of thirteen. There was some little improvement when he ran for the second time on the same course two weeks later and was sixth in a field of similar size, but it was only too evident that time would have to be his ally if he were ever to play anything better than a supporting role on the Turf.

Three developments affecting the career of Alycidon happened during the winter. The first was that Lord Derby, the rotund and immensely popular 17th Earl who had built up perhaps the most influential thoroughbred stud in the world, died and was succeeded by his grandson. The second was that Alycidon matured at an exceptionally rapid rate and was taking shape as a real racehorse by the spring of 1948. The third was that the Stanley House stable jockey, thirty-year-old Doug Smith, became ill and had to go into a hospital for a serious internal operation which meant that he would be out of action until the middle of the summer. Smith, though still playing second fiddle to Gordon Richards and yet to gain the first of his five jockeys' championships, had been riding brilliantly and had 173 wins to his credit in 1947. There is no doubt that Smith's illness had a profound yet inscrutable effect on the career of Alycidon.

In Doug's absence the mount was given to his brother Eph when Alycidon made his first appearance as a three-year-old in the Christopher Wren Maiden Stakes at Hurst Park in April. The race revealed none of the colt's growing ability, but it did expose his besetting sin, laziness. The 1¼ mile start at Hurst Park was close to the racecourse stables and Alycidon, sensing the proximity of a comfortable loose-box, backed away from the tapes. Eph gave him an admonitory cut with the whip, but Alycidon, not to be intimidated, then dug in his toes and refused to co-operate altogether. He took no part in the race; and Walter Earl, called before the Stewards to explain such unseemly behaviour by one of his charges, could only plead that he would try him in blinkers in future.

Alycidon ran in blinkers for the rest of his career. In his case they were certainly not, as they are sometimes called, the "rogue's badge". No braver or more determined battler has ever run, but he was an intelligent horse and enjoyed looking about him, and the blinkers had the effect of concentrating his attention on the business ahead. The stable apprentice Dick Shaw was given the mount in his next three races. In the first of these, the mile Thirsk Classic Trial, he won by a neck from Free Dip, though the runners were not really of Classic calibre at all. Then, in the first week of May, he was beaten into third place by Valognes and Wainwright in the Chester Vase, but there is little doubt that he would have won with an experienced jockey such as Smith on his back. The dead flat track at Chester, less than a mile in circumference and continually on the turn, is one of the hardest in the country to ride, and Shaw was frankly outmanœuvred. A fortnight later Alycidon was at Manchester to win the $1\frac{1}{4}$ miles Royal Standard Stakes, but it was only by a neck that he beat the second class Nathoo. The Derby was only sixteen days away and an immediate decision about running had to be made. That decision, based on Alycidon's backward condition and the fact that Smith was still unavailable, was in the negative.

In the years that followed there was much inconclusive discussion of what the outcome would have been if Smith had been riding from the beginning of the season. One school of thought, of which Lord Derby himself was an adherent, was that Alycidon would have won the Chester Vase so convincingly that a decision to run at Epsom would have been inevitable, and that Alycidon would have won the Derby. The other school of thought was that he was too immature to stand a full scale Derby preparation and that he might have been ruined; in other words, his subsequent development into a truly great stayer was made possible by the relatively easy time he had during the early summer of his three-year-old season. The opposing views can only be recorded without comment.

Alycidon ran one more unexceptional race before he began to show the form that was to take him to the heights. That was in the

King Edward VII Stakes at Royal Ascot, in which he ran lazily and finished only third. Tommy Lowrey, who had won the St. Leger on Chamossaire and the Derby and St. Leger on Airborne in recent years, rode him at Ascot. Lowrey had the mount again in the Princess of Wales's Stakes at Newmarket two weeks later, when he understood Alycidon's idiosyncrasies much better and drove him home two lengths in front of the last St. Leger winner Sayajirao. It is true that Sayajirao was not quite the horse he had been as a three-year-old and was giving away more weight than the age allowance, but Alycidon won with real authority and the performance gave more than a hint of great things to come.

Doug Smith was in the final stages of convalescence at the time of the Princess of Wales's Stakes, was fit to ride him in the next race, the St. George's Stakes at Liverpool at the end of July, and was not parted from him for the rest of his career. The St. George's Stakes was run in a thunderstorm and such torrential rain that the remaining race on the programme had to be abandoned. Alycidon, after seeming to be winning easily, practically stopped when there was a terrific clap of thunder directly overhead a furlong from the finish, and only scraped home by a head from Riding Mill, a dogged stayer who was to be a frequent adversary in the future.

Alycidon's improving form had earned him a place in the last of the Classic races, the St. Leger, but his form had impressed the public so little that he was allowed to start at 20-1. The hot favourite for the last of the 1948 Classic races was My Love, who had the solid recommendation of victories in the Derby and the Grand Prix de Paris. Other notable members of the field of fourteen were Solar Slipper, Noor, Royal Drake, Vic Day, Angelola and the American-bred Black Tarquin, who had shown his class by running the tough Italian four-year-old Tenerani to a short head at Ascot in July. The Aga Khan had provided My Love with a pacemaker, Somali, in an attempt to ensure that this proven stayer was not put at a disadvantage by a dawdle in the early stages. But expectations of a truly run race were dashed when Somali whipped round as the tapes rose and took no part. The runners went off at a canter, and after a couple of furlongs Smith had to make up his mind to send Alycidon ahead. Although Alycidon looked about him continuously and had to be pushed along the whole way, he had galloped most of his rivals silly by the time they were half way up the straight; and Black Tarquin alone had the reserves of speed and energy to tackle him a furlong from home and sprint past to win by one and a half lengths. The rest were well beaten, and My Love came in an ignominious straggler in sixth place.

The St. Leger had proved two things about Alycidon. One was that he was a colt of true class. The second was that he must have a pacemaker if his stamina was to be properly exploited. There was no time to find a pacemaker for his next race, the Jockey Club Stakes over 1¾ miles at Newmarket less than three weeks later. He had to make all his own running once more, and again showed little inclination to concentrate, but his superiority to his four rivals was such that he beat the French horse Cadir easily enough. Benny Lynch, a charming little horse that Lord Derby had bought for 500 guineas as a yearling to represent him in the Arundel Castle Stakes at Goodwood, was called up to make the pace in Alycidon's last race in 1948, the two miles King George VI Stakes at Ascot in October, and did the job so well that he became Alycidon's indispensable ally in his triumphant campaign the following year. The field for the King George VI Stakes was very strong, and included the French Two Thousand Guineas winner Rigolo, the French Derby third Flush Royal, the Oaks third Folie II and Djeddah, who was to win the Eclipse Stakes the next year. With the help of the fast pace set by Benny Lynch, Alycidon simply lost this distinguished collection of horses in the last half mile to beat Djeddah by five lengths.

During the winter Lord Derby, Doug Smith and Walter Earl went into conference to decide Alycidon's plan of campaign for 1949. Clearly a relentless gallop from end to end of the Ascot Gold Cup must be assured and a single pacemaker, even one as capable and courageous as Benny Lynch, could not be given the whole responsibility for a race as long as 2½ miles. The need for two pacemakers to operate in relay was inescapable, and accordingly Stockbridge, who had won a race over nearly two miles at Hurst Park in 1948, was purchased during the winter to make up the team.

The plan was for Stockbridge to make the early running, with Benny Lynch and Alycidon close behind him. Smith, on Alycidon, was to be the general in charge of the operation. As soon as he detected any sign of flagging in Stockbridge, or felt the pace was not fast enough, he would order Benny Lynch into the lead, continuing to keep in touch himself so that Alycidon could move ahead at the crucial moment to maintain the pressure on his opponents' stamina. The plan produced such a dramatic and decisive victory that it is

tempting to assume that there was never any doubt of the outcome.
But in fact, as in the most classically conceived battle plans, as
indeed in any plan involving creatures of flesh and blood and spirit,
things were not so simple as they seem in retrospect, and the period
between conception and execution was by no means free of anxiety.

The most serious worries sprang from the state of Earl's health,
the character of Alycidon and the prevailing state of the going. The
dapper Earl, a perfectionist in every aspect of the trainer's craft, was
a sick man, suffering from an incipient tumour of the brain which was
responsible for his death the following year; and he had to overcome
Alycidon's growing reluctance to exert himself at home and get him
fit in a dry spring and early summer when the horse was prone to jar
himself badly on anything like firm ground. That Alycidon was
able to overcome these disadvantages and prove himself one of the
greatest of stayers was a tribute both to his own inherent quality and
the skill, will-power and invincible courage of his trainer.

Earl made an early decision that long gallops were superfluous in
the case of such a true stayer, and all that was needful was to
sharpen his speed and keep his wind clean by dashes of six or seven
furlongs on the Limekilns summer gallop and on the peat moss
gallop of the Stanley House private training ground. As long as he
was kept between two stable companions his innate spirit of competition was strong enough to make him work, and these short, sharp
gallops, combined with his public outings in the Ormonde Stakes at
Chester, accompanied by Benny Lynch, and the Corporation Stakes
at Doncaster, accompanied by Stockbridge, brought him to the peak
of fitness for Royal Ascot.

Black Tarquin sailed successfully through his three preliminary
races. The betting public were so dazzled by the qualifications of the
two outstanding English-trained horses in the Gold Cup and by the
prospect of a settlement of the controversy provoked by the St. Leger
that they ignored Turmoil II, the recent winner of the corresponding
race in France, the Prix du Cadran. Black Tarquin started at 11–10,
Alycidon at 5–4, and Turmoil II at 100–6. From the moment
Alycidon stepped on to the track at Ascot he seemed a horse geared
mentally and physically for a supreme effort. Stockbridge and Benny
Lynch played their supporting roles to perfection, and five furlongs
from home Smith sent Alycidon past Benny Lynch into the lead.
Black Tarquin moved up to join Alycidon as they turned into the
straight, and seemed to be going ominously well for a few strides.

But Alycidon galloped on remorselessly, and in the end it was Black Tarquin who cracked, leaving Alycidon to pound ahead to win, with ears pricked, by five lengths. Turmoil II never got into the picture, and trailed in fourth, nearly twenty lengths behind the winner.

Black Tarquin had given his all, and the effort broke him. He ran once more, finishing only fourth in the Princess of Wales's Stakes at the Newmarket July meeting, and then retired.

The superiority of Alycidon to the best of the other available stayers in the Ascot Gold Cup was so overwhelming that the other two races of the "Cup" Triple Crown were at his mercy. Even so he did not complete his mission without alarm. The going was terribly hard at Goodwood and Alycidon, for all Stockbridge and Benny Lynch could do to soften up the opposition, was so stumped up that he had to struggle his hardest to beat his old rival Riding Mill. This chastening experience might have disheartened a horse less tough and resilient, but Alycidon came back fighting fit for his final venture in the Doncaster Cup in which, aided by a new pacemaker Amiris, he gave one of his most devastating performances to beat Aldborough by eight lengths. Aldborough paid the most explicit of compliments to his conqueror when he beat a good field for the Doncaster Cup in convincing fashion a year later.

The stud careers of Black Tarquin and Alycidon wrote a revealing tail-piece to the story of their racecourse rivalry. Black Tarquin, supposedly the more brilliant of the pair, was a comparative failure as a stallion, though most of his progeny stayed and many did well as jumpers. Alycidon, on the other hand, was one of the most success-ful stallions of his time. He headed the list of winning sires once, was second twice, and was in the first eight six times. He got Classic winners and animals who excelled over all racing distances. Slow horses do not achieve such success as sires of top class performers on the flat, and the stud record of Alycidon exposed the criticism that he was a one-paced plodder as a baseless calumny. Alycidon may have been the last of the great stayers; but he would have achieved great-ness as surely in the age of the glorification of the middle distance horse.

Native Dancer

Native Dancer was one of the greatest American horses of the post-war era. Defeated only once, and unluckily at that, he became a nation-wide sporting hero owing to the fact that his racing career happened to coincide with the rapid spread of television; moreover, being a grey, he was an easy horse for any viewer to follow on the screen. Through his many television appearances he made for American racing thousands of friends who might otherwise have remained totally indifferent to the sport. Arkle performed the same service for National Hunt racing over here.

He was foaled on March 27th, 1950 at the Dan W. Scott Farm in Lexington, Kentucky, directly across the road from the Gallaher Farm where the stallion Polynesian stood. He himself was bred and owned by Mr. Alfred G. Vanderbilt and was a grey colt by Polynesian out of Geisha, by Discovery. Polynesian was by Unbreakable, a son of Hyperion's half-brother Sickle. Unbreakable raced in England, where he was trained by Captain Cecil Boyd-Rochfort and his most important success was in that popular seven furlong handicap, the Victoria Cup at Hurst Park. Polynesian was a brilliant though rather crotchety performer. As a two-year-old he suffered from a form of blood-poisoning that at times almost paralysed him. He is said to have been cured of this when his trainer's small son knocked a wasps' nest out of a tree under which Polynesian happened to be standing. The stings sent Polynesian almost mad with pain and irritation, and rushing madly about the paddock, he sweated the poison right out of his system. He must have had a tough constitution as he ran fifty-eight times and was only ten times unplaced. Although he won the Preakness of just over nine furlongs, he was probably more effective still over shorter distances and he equalled the then world record for six furlongs of 1 minute 9⅕th seconds.

Geisha, dam of Native Dancer, won one race and was a sprinter who came from a sprinting female line. Her sire Discovery was a tough performer who stood up to plenty of hard racing and won twenty-seven of his sixty-three outings. Miyako, dam of Geisha, was bought by Mr. Vanderbilt after winning a stakes race. She only produced two other foals, neither of any account, before her death in 1948. However Miyako's dam La Chica was a notably successful brood mare, among her offspring being El Chico, the leading two-year-old of 1938. La Grisette, dam of La Chica, was by Roi Herode, sire of another brilliant grey horse, The Tetrarch.

Physically Native Dancer, when full-grown, was one of the most impressive horses seen on the American Turf in modern times. Standing 16.3 hands, there was no suggestion of legginess about him and he was tremendously powerful. His massive build, his iron-grey colour and the relentless manner in which he so often crushed his opponents often earned him comparison to a battleship. His temperament was fundamentally kindly, but he could sometimes be playfully rough to the point of being rumbustious. He was broken at Mr. Vanderbilt's Sagamore Farm in Maryland, hence his eventual and typically American nickname of "the grey ghost of Sagamore". His trainer was Bill Winfrey who had begun his professional racing career by "walking the hots" for his father; in other words he walked horses round to allow them to cool off after a race or a work-out. For a brief period Winfrey was a jockey but in his own words he was "long on weight and short on ability".

In his first season's racing Native Dancer ran nine times and remained undefeated. It can be claimed that he was never seriously extended as he won every one of his races by open daylight. Seven of his successes were stakes—the Youthful, Flash, Saratoga Special, Grand Union Hotel, Hopeful, Futurity and East View—and altogether he won $230,495, a record sum for a two-year-old. By and large he gave the impression of smooth, high-class, professional competence rather than of sheer brilliance. In the Futurity, though, he equalled the course and world record of 1 minute 14⅔ths seconds for a straight six and a half furlongs. He won from five furlongs to a mile and half a furlong and no matter the distance, he left onlookers with the feeling that he had scored with a nice bit in hand. Except that he was inclined to take a strong hold at the start of his races, he took no more out of himself than was strictly neccessary. In the Experimental Free Handicap he was given 9 st. 4 lb., 7 lb. more than his nearest rivals, Laffango and Tahitian King. When the season was concluded, in two of the three polls taken he was voted over-all champion, an honour never before accorded to a two-year-old. In the third poll he was second in the voting for the Horse of the Year and a unanimous selection for the position of champion two-year-old.

After his two-year-old season Native Dancer was shipped to California and his ankles were fired. This caused rumours that he was basically unsound and unlikely to stand further training. In fact the only crisis during his Californian sojourn was when he broke loose one morning and jumped a big fence, luckily without doing himself an injury. In the meantime he put on a lot of weight and as a three-year-old he looked a typical, massive, heavily muscled sprinter. A good many people reckoned he was certain to have stamina limitations as apart from his appearance, his pedigree indicated he might not stay.

Returning to the East in the spring, Native Dancer won the one mile Gotham Stakes at Jamaica by two lengths and a week later the Wood Memorial in which he beat Tahitian King and Invigorator with ease. He then moved on to Louisville for his main target, the ten furlong Kentucky Derby, and this, of all races, was the one he was destined to lose.

The Kentucky Derby was won by Cain Hoy Stable's Dark Star who led from start to finish and beat Native Dancer by a head in the fifth fastest Derby on record at that time. There is no doubt that Native Dancer ought to have won. He was badly interfered with on the first bend and had to be checked. His jockey Eric Guerin seemed to lose his head after this and took him unnecessarily wide. In the last two furlongs the grey, though he had improved his position considerably, still had two and a half lengths to make up on Dark Star and he just failed to close the gap, the winning post coming a couple of strides too soon. He had started a hot favourite at 7–10 and his defeat caused a tremendous sensation. After the race Guerin addressed some lively remarks to Money Broker's jockey, an individual with the unusual name of Al Popara, while a good many spectators had unflattering comments to make on the way that Guerin had handled the favourite. One member of the Churchill Downs board of directors observed in deep disgust: "He took that colt everywhere on the track except the ladies' room." Dark Star in due course sired that good filly Gazala, winner of the French One Thousand Guineas and the French Oaks in 1967.

None the worse, Native Dancer next won the Withers Stakes by four lengths. On May 23rd he clashed again with Dark Star, this time in the Preakness. Dark Star bowed a tendon after leading for a mile and Native Dancer, a 5–1 on favourite despite his Derby defeat, won by a neck from Jamie K. The narrow margin of his victory caused renewed misgivings on the score of his stamina, but he routed his critics a fortnight later by winning the mile and a half Belmont Stakes in 2 minutes 28⅖ths seconds, a time only bettered by Count Fleet and Citation. Again Jamie K. was the runner-up and again the winning margin was only a neck. Native Dancer, though, appeared to be increasing his lead at the finish and at one point in the straight Jamie K. had only been a head behind the grey.

The remainder of Native Dancer's three-year-old career has been described as a "triumphant romp". He won the Dwyer, the Arlington Classic by nine lengths, the Travers by five and a half lengths, and the American Derby. Unfortunately in the American Derby, in which Arcaro rode him in place of Guerin who was under suspension, he bruised a foot badly. Thus his eagerly awaited autumn meeting with the handicap champion, Tom Fool, never took place. Tom Fool it was who was voted Horse of the Year. Native Dancer had won nine races as a three-year-old and earned for Mr. Vanderbilt $513,425.

Native Dancer's campaign as a four-year-old took place entirely in New York. He only ran three times but was nevertheless voted Horse of the Year and the best handicap horse. He began by winning a six furlong event at Belmont Park, easily defeating two good sprinters, Laffango and Impasse, who were receiving 5 lb. and 13 lb. respectively. Eight days later, carrying 9 st. 4 lb. in the Metropolitan Mile and conceding from 13 lb. to 23 lb. to his rivals, he just got up to beat Straight Face, who had recently won the Dixie Handicap in great style, by a neck. Seven lengths behind Straight Face on the turn for home, he showed superb courage and acceleration to snatch the lead in the last few strides. In his next race Straight Face won the Suburban Handicap.

Native Dancer developed soreness in his off fore-foot soon afterwards and did not run again for three months. He reappeared in the Oneonta Handicap, an overnight race at Saratoga. Carrying 9 st. 11 lb. he beat his two opponents with contemptuous ease. In the Metropolitan Mile Native Dancer had caused a "minus pool" on the Tote. Fearing another "minus pool", the Saratoga management

staged the Oneonta Handicap as a betless exhibition. In this contest
Native Dancer wore a bar-plate shoe with a clipper to protect his
tender foot. Unfortunately, though, the injury recurred in a
training spin a few days later and Mr. Vanderbilt reluctantly decided
to send his champion to the stud. Native Dancer had won $785,240
in prize money and at the time only Citation, Stymie and Armed had
won more.

   Native Dancer died in the autumn of 1967. Possibly, considering
how good he was himself, he did not quite fulfil expectations at the
stud and he was never champion sire. However, apart from many
fast two-year-olds, he sired Kauai King, winner of the Kentucky
Derby and the Preakness in 1966, in which year he finished second
in the list of winning sires. In Europe he is best remembered by the
brilliant grey filly Hula Dancer, whose victories included the Grand
Criterium, the One Thousand Guineas and the Champion Stakes.
He also sired the English-trained Secret Step, a top-class sprinter,
and the French-trained Dan Cupid, sire of Sea Bird, winner of the
Derby and the Prix de l'Arc de Triomphe and undoubtedly one of
the outstanding horses of this century.

Swaps

The years 1955 and 1956 were among the most exciting in American
racing history, because they were graced by not one but two
champions of the very highest grade—Swaps and Nashua. Horses
of their class, which is world class, usually come singly, and at
intervals of several generations. The coincidence of Swaps and
Nashua aroused feverish and unprecedented interest among racing
fans in all parts of the United States. Every detail of their training
routines, their ailments, their characters, their plans and performances, were chronicled, mulled over and debated. The merits of each
were argued with passion by his own partisans, but when they had
done racing no impartial observer of the American racing scene would
have cared to state with absolute conviction, which was the better of
the pair. They met twice in racecourse competition with a resulting
score of one-all; they were elected "Horse of the Year" once each;
they had similar success ratios, Swaps winning nineteen of his
twenty-five starts and Nashua twenty-two of his thirty starts. There
was little enough to choose between them on these counts, and
preference has been given to Swaps for the purpose of this study not
through conviction that he was the better, but because the fortitude
he displayed in overcoming pain and physical handicap made him
unique among great racehorses. Moreover Swaps was the product of
a revolutionary system which shook traditional concepts of the way
thoroughbreds must be bred and raised, and this factor, with the
controversy that followed, added spice to his triumphs on the
racetrack.

It is even possible that Swaps's most enduring achievement was to
shatter the old mystique of the Kentucky breeders. It had been
almost an article of faith that high-class thoroughbreds could only
be reared in spacious paddocks on the blue grass lands of Kentucky,

watered by subterranean springs of limestone water. Rex Ellsworth, the owner-breeder of Swaps, maintained that the Kentucky mystique was nonsense. To prove his point he set out to breed thoroughbreds on the semi-desert lands of California. Whereas the Kentucky breeders calculated that ten acres of rich pasture were required for each thoroughbred, Ellsworth kept up to 700 horses on 300 acres. Instead of spacious paddocks of lush grazing, the Ellsworth horses had small pens, enclosed by wire fences, and instead of traditional fodder they were fed pellets of grain, molasses, hay, grass, vitamins and minerals mixed in electronically controlled machines with different proportions for foals, brood mares, yearlings and horses in training. "Why, they raise horses like we raise dogs," remarked one Kentucky breeder in disgust after hearing a description of Ellsworth's methods. But the proof of the pellets is not in the eating but in the racing form of the consumers, and Swaps demonstrated that Ellsworth's methods could produce a champion, and left the Kentucky myth in decidedly threadbare condition when he travelled east to Louisville in May 1955 to beat the locally bred star Nashua and become the first California-bred winner of the Kentucky Derby.

The Swaps story really began in 1933 when Rex Ellsworth, accompanied by his brother Heber, visited Lexington, Kentucky, with a hired horse-box and drove back to his native Arizona with eight fillies and mares purchased for a grand total of 600 dollars. They were cheap animals even at depression prices, and Ellsworth had been compelled to ignore pedigree and select purely on conformation. "Conformation rather than pedigree" remained his guiding principle as he built up his racing and breeding empire in the years that followed. His partner in the enterprise was Meshach ("Mish") Tenney, who was officially the trainer. They were devout Mormons; each saw service as a missionary, Tenney in Colorado and Ellsworth in Africa, and when the stable began to enjoy success their Church received the customary 10 per cent of earnings. Johnny Burton, who rode Swaps in his races as a two-year-old, also was a Mormon, and left the stable to go on a mission.

By occupation Ellsworth and Tenney were ranchers and cowboys. Ellsworth was brought up to ride the range and was expert in all aspects of horsemastership which are essential to the profession of cowboy, including practical veterinary work, saddlery and shoeing. This last-named aptitude served him in good stead at one time when there was a nation-wide strike of racecourse farriers, though he made himself unpopular with the union by doing his own shoeing. The decisive moment in the development of Ellsworth's breeding interests came shortly after the second world war when he toured Europe in search of a top-class stallion. He negotiated for, but failed to obtain, Nasrullah, who later was exported from Ireland to Kentucky, where he sired Swaps's great rival Nashua. Instead Ellsworth paid 146,000 dollars for Khaled, another horse of the Aga Khan's breeding. Khaled was a high-class miler who had won such important races as the Coventry Stakes, the Middle Park Stakes and the St. James's Palace Stakes and been second in the Two Thousand Guineas. He was by Hyperion whose sons Heliopolis and Alibhai had already become stud successes in the United States.

Having installed Khaled at the Ellsworth Ranch at Chino, California, for the 1948 stud season, Ellsworth began to acquire mares by Beau Pere to mate with him. Beau Pere, by the great stayer Son-in-Law, had been located in England, Australia, New Zealand and the United States during an extraordinarily varied stud career, and was then the leading stallion in California. Thus he bought the Beau Pere filly Iron Reward, together with two other yearlings, for 45,000 dollars. Iron Reward had bad joints and was so inadequate a racer that the best she could do in eight attempts was to finish fourth twice in the lowest class. But she paid a rich dividend when in 1952, as a result of one of her planned matings with Khaled, she produced the chestnut colt who was to become famous as Swaps.

Although Swaps lacked the rolling grassy paddocks in which Kentucky youngsters built up muscle and sinew, he did not want for healthy exercise or schooling in his early days. In conformity with the practice at the Ellsworth Ranch, he was taught to walk, trot, turn and canter slowly in hand even before he was weaned, and as a yearling was ridden regularly in an enclosed school. The Ellsworth early training methods produced horses who were noted for their excellent behaviour and discipline. Swaps was no exception to the rule. Though eager, fiery even, in action, he was quiet as an old sheep at all other times. When he was brought up to Kentucky for his Derby venture, Tenney provided a news story which endeared horse and trainer to the public by sleeping in his box.

Swaps grew up a model of deportment and also, in most respects, a model of thoroughbred conformation. He was long and deep in the body, with a beatifully placed shoulder, short cannon bones and perfectly sloped, springy pasterns. If he could be faulted it was on account of his rather light quarters, but his owner, a student of conformation, thought them even and well shaped. That he was fighting against pain and recurrent lameness for most of his active life was certainly not due to physical malformation, but to the misfortune of splitting the sole and heel of his off forefoot. The injury occurred in January of his three-year-old season, the wound became infected, and gave him practically constant trouble until his enforced retirement twenty months later.

Swaps, who was so called because Ellsworth and Tenney were continually swapping ideas on how to name him without being able to reach a decision, had not raced much as a two-year-old or given any real indication of his future excellence. Most of his juvenile racing took place in a period of less than two months at Hollywood Park in the middle of the year. He won a maiden race by three lengths and beat a useful horse called Trentonian by two and a half lengths in the June Juvenile Stakes, but was beaten into third place in the Westchester and the Haggin Stakes, and was unplaced in the Charles S. Howard Stakes. He was found to have a high temperature after his failure in the last-named race, and was not fit to run again until six months later, when he returned to win a small race at Santa Anita on December 30th. He beat much stronger opposition in the San Vicente Stakes on the same course on January 19th, but it was during that race that he first sustained his foot injury. Tenney designed a soft leather pad to fit under the shoe and protect the foot; but, although this enabled him to continue racing, he was limited to running on good ground because mud tended to aggravate the infection.

The trouble did not prevent Swaps winning his first race of major importance exactly a month later. This was the Santa Anita Derby in which he showed his inexperience by shying at a starting gate parked on the inside of the course one hundred yards from the finish. He nearly threw the race away, but recovered in time to hold off Jane's Joe and win by half a length.

After one small preliminary race, Swaps then faced Nashua in America's foremost Classic race, the Kentucky Derby. At first the tendency at Churchill Downs was to disparage the Californian upstart colt and regard Nashua as a sure winner, but opinion began to shift in favour of Swaps shortly before the race. Willie Shoemaker, who rode Swaps in most of his races after his two-year-old days, got him away very quickly, took the inside rail at the first bend, and never lost the lead. Nashua almost drew level on the last turn, but Shoemaker only needed to ride Swaps with his hands to send the Ellsworth colt clear again in the straight to win by one and a half lengths.

Swaps was not entered in the Preakness or the Belmont Stakes, so he returned to California after the Derby, leaving the other two races of the Triple Crown to Nashua. He carried all before him in his native State, and gained one of his most significant successes in the Californian Stakes at Hollywood Park, in which he beat Determine, the winner of the Kentucky Derby the previous year, comfortably by one and a quarter lengths. In August Swaps moved to Chicago to win the American Derby at Washington Park, and it was on the same course eleven days later that the match between Swaps and Nashua, which enterprising racecourse executives all over the United States had been trying to arrange ever since the Kentucky Derby, at last materialized. A great deal of prestige, as well as a "winner-take-all" prize of 100,000 dollars, depended on the result, and the meeting of the two brilliant colts generated intense nationwide interest. The race itself was an anticlimax. Catching his rival by surprise, Eddie Arcaro whipped Nashua out of the gate and opened up a clear lead immediately. Try as he would, Swaps could never get properly on terms, and collapsed in the last furlong to suffer a seemingly ignominious defeat by six and a half lengths.

Nashua was acclaimed three-year-old champion, and was elected "Horse of the Year" in due course. He was entitled to the honour, though it transpired subsequently that the Washington Park Match did not reflect fairly the relative merits of the two runners. Swaps's heel was so bad after the match that an operation was necessary, and his joints and coronets had to be blistered. He was not fit to run again that year and there is no doubt that he had been unable to do himself justice in the match.

Several attempts were made to arrange a rubber match between Swaps and Nashua as four-year-olds; but although Ellsworth uttered challenging sounds and announced his intention of following Nashua into the Atlantic if necessary, satisfactory arrangements were never completed. American owners as a rule are willing to put their horses to the most searching tests and accept victory and defeat as they come, but in this case the two outstanding four-year-olds were able to pursue profitable but separate campaigns. Nashua did little wrong and won six of his ten races, but at the end of the day it was

agreed that his efforts had not compared with the sheer brilliance
shown by Swaps. The performances of Swaps in 1956 were described
as the finest example of sustained greatness by any four-year-old in
American racing history, and he was elected "Horse of the Year"
almost unanimously. He broke or equalled no fewer than five world
records while conceding lumps of weight to other class horses and
captured races of the importance of the American Handicap ($1\frac{1}{8}$
miles), the Hollywood Gold Cup ($1\frac{1}{4}$ miles) and the Sunset Handicap ($1\frac{5}{8}$ miles), all at Hollywood Park, and the Washington Park
Handicap (1 mile) on the Illinois track. Different distances came
alike to him and failed to dim his brilliance, and the only real
advantage he enjoyed was the limitation of the top weight to 130 lb.
in the races he contested. He was beaten in only one of his ten races
as a four-year-old, and an uncharacteristic lapse of concentration
by Shoemaker was responsible for his defeat in the Californian
Stakes, the race in which he had beaten Determine the previous
year.

A second operation, involving the removal of infected tissue from
his heel, had been necessary in February. Shortly before the
American Handicap tetramycin was administered to combat infection which was spreading up the pastern, and in September, shortly
before he was due to take part in the United Nations Handicap at
Atlantic City, his troubles finally caught up with him. Fresh infection of the heel prevented him running, and a few weeks later, when
he was back in training at Garden State Park, he sustained two
lineal fractures of his near hind cannon bone during a gallop. Four
days later, trying to get up in his stall, he broke the plaster cast and
extended the fracture to the fetlock. The vets were doubtful whether
he could be saved, but "Sunny Jim" Fitzsimmons, the trainer of
his great rival Nashua, lent a special sling in which he was suspended
for six weeks in order to keep the weight off the injured leg.

By early September he was able to be flown home to California.
At the airport a large and emotional crowd watched him hobble
from the aircraft to the horsebox which was to take him to the Ellsworth Ranch. The magnificent thoroughbred, 16 hands 2 inches
tall, had lost 300 lb. of his normal weight of 1,200 lb., but he had
not lost his proud bearing or the docility that had made him such a
wonderful patient. Ellsworth announced that he would race again
when he was fully sound, but this was never within the bounds of
possibility. He had sold a half share in Swaps to John Galbreath "for

an exchange of thoroughbred stock, breeding seasons and other personal considerations" after the Washington Park Handicap, and sold the other half to Mrs. Galbreath for a further consideration of 1,000,000 dollars about a year after the horse's retirement. Swaps went to stud at the famous Spendthrift Farm in the State of Kentucky where he had gained his historic Derby triumph; and in 1963 his son Chateaugay followed his shining example by winning America's premier Classic race.

Ribot

If the reputation of Ribot depended entirely on his solitary appearance in England in the King George VI and Queen Elizabeth Stakes of 1956 he would hardly be regarded as one of the greatest racehorses who ever trod the Turf. Of course he won all right. He never was beaten in any of the sixteen races in which he took part; but for much of the distance of $1\frac{1}{2}$ miles he seemed to be making heavy weather of the task of getting the better of one of the poorest collections of horses, apart from his august self, who have ever turned out for England's most important international race. The runner-up was the Queen's colt High Veldt, a three-year-old who had won two of the early Classic Trials but could be called top-class only by courtesy and found his right mark when finishing fifth in the St. Leger; and the third horse was the Belgian champion Todrai, who did not quite measure up to the highest international standards and had compromised his chance by charging the starting gate, dislodging his rider and galloping loose for several minutes before he could be caught.

Ribot's invariable partner Camici had to push Ribot repeatedly to hold his place as they galloped through the Swinley Bottom and began the long ascent from the Old Mile start towards the straight. Todrai led round the last bend, and it was not until this stage had been reached that Ribot began to dominate his opponents in the masterful manner to which his admirers were accustomed. In the final quarter mile he produced the acceleration for which he was famous on the Continent of Europe, and streaked away from the others to beat High Veldt by five lengths.

The final victory was conclusive, but the performance as a whole was not impressive enough to satisfy the English critics who had been led to expect the easy mastery of a world champion. The explanation is clear. The Ascot course had been saturated by heavy rains which had overtaxed the existing drainage system and left boggy patches to interrupt the normal even tenor of Ribot's stride. Afterwards Camici, an Italian jockey as dour as an Aberdonian, broke his habitual silence to state that Ribot seemed to resent the sticky ground. Only when he reached the higher, drier ground in the straight was he able to bring his superb action into play.

To find the most majestic performances of Ribot, the performances which proved him indisputably a world-beater, it is necessary to turn to his two ventures in the Prix de l'Arc de Triomphe and to some of his races in Italy, notably the Gran Premio del Jockey Club. Nevertheless the significance of his victory in the King George VI and Queen Elizabeth Stakes should not be missed, for one of the surest indications of true greatness in a racehorse is the ability to rise above disadvantages and win in unfavourable circumstances.

Ribot was foaled at the English National Stud at West Grinstead, in Sussex, on February 27th, 1952. His dam Romanella was on a visit to Tenerani, who was also the sire of Ribot but had been standing in his native Italy the previous stud season. Thus Ribot was not in England for the first time when he came to win the King George VI and Queen Elizabeth Stakes four years later, but the entire credit for the greatness of Ribot, so far as human agency may determine these inscrutable matters, belonged to his breeder Federico Tesio, who was also responsible for the breeding of Tenerani and Romanella.

Tesio, a former Italian cavalry officer, had founded his stud at Dormello in lovely surroundings on the shores of Lake Maggiore in 1898. As he was not a rich man, he had to seek his foundation stock in the bargain sections of the thoroughbred market, but such was his flair, his industry, his horsemastership, his judgment, indeed his genius, that he was able to build up one of the most influential studs the world has ever known in a country whose thoroughbred population was only a fraction of that of England and Ireland combined, or France, or the United States, or Argentina. He bred a score of winners of the Italian Derby, the two unbeaten world-beaters Nearco and Ribot, and at least half a dozen other horses of world class including Donatello II, Tenerani, Botticelli, Toulouse Lautrec and Niccolo Dell' Arca.

One of the secrets of Tesio's success was close supervision of every aspect of his racing empire. The cluster of small farms that made up the Dormello stud was centred on his own house, and he trained his own horses at Milan forty miles away. In this way he had intimate knowledge of the characteristics of all his animals in the stud and the stable, and based his mating plans on that knowledge rather than any breeding theories. He liked to mate his mares with a variety of stallions. For this reason he seldom kept a stallion of his own; he preferred to sell his best horses when their racing was done and to patronize them, together with many other foreign stallions, from time to time if they were standing abroad.

The breeding of Ribot illustrated several aspects of Tesio's policies and his genius for the cheap acquisition of breeding stock destined to prove its worth many times over. He bought the granddams of both Ribot's sire Tenerani and Ribot himself in England for exiguous sums. Try Try Again, the granddam of Tenerani, was bought at the Doncaster Yearling Sales in 1932 for 140 guineas, and Barbara Burrini, the granddam of Ribot, was bought as a foal at the Newmarket December Sales in 1937 for 350 guineas. If these were fantastically cheap animals on which to base the production of a world-beater, let it be added that Tenerani and Ribot's dam Romanella showed high-class form. Tenerani, a horse of supreme toughness and courage, was not only one of Tesio's twenty Italian Derby winners but also his first winner in England when he beat the subsequent St. Leger winner Black Tarquin in the Queen Elizabeth Stakes at Ascot and went on to beat the Ascot Gold Cup winner Arbar, who broke down near the finish, in the Goodwood Cup. Romanella was fast and precocious. She won one of Italy's most important two-year-old races, the Criterium Nazionale, but developed a ringbone and did not run after her first season. The union of the tough, sound, staying Tenerani and the speedy Romanella produced the incomparable Ribot.

Tesio always maintained that Tenerani was an underrated horse and would sire a champion. He was proved right when Tenerani got Ribot in the last of his three stud seasons in Italy before being sent to England, where he was a great failure, perhaps for lack of the right mares.

Ribot showed little distinction in his earliest days. He was far the smallest of the Dormello crop of foals of 1952 and was nicknamed "il piccolo"—the little one. However he was alert and intelligent, and when he went into training quickly gave his owner-trainer-breeder the idea that he had a brilliant future. "This little one will be somebody one day; he is full of quality and remarkably well shaped," Tesio told his wife. Nevertheless his small stature was responsible for his omission from the entries for the Italian Two Thousand Guineas, Derby and St. Leger.

Unfortunately Tesio did not live to see Ribot fulfil his hopes. The great breeder died at the age of eighty-five in May 1954, just two months before the colt made his first public appearance in Milan. For the rest of his career Ribot was the joint property of Tesio's widow, Donna Lydia, and Marchese Mario Incisa della Rochette, who had become Tesio's partner before the second world war when more capital was needed for the proper development for the whole racing and breeding empire, known as the Razza Dormello-Olgiata. He was trained by Ugo Penco for all his races and ridden by Enrico Camici.

Ribot won his first race, the Premio Tramuschio over five furlongs at Milan on July 5th, by a length from his stable companion Donata Veneziana. The outing was primarily educative, and it was not until he won the Criterium Nazionale, the race in which his dam had made her name, over an additional furlong on the same course in September that he established himself as one of the leaders of his age. His third and last race that season was the Gran Criterium, Italy's greatest two-year-old race, a month later. On that occasion Ribot had to struggle harder than in any of his other races, and got the better of Gail by no more than a head. Afterwards Camici blamed himself for faulty tactics. Ribot had made all the running in his two previous races, but Camici rode a waiting race in an attempt to help him stay the $7\frac{1}{2}$ furlongs of the Gran Criterium, and this evidently did not suit him. In all his subsequent races Ribot was allowed to keep in close touch with the leaders the whole way, for the great horse was a free runner. Yet Gail, who went on to beat another high-class two-year-old Zagros, besides good older horses, in the Premio Chiusura three weeks later, was a brilliant and precocious colt who was a very formidable opponent for Ribot in his immaturity.

Ribot spent the close season at the splendidly equipped Barbaricina winter training quarters at Pisa near the west coast of Italy, and it was on the little Pisa track that he had his first race as a three-year-old in the $7\frac{1}{2}$ furlongs Premio Pisa, in which he beat Donata

Veneziana for the second time, though in a canter by the greatly increased margin of six lengths. As he was not engaged in the principal Italian Classic races he simply free-wheeled through minor races in the spring and summer, though the $1\frac{1}{4}$ miles Premio Emanuelo Filiberto at Milan in April, when he enlarged his previous narrow margin of superiority over Gail to an overwhelming ten lengths, ranks as a Classic race in Italy. For this reason he had the advantage of reaching his main objective, the Prix de l'Arc de Triomphe at Longchamp on October 9th, in fresh condition compared to his rivals who had had arduous programmes throughout the season. Ribot tuned up for his Longchamp expedition by running in the Premio Besana at Milan a month earlier and gave a convincing demonstration of his fitness and his superb quality by beating Derain, who was to win the Italian St. Leger little more than a week later, by ten lengths.

There have been better fields for the Prix de l'Arc de Triomphe than the horses who turned out against Ribot in 1955, but they were very far from negligible. They included the French Derby winner Rapace and the Irish Derby winner Zarathustra; Macip and Bewitched, the first and second in the French St. Leger; the Irish Two Thousand Guineas winner Hugh Lupus; and the fillies Douve and Picounda, who had been first and second in the French Oaks. Ribot disposed of them all summarily. His confirmed tactics of running in the leading group from the start kept him out of trouble, for there was a scrimmage in the early stages in which Hidalgo fell and several other horses, including Rapace and Bewitched, were badly hampered. In the straight Ribot drew away from all the others in a commanding fashion which invalidated any excuses that might be put forward on behalf of his opponents and passed the winning post three lengths in front of Beau Prince II, who had been third in the Grand Prix and the St. Leger, with Picounda in third place.

After he had had such an easy season Ribot was probably improved by his race in the Prix de l'Arc de Triomphe. At any rate, he gave an even more masterful performance in his one remaining race as a three-year-old, the Premio del Jockey Club over $1\frac{1}{2}$ miles at Milan a fortnight later. The opposition lacked the all-round strength of the field at Longchamp, but it did include the good French seven-year-old Norman, who had won the race twice already. Ribot's old rival Gail and Damina set a fast pace, but Ribot kept effortlessly in touch. In the straight he swept to the front, increased his lead with every stride and completely outclassed Norman to win by fifteen lengths.

The Premio del Jockey Club concluded Ribot's activities for 1955 and he retired to winter again at Barbaricina in preparation for a four-year-old campaign which was to set the seal on his fame. It is impossible not to admire the restraint and the realism with which his career was planned. As a four-year-old he was given three important objectives, the Gran Premio di Milano over one mile seven furlongs in June followed by the two principal European international races, the King George VI and Queen Elizabeth Stakes and the Prix de l'Arc de Triomphe. His other outings, three in the spring and one in September, were mere pipe-openers designed to ensure that he would be fighting fit on the days that mattered. In the Gran Premio di Milano, the biggest event in the Italian calendar, he beat by eight lengths his stable companion Tissot, who had won another big race, the Premio d'Italia, in runaway fashion; his victory at Ascot has been described already. The 1956 Prix de l'Arc de Triomphe provided him with his sternest test of all. The field at Longchamp included the high-ranking American horses Fisherman and Career Boy; Fisherman was a past winner of the Washington International and another runner, Master Boing, was a future winner of the Laurel Park race. Zarathustra took part again, and other runners were the Irish Derby winner Talgo, the French St. Leger winner Arabian, the Grand Prix winner Vattel and the two Classic fillies Apollonia and Sicarelle, the winners of the French Oaks and the Oaks respectively. Fisherman made the running in true American style, but was never far in front of Ribot, who moved up to the leader approaching the last turn and shot ahead in the straight to open up an ever-increasing gap, without Camici needing even to feel for his whip, and win by six lengths from Talgo. Tanerko, who was to win the Grand Prix de Saint-Cloud in each of the next two years, was two more lengths away in third place.

Ribot won his second Prix de l'Arc de Triomphe by an even wider margin than Vaguely Noble was to do twelve years later. Sir Ivor, the runner-up to Vaguely Noble, was without much doubt a better horse than Talgo, though Talgo excelled himself at Longchamp and there may not have been a great deal to choose between the overall strength of the opposition in 1956 and in 1968. The comparison need not be stretched to invidious lengths; Ribot and Vaguely Noble were both great racehorses, and Ribot at least could claim the superior merit of having a flawless record.

"Il piccolo" did not remain small or insignificant. When fully developed he stood 16 hands, squarely built with exceptional depth through the body and powerful quarters. For all his strength, he did not lack quality, and his light bay frame had tremendous individuality. He had a most gentle, though playful, disposition while he was in training. At exercise he frequently got rid of his lad through sheer high spirits, and actually had the effrontery to throw his old friend Camici when he was shown to the public in an exhibition gallop on Milan racecourse before he finally retired to stud.

Ribot spent his first stud season at Lord Derby's Woodland Stud at Newmarket, and then returned to Italy. Three years later he was leased to the American John W. Galbreath, who paid 1,350,000 dollars to stand him for a five year period at the Darby Dan Farm at Lexington in Kentucky. When the lease expired in 1965 satisfactory arrangements, particularly in respect of insurance, for his transport back to Italy could not be made, and he remained in Kentucky.

Ribot became the outstanding Classic sire in the world. He sired the Prix de l'Arc de Triomphe winners Molvedo and Prince Royal II, and three of his sons—Ragusa, Ribocco and Ribero—brought off the double of victories in the Irish Sweeps Derby and the Doncaster St. Leger; of his daughters, Alice Frey won the Italian Oaks and Long Look the Oaks at Epsom. He also sired top-class horses like Tom Rolfe, Dapper Dan, Arts and Letters and Graustark in the U.S.A. Nevertheless the majority of his progeny, who required time to mature, were more suited to a European than an American racing system, and by 1968 he had been champoin sire twice in England.

The progeny of Ribot came in many shapes and sizes. Some, like Ribocco, were perfect little models of the thoroughbred; others, like Ribocco's brother Ribero, were a hand taller and less elegant in outline. The characteristic which most of them had in common was a willingness to idle through a race, if permitted to do so, combined with an indomitable will to win once persuaded to enter the fighting line. Very few Ribots lost races by small margins, and that fact gives the measure of the Ribot spirit.

Tulloch

The 1956–57 season produced one of the finest vintage collections of two-year-olds ever seen in Australia. At the end of the season the official handicapper could not separate the two leaders of that age group, Tulloch and Todman, and allotted them 9 st. 5 lb. each in the Free Handicap. It was an assessment that could not be criticized, because they had met twice and emerged with one victory each. Tulloch had outstayed Todman in the Australian Jockey Club Sires Produce Stakes over seven furlongs, but Todman got his revenge in the Champagne Stakes over a furlong less four days later, when he outpaced his famous rival by six lengths. Thus they were inseparable on merit as two-year-olds, but the distances over which they gained their respective victories were the vital clues to the future. For Todman turned out to have distinct stamina limitations, although he won the Canterbury Guineas at nine furlongs, and was essentially a sprinter, if a very brilliant one; whereas Tulloch became a middle distance performer and stayer on whose behalf it could be claimed without demonstrable exaggeration, at the height of his three-year-old career, that he was the best horse in the world.

Records fell right and left while Tulloch was racing. His earnings of £18,088 as a two-year-old were a record for a horse of his age in Australia, and he was the first horse to make a clean sweep of the three big two-year-old races, the Australian Jockey Club Sires Produce Stakes, the Victoria Racing Club Sires Produce Stakes and the Queensland Turf Club Sires Produce Stakes. His total earnings of £66,148 at the end of his second season were the highest ever for a horse at two and three years of age and, by the time he retired at the age of six, he had become the first horse to earn more than £100,000 in Australia. He was the first horse since Florence in 1870–71 to bring off the Classic treble of the A.J.C., V.R.C., and

7

Q.T.C. Derbys. Finally he smashed the record of the mighty Phar Lap by more than two seconds when he won the A.J.C. Derby in 2 minutes 29.1 seconds, and set a new Australian record for 1½ miles when he won the Caulfield Cup as a three-year-old. With this string of records and achievements to his credit, it is no wonder that Tulloch was the idol of the racing public.

Australian horses are famed for their speed, New Zealand horses for their stamina. Tulloch could never be accused of lacking speed, but the stamina which he also possessed in abundant measure was an indication of his New Zealand origin. He was bred by Mr. D. H. Blackie and was foaled at the lovely Trelawney Stud at Cambridge in the Waikato district of the North Island, and was by Khorassan out of Florida by Salmagundi. His sire and maternal grandsire were both British bred. Khorassan, who had replaced one of New Zealand's most successful stallions Foxbridge at the Trelawney Stud, was by the Two Thousand Guineas winner Big Game out of Naishapur, who was second in the Oaks and was a daughter of the Oaks winner Udaipur. He won the Dee Stakes at Chester and the Classic Trial Stakes at Kempton Park. Salmagundi, who never won a race, was a half-brother of the St. Leger winner Salmon Trout. Florida, on the other hand, belonged to a thoroughbred family that had been in New Zealand for nearly a century—since 1861, to be precise, when Tulloch's eighth dam Mountain Nymph was imported from England as a six-year-old. Although collateral branches of the family had produced some high-class horses in the Dominion, the branch from which Tulloch sprang had remained in relative obscurity until the experiment of blending it with classically bred imported stallions was tried.

Florida herself was in training for six seasons, won £6,960 in stakes races and stayed about 1½ miles. She was useless except on soft ground, and had the curious habit of tailing herself off in the early stages of her races and coming with a whirlwind finish. She was a plain little mare and her son Tulloch was not the sort of colt to catch the eye of the undiscriminating observer, because he was small and had a slight dip in his back. But there was no keener judge of a yearling than the leading Sydney trainer Tommy Smith, and he made up his mind to have Tulloch the moment he saw him at the New Zealand National Sales at Trentham, near Wellington, in January 1956, and bought him for 750 guineas. "I liked his game head and his beautiful swinging walk," Smith said by way of explanation of his purchase after Tulloch had demonstrated his excellence. But many people at the time could not understand why Smith had bought so unprepossessing a colt and told him bluntly: "You've made a mistake."

Smith took a lot of yearling purchases back from the New Zealand Sales that January, and none of the others was as difficult to place as Tulloch. In the end he persuaded Mr. E. A. Haley, an octogenarian Sydney sportsman and breeder, to take him, and before long Tulloch proved himself one of the bloodstock bargains of all time. His racing career began early, as he made his debut in the Breeders Plate, the first two-year-old race at Randwick, in September 1956, and was second to Flying Kurana. Horses in Australasia take their ages from August 1st, so Tulloch was officially two-years-old, though his real second birthday did not come round until October. He had just passed that landmark when he won his second race, the five furlongs Canonbury Stakes, in which he beat Prince Darius, who was to be his principal rival in the Classic races the following year. Although he continued to hold his own and never finished out of the first two as a two-year-old, Tulloch did not show that he was anything out of the ordinary until he began to race over longer distances in the autumn. It was then that he gained his three convincing victories in the Sires Produce Stakes and slammed Prince Darius in a six furlong race at Warwick Farm, Sydney, though his defeat by Todman in the Champagne Stakes left the question of the two-year-old championship wide open.

Tulloch was in action again early as a three-year-old when he beat some good sprinters in the seven furlong Warwick Stakes. But the race that everyone was waiting for was the Rosehill Guineas over $1\frac{1}{4}$ miles at Randwick, because this was expected to produce a dramatic and decisive confrontation between Tulloch and Todman. Like so many eagerly awaited events, this did not materialize, because Todman cracked a sesamoid bone running in a preliminary race and did not return to the racecourse until two seasons later. In the absence of Todman, Tulloch had little difficulty in winning the Rosehill Guineas from Prince Darius. He was then aimed at the A.J.C. Derby in which the only doubt concerned his stamina. Some of the critics were inclined to question whether a grandson of Big Game could be relied on to stay $1\frac{1}{2}$ miles, and Neville Selwood, whose mount Ranchipur was the only member of the field of five to have already won over the distance, resolved to put Tulloch's stamina to a searching test. Selwood set a blistering pace, but Ranchipur had had enough five furlongs from home, where Ward, also intent on exposing any weakness in Tulloch, sent Prince Darius into the lead. George Moore, on Tulloch, never had the least cause for concern as these manœuvres unfolded. Tulloch kept in touch without effort, swept past Prince Darius leaving the dip 1½ furlongs from the finish and sprinted away to beat Prince Darius by six lengths in record time.

Top-class three-year-olds seldom take part in the Caulfield Cup, run over 1½ miles at Melbourne in mid-October, but the manner in which Tulloch had won the A.J.C. Derby had convinced his connections that he could win that coveted race with his handicap weight of 7 st. 8 lb. There was a scare on the eve of the race when Tulloch grazed a leg rolling in a sand bath, but no serious harm was done. His usual jockey Moore could not do the weight, so Selwood was given the responsibility of riding Tulloch. There were some anxious moments in the middle of the race when Tulloch seemed to be badly shut in, and Mac's Amber, ridden by Bill Williamson, looked the probable winner as he turned into the straight with a clear lead. However Selwood succeeded in extricating Tulloch soon enough, and in the last furlong the brilliant three-year-old went by Mac's Amber as if he were standing still and won by two lengths.

After that staggering performance Tulloch seemed to have the even more important Melbourne Cup at his mercy, although he would have had to carry 8 st. 4 lb., 5 lb. more than the record weight carried to victory by a three-year-old in the Flemington race. But Tulloch's owner put his foot down. He stated his firm opinion that it was too much to ask the colt to carry such a big weight against older rivals over two miles after what he had already accomplished, and nothing would make him change his mind, even though Tommy Smith flew from Melbourne to Sydney in an attempt to persuade the old man that Tulloch could win. While the racegoing public were bitterly disappointed at the decision, they had to acknowledge Mr. Haley's humane consideration for the horse.

Although he missed the Melbourne Cup, Tulloch did not lack further tasks as a three-year-old. He beat the luckless Prince Darius again, this time by eight lengths, in the Victoria Derby, and outclassed another good horse, the subsequent Washington International winner Sailor's Guide, in the C. B. Fisher Plate at Flemington. Shortly afterwards he was flown the 1,000 miles to complete his Derby treble as Brisbane, where his victory cost him very little effort.

Tulloch was allowed a well-earned midsummer rest after his Brisbane trip, and did not look quite as robust or bright in his coat as usual when he returned to racing in February. He took a little time to recover his form, and suffered two defeats before he picked up the winning thread again. The first was in the St. George's Stakes over nine furlongs at Caulfield, in which Prince Darius at last got partial revenge for several defeats by winning comfortably, and the second was in the Queen Elizabeth Stakes at Flemington. This 1¾ miles race was run in the presence of the Queen Mother and produced a real thriller in which Sailor's Guide scraped home by a short half head from Prince Darius, with Tulloch a half head further behind in third place. Unhappily there had been some scrimmaging in which Prince Darius was the sufferer and had to be checked on the rails a furlong from home. There was an objection, but Sailor's Guide was allowed to keep the £6,650 first prize.

Although narrowly beaten, Tulloch had shown in the Queen Elizabeth Stakes that he was rapidly approaching his best, and he won all his six remaining races as a three-year-old, which included the V.R.C. and A.J.C. St. Legers. Whereas Tulloch thrived on racing, both Sailor's Guide and Prince Darius took some time to recover from their exertions in the Queen Elizabeth Stakes. Tulloch twice beat Prince Darius with ease, and after doing so by twenty lengths in the A.J.C. St. Leger came out again three days later to beat the top class older miler Grenoble in the eight furlongs All Aged Stakes. His performance in the latter race gave incontrovertible proof of his pluck and versatility. He had several lengths to make up in the straight and for once Moore had to touch him with the whip, but then his celebrated burst of speed was forthcoming and in the end he was a decisive winner.

Tulloch's reputation was sky-high when he had finished racing as a three-year-old. The big Australian weight-for-age races of the following season seemed to be his for the taking, but at that stage his horizons had expanded far beyond the confines of the Australian continent. His owner refused tempting offers to export him, including one of 150,000 dollars from the United States, but was entertaining plans to send him to race abroad. The most ambitious plan was to send him first to the United States and then on to England to take part in the Ascot Gold Cup. These visions of world conquest were frustrated by an unpredictable and mysterious internal ailment which prevented Tulloch racing again for nearly two years. During that period four separate attempts were made to get him fit to run, but each time he began scouring as soon as he was put into strong work. In the autumn of 1959–60 his physical condition at last took a definite turn for the better, but his work in home gallops was so in-and-out that Tommy Smith finally decided that the only way to find out whether it was worthwhile keeping him in training was to run him. The race chosen for his comeback was the Queen's Plate at Flemington in March 1960, and there were scenes of wild enthusiasm on the track when he answered the question of his fitness by beating the Victorian champion Lord. Nor was he beaten in any of the other four races he contested before the end of the season, though he had to struggle hard to beat the 1958 Caulfield Cup winner Sir Blink in the Queen Elizabeth Stakes at Randwick.

By coincidence Tulloch's famous contemporary Todman had made a comeback a few months before Tulloch, after spending two years on the shelf, and won all his three races before signs of further leg trouble led to his retirement to stud. Tulloch, on the other hand, was kept in training for another season with the twin objectives of winning the £25,000 Melbourne Centenary Cup and reaching the £100,000 mark in total earnings. He was allotted 10. st. 1 lb. in the Melbourne Cup, and only Carbine and Archer, way back in the nineteenth century, had ever carried so much weight successfully in that great race. Nevertheless he seemed to have worked his way back to his very best and had broken the Australian record for 1¼ miles when winning the Cox Plate at Moonee Valley, with the result that he started favourite. In the event his running was a sad anti-climax, because he was outpaced in the early stages and could make no real progress later in the race, with the result that he never got out of the middle division of the field. Tulloch never stood higher than 15 hands 2 inches while in training, and the weight may have been just too much for him.

In the second half of the season Tulloch inched his way laboriously towards the £100,000 target like a class but out of form batsman struggling to a century. At one moment an oil company, with a shrewd eye to publicity, sponsored a £4,000 race at Rosehill to help him to his target, but Tulloch let them down when he was beaten by a half head by the six-year-old gelding Savage. He had to move on to Adelaide, 800 miles away, to push his earnings into six figures.

Tulloch went out in a blaze of glory. His last two races were in Queensland, and he won them both. His final performance—and it was surely one of his greatest efforts—was to carry 9 st. 12 lb. to victory in the two miles Brisbane Cup, in which he turned the tables on Sharply, who had beaten him in the Sydney Cup.

Tulloch had found it tough going in his last season, but had triumphed in the end. At one time there was an outcry that he ought to be retired, and after he had been beaten into third place by Lord and Dhaulagiri in the Queen Elizabeth Stakes at Flemington in March 1961, George Moore dismounted and expressed the opinion that he had broken down. "Probably another horse trod on his foot," commented Tommy Smith laconically. The trainer never lost faith that Tulloch would prove himself a great horse again, and the result of the Brisbane Cup vindicated his judgment.

It is a thousand pities that illness cut out the middle, and what might have been the most productive, part of his racing career. Circumstances deprived him of the chance to prove himself in international racing, but on the balance of Australian form he was so superior to Sailor's Guide, who was awarded the Washington International on the disqualification of Tudor Era, that there is no reasonable doubt that he was a great horse by world standards. Tommy Smith was quoted as saying of him: "Tulloch is a freak. The secret of his greatness is that he is a stayer who can go like a sprinter in big races." No better definition of an outstanding race-horse could be made.

Tulloch's racing record testifies eloquently to his courage, class and marvellous constitution. He ran in fifty-three races and won thirty-six of them. He was second twelve and third four times, and the only time he was unplaced was in the Melbourne Centenary Cup.

Ballymoss

Ballymoss was bred by Mr. Richard Ball at his stud at Naul in Co. Dublin. Mr. Ball, therefore, can claim the distinction of having bred the best flat-race horse trained in Ireland this century. He also bred a great steeplechaser in Reynoldstown. Ridden by Mr. Frank Furlong, Reynoldstown won the Grand National with 11 st. 4 lb. in 1935, and ridden by Mr. Fulke Walwyn, he won again with 12 st. 2 lb. the following year.

Ballymoss is by Mossborough out of Indian Call, by Singapore. Mossborough, bred by the late Lord Derby, is by Nearco out of the Bobsleigh mare All Moonshine, a three-parts sister to Hyperion. Mossborough himself was some way short of true classic quality, but he was a good horse, nevertheless, winning five of his sixteen races including the Churchill Stakes at Ascot and the Liverpool Autumn Cup. Probably his best performance was to finish close up second in the Eclipse Stakes conceding the winner, Mystery IX, 12 lb. He was champion sire in 1958 and second in 1957. Another outstanding winner he sired was the English-bred, Irish-trained Noblesse, who won the Timeform Gold Cup and the Oaks.

Indian Call, foaled in 1936, was bred by that lavish supporter of the Turf, Lord Glanely, and was by Singapore out of Flittemere, by Buchan out of Keysoe. In the four nearest generations of Ballymoss's pedigree there are five St. Leger winners—Singapore, Gainsborough, Bayardo, Keysoe and Swynford. In addition, there are the undefeated Grand Prix winner Nearco; Buchan, first past the post in the Ascot Gold Cup only to be disqualified; Rabelais, winner of the Goodwood Cup; Sunstar, winner of the Derby; and Rosedrop and Keystone II, winners of the Oaks. No one could complain, therefore, that Ballymoss's breeding suggested insufficiency of stamina.

Flittemere, grandam of Ballymoss, was bred and raced by the late Lord Derby for whom she won the Yorkshire Oaks. When her racing career was over she was sold at the Newmarket December Sales for 3,500 guineas to Sir Alec Black. Two years later, in 1931, Sir Alec decided to get rid of all his bloodstock and sent thirty-four mares up to Newmarket to be sold. Flittemere, barren to Diophon, was one of twelve mares that failed to reach their respective reserves. The following year what was left of Sir Alec's bloodstock was bought, Flittemere included, by Lord Glanely. Flittemere was a sad disappointment to her new owner as she never bred a winner in this country although her son Grand Flit won fifteen races in Belgium.

Indian Call gave no proof of racing ability. She ran a couple of times without distinction and after the declaration of war in 1939 she and Flittemere were members of a large draft sent by Lord Glanely to the December Sales. Not unnaturally the market was in a depressed condition; Flittemere went for ten guineas and Mr. Richard Ball was able to purchase Indian Call for fifteen guineas. Indian Call proved a marvellous bargain as altogether she bred seven winners, the next best after Ballymoss being Guide, by Chamossaire, who won eight races and over £5,000 in stakes.

In September 1955 Mr. Ball sent Ballymoss to the Yearling Sales at Doncaster and for 4,500 guineas Ballymoss was bought by Vincent O'Brien on behalf of an American patron, Mr. J. McShain. O'Brien was then in the process of transferring his main interests from jumping to the flat. This quiet, trim, immensely shrewd Irishman had established his racing reputation as a remarkably successful trainer of hurdlers and steeplechasers, and from his stable at Cashel in Co. Tipperary he had sent out the Grand National winners Early Mist, Royal Tan and Quare Times; Hattons Grace, winner of the Champion Hurdle three years running; Cottage Rake, winner of the Cheltenham Gold Cup three years running; and another Gold Cup winner, Knock Hard. Ballymoss was to be the first winner of an English classic he trained. However, he had won the Irish Derby in 1953 with Chamier. Chamier had in fact finished second to the English horse Premonition, but Premonition had suffered disqualification, a fate that seemed to many who watched that race to be totally unjust. Mr. McShain is head of a large firm of building contractors, one of whose major constructions is the Pentagon at Washington. A resident of Philadelphia, Mr. McShain races in the United States under the "nom de course" of "Barclay Stable"—hence the red "B" on the front and back of the white jacket of his racing colours.

Ballymoss was slow to develop and his record as a two-year-old gave little indication of future greatness. He ran four times, his one success being in the seven furlong Laragh Maiden Plate at Leopardstown, worth £202 to the winner. A month later he was second in the seven furlong Stayers Plate at the Curragh. At this stage of his career he hardly seemed likely to become more than a useful long distance handicapper. Certainly, when the Derby was discussed during the winter, the name of Ballymoss was never afforded a mention.

The Madrid Free Handicap run over seven furlongs at the Curragh was Ballymoss's first target as a three-year-old, but at the beginning of April, when the race was run, he was still backward physically and in any case the distance was too short for him. He finished unplaced. A month later, considerably straighter in condition, he showed vastly improved form to win the mile and a half Trigo Stakes at Leopardstown. This performance, though, hardly entitled him to serious consideration for the Derby for which he continued to be on offer at 100-1. He was by now, however, beginning to make rapid and impressive improvement and reports of his progress were such that he eventually became quite a popular each-way choice and started at 33-1.

The favourite for the Derby was Sir Victor Sassoon's Crepello, winner of the Two Thousand Guineas, and this big, handsome chestnut by Donatello II dominated his rivals in the paddock at Epsom. It was generally considered, though, that there was a great deal to like about Ballymoss. A chestnut standing 15 hands 3½ inches, he looked powerful and compact and stood on the very best of legs. He certainly gave the impression that he meant business.

Ridden by Irish jockey T. P. Burns, Ballymoss was in a handy position from the start. He was in the leading half dozen coming down the hill and never met with any interference. Fifth at Tattenham Corner, he quickened in the straight and moved smoothly into the lead a quarter of a mile from home. At that point Burns thought he was going to win, but almost immediately Lester Piggott challenged on Crepello. Accelerating in the way that only a top-class horse can, Crepello swept past Ballymoss and in less than no time was two and a half lengths clear. Piggott eased him in the final fifty yards and he won "a bit cheekily", as Burns put it afterwards,

by a length and a half from Ballymoss, with Pipe of Peace a length
away third. After the race the ever-confident Charlie Smirke
declared it was one of the slowest Derbys he had ever ridden in;
actually the time was 2 minutes 35⅖ seconds, the fastest since
Mahmoud won in 1936.

Ballymoss had run a magnificent race against a horse widely
reckoned to be one of the best Derby winners of the century.
Ballymoss, moreover, had one great advantage over Crepello; he
was a sound horse and Crepello was not. Ballymoss went on from
strength to strength; Crepello never saw a racecourse again.

The next race for Ballymoss was the Irish Derby on June 26th.
His task there was a simple one. In a field of eight he started favourite
at 9–4 on and won as he pleased from Hindu Festival and Valentine
Slipper.

With Crepello already in retirement, the joint favourites for the
St. Leger before the August meeting at York were Ballymoss and
Colonel Giles Loder's Eclipse Stakes winner Arctic Explorer.
There was intense interest, therefore, in the 1½ mile Great Voltigeur
Stakes at York in which they met. As a matter of fact neither of
them won, Ballymoss finishing second, four lengths behind Brioche,
while Arctic Explorer ran poorly and was fifth of seven, sixteen
lengths in rear of the winner.

Supporters of Ballymoss were not unduly downcast by the colt's
defeat. He blew a lot after the race and it was assumed that O'Brien
had wisely left something to work on. Moreover there had been a
lot of rain the night before; the going was very dead and Ballymoss
did not appear to like it.

At the final call-over the day before the St. Leger, Ballymoss was
a clear favourite at 5–1. However rain fell throughout the night and
the following morning as well. Confidence in the Irish colt began to
ebb, and because of the conditions nobody seemed to want to back
him. He drifted out to 8–1, the first and second favourites being
Captain Elsey's pair Brioche and Tenterhooks, the latter of whom
had won the Goodwood Cup.

Throughout the race, the early pace of which was distinctly
moderate, Ballymoss was going exceptionally well and Burns's chief
worry was to prevent him from taking the lead too soon. Fifth into
the straight just behind the leaders, Ballymoss struck the front a
good two and a half furlongs from home. At that point it looked as
if he was going to win very easily indeed, but he was unable to draw

clear and in the end he had to fight back hard to withstand a resolute late challenge from Court Harwell. He passed the post a length ahead of Court Harwell with Brioche three-parts of a length away third. It was the first victory of an Irish-trained horse in the St. Leger and the first Irish success in an English Classic since Orby's Derby victory fifty years previously. Mr. and Mrs. McShain had flown over from the United States the previous morning. They had not come over for the Derby as O'Brien had warned them that Ballymoss might not be quite as fit as he liked, having missed a little work through an injured foot.

Ballymoss's final appearance as a three-year-old was in the ten furlong Champion Stakes at Newmarket on October 17th. Favourite at 11–8, he ran deplorably and finished seventeen lengths behind the winner, Rose Royale II. His running was really too bad to be true. Possibly he had gone over the top; conceivably he had hurt himself more severely than was thought at the time when he lashed out in the paddock and struck the rails. Thereafter he was always ridden by a lad in the parade ring.

Ballymoss ran six times as a four-year-old; he was beaten in his first and last races and won the remainder. His first outing was in the one mile five furlong Ormonde Stakes at Chester early in May. He gave the impression in the paddock of being still a bit backward, and starting at 9–4, he was beaten a length and a half by the favourite, the Queen's good four-year-old Doutelle whom he was meeting at level weights. It was generally agreed afterwards that the race was just what he needed. He undoubtedly looked straighter in condition when he lined up for the Coronation Cup at Epsom, and starting favourite at evens, he won comfortably enough by two lengths from the French six-year-old Fric in a field of four.

The next task allotted to Ballymoss was to bring off the double of the ten furlong Eclipse Stakes at Sandown and the mile and a half King George VI and Queen Elizabeth Stakes at Ascot the following week. At that time Tulyar was the only horse to have achieved this particular double, but Busted pulled it off in 1967 and Royal Palace in 1968. As it happened Ballymoss was not severely tested at Sandown as the opposition was far from formidable. Favourite at 11–8 on, he won as he pleased by six lengths from the Queen's Restoration in the fast time of 2 minutes 8⅗ seconds.

A tougher contest faced him at Ascot and among his opponents were the Derby winner Hard Ridden; Thila, winner of the Prix du

Conseil Municipal and nine races in Germany; Brioche; and the Queen's pair Almeria and Doutelle. Ballymoss was favourite at 7–4 and it is no exaggeration to say that he completely outclassed the opposition. As soon as Breasley asked him to accelerate in the straight, he went past the leader, Almeria, like a Rolls-Royce passing a station cab and he won by three lengths with his ears pricked. Almeria was second and Doutelle third. Hard Ridden failed to stay, thereby confirming the widely-held view that he had been singularly fortunate in running in one of the very few Derbys that was not a true test of stamina.

Ballymoss's final European race, and his supreme triumph on the Turf, was the Prix de l'Arc de Triomphe at Longchamp on October 5th. The field of seventeen included that great filly Bella Paola, winner of the One Thousand Guineas, the Oaks and the Prix Vermeille; San Roman, who had won the Grand Prix; Wallaby, winner of the French St. Leger; Sedan, the best three-year-old in Italy; Tanerko, a five-year-old that had won the Grand Prix de Saint-Cloud; Scot, winner of the Prix du Cadran; and Fric, winner of the Coupe de Maisons Laffitte. Although the going was considerably softer than he really liked, Ballymoss proved himself indisputably the best horse in Europe, winning decisively by two lengths from Fric to the unrestrained delight of the many Irish and English spectators who were present. Cherasco was two and a half lengths away third. Breasley rode a typically cool and well-judged race. He made no attempt to hurry Ballymoss in the early stages when he took his position in the rear half of the field. Approaching the final bend Ballymoss began to make up ground on the bit. He struck the front entering the straight and from that point he was never for one second in danger of defeat. His price was the generous one of 39–10 and his victory earned £46,439 for Mr. McShain.

Doubtless it would have been wise to retire Ballymoss at this juncture, but understandably Mr. McShain was keen to display his great horse in America. Accordingly it was decided to run him in the Washington International at Laurel Park, despite the fact that the sharp bends and short run-in on that track were thoroughly unsuitable for a horse of Ballymoss's type.

After seven false starts, it proved a rough and unsatisfactory contest in which Ballymoss finished third behind the English bred Tudor Era and Sailor's Guide. The Stewards subsequently reversed the order of the first two after examining the patrol films of the race.

Controversies and recriminations abounded subsequently and it was regrettable that Ballymoss's fine racing career terminated on a distinctly sour note. He had won £107,165 in stakes, easily surpassing the stakes record for a British horse previously held by Tulyar.

Throughout the summer there had naturally been a good deal of speculation on the plans that would be formulated for Ballymoss's career at the stud. Mr. McShain generously decided that he would like Ballymoss to stand in England although he could, of course, have obtained a far greater financial reward if he had chosen to stand his horse in America. The difficulty was that he stipulated payment in dollars which made it quite impossible for an individual English breeder, or for a group of English breeders for that matter, to obtain the horse. Moreover negotiations with the National Stud came to nothing. However eventually Mr. McShain agreed to accept payment in sterling and the following announcement was made on September 15th:

"Mr. McShain has authorized the announcement that, in the interests of British bloodstock, he wishes Ballymoss to remain in England at stud.

"He has arranged to syndicate the horse on completion of his 1958 programme—40 shares at £6,250 a share, of which Mr. McShain retains ten.

"The remaining 30 shares have been guaranteed by Sir Victor Sassoon and Mr. William Hill.

"Details regarding the application for shares and/or nominations will be announced later. The stud at which the horse will stand is not yet decided.

"Mr. McShain has refused two vastly bigger offers from the U.S.A., including one from Texas.

"In view of Ballymoss's Turf successes, the owner wishes him to be at stud in England."

It was eventually decided that Ballymoss should stand at the Banstead Manor Stud, Cheveley, Newmarket. He had his first runners in 1962 and he was leading first-season sire that year. He was fifth on the list in 1964, tenth in 1965, fifth in 1966, while in 1967 he firmly established his reputation by siring Royal Palace, winner of the Two Thousand Guineas and the Derby.

Bella Paola

Germany is entitled to point with pride to Bella Paola, as this great filly, although owned and bred by M. Francois Dupré and trained in France by F. Mathet, is at least three-quarters German in origin and was the first animal of predominantly German blood to win an English classic. Her first four ancestors in direct male line all won the German Derby—Ticino in 1942, Athanasius in 1934, Ferro in 1926 and Landgraf in 1917. Landgraf was by the English horse Louviers, second in the sensational Derby of 1913. He was exported to Russia and disappeared there during the Revolution.

Ticino, foaled in 1939, won fourteen of his twenty-one races, including the Grosser Preis von Berlin on three occasions. In 1946 he was retired to the Erlenhof Stud, Frankfurt-on-Main, where he had been bred, and when his oldest runners were but three years of age, he was leading sire in Germany, a position he successfully maintained until 1958. He became infertile after the covering season of 1955 and was put down in 1957. One of his sons, Neckar, who won the German Derby and the Prix de Chantilly among other successes, sired Peseta II, dam of the 1967 Oaks winner Pia. Despite his admirable stud record, Ticino was used by only two non-German breeders, M. F. Dupré and Mr. Clifford Nicholson. Mr. Nicholson was far less fortunate in the results he obtained than M. Dupré.

The story of Rhea II, dam of Bella Paola, is a somewhat involved one. The fourth dam of Bella Paola was Hesione, by the French Derby winner Alcantara II. M. Dupré bought Hesione for 1,200 guineas in 1929 and had her covered by Pharos who was then standing at his stud at Ouilly. The produce of the mating, a filly called Princess d'Ouilly, raced in the colours of the glamorous Miss Pearl White, whose hectic adventures, portrayed largely in serial films, kept the less discriminating patrons of the cinematograph glued to their seats during the early nineteen-twenties. Reine d'Ouilly, after winning once and being placed on several occasions, reverted to M. Dupré and in 1940 he sold her to a Commission of the German Supreme Racing and Breeding Authority, thereby being more fortunate than many French owners and breeders whose bloodstock was ruthlessly confiscated. In Germany Reine d'Ouilly, whose son Aristocrate had finished third in the Prix du Jockey Club, produced two colts of no significance and then a filly by the French sire Indus called Regina IV. Reine d'Ouilly, in foal to Gundomar, was returned to France in 1947. Having sold her to the Germans, M. Dupré felt that he was unable to take her back again, so the French Mission of Restitution put her up for auction and she was bought by the Haras de St. Jacques.

The Gundomar foal that Reine d'Ouilly was carrying on her return to France was sold as a yearling and bought by M. Dupré. Named Prince d'Ouilly he won six races in England, Germany and Belgium including the Granville Stakes at Ascot, the Gordon Stakes at Goodwood and the Grosser Preis von Baden. At the stud he stood in Belgium, France and finally in Colombia. Gundomar, by the German horse Alchimist, traces to Dark Ronald, whose export from England to Germany in 1913 proved of the utmost benefit to Germany. Gundomar never ran as a three-year-old as there was no racing in Western Germany at that time. He only sired three crops of foals before meeting with a fatal accident but even so he was highly successful, thirty-five of his forty-five foals proving winners.

In 1950, doubtless encouraged by the promise of Prince d'Ouilly, then a two-year-old, M. Dupré went to Germany and bought from the Waldfried Stud, Rhea II, a filly by Gundomar out of Prince d'Ouilly's half-sister Regina. The following year Regina herself came to M. Dupré's stud to be covered by Tantième's sire, Deux Pour Cent. M. Dupré took a fancy to her and bought her. Her owner Count Spreti was in fact reluctant to part with her, but at that time his foreign assets were blocked and he needed money to purchase a stallion in France. Regina proved a sad disappointment to M. Dupré as she never once produced for him a live foal. Rhea II, therefore, was her only living produce. Rhea II won a couple of races as a three-year-old, one over 1500 metres, the other over 1600, and then had her covered by Ticino. The result of this union was Bella Paola.

Plate 26 Swaps

Plate 27 Ribot

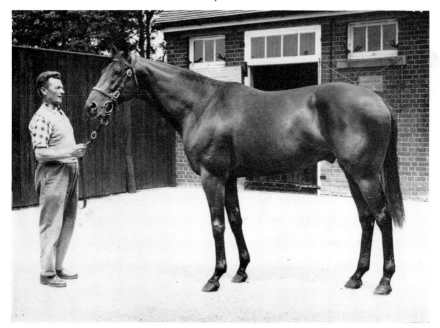

Plate 28 Tulloch

Plate 29 Ballymoss

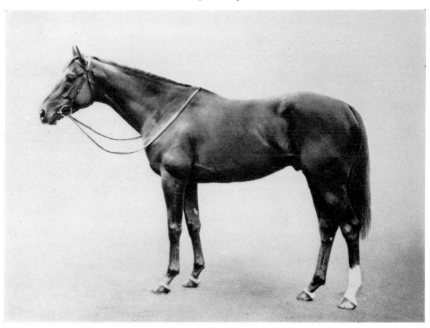

Plate 30 Bella Paola

Plate 31 Arkle

Plate 32   Sea Bird II

Plate 33   Vaguely Noble

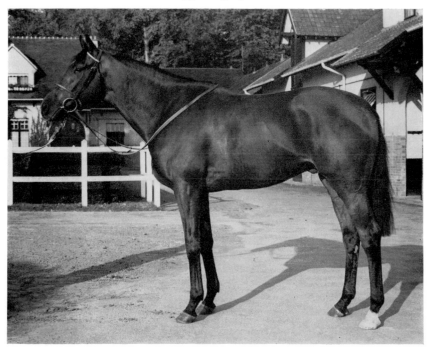

Bella Paola was a big filly even as a two-year-old, but she came to hand reasonably early and succeeded in winning three of her four races. She made a highly promising first appearance in the Prix Yacowlef, finishing a creditable third to the speedy American-bred filly Shut Out. Her second outing was the seven furlong Prix Georges de Kerhallet at Clairefontaine on August 14th and this she won without the slightest difficulty. A sterner test awaited her in the seven furlong Criterium de Maisons Laffitte but she defeated her rivals with an ease that verged on the contemptuous. Finally, on October 13th, she lined up for the most important of French two-year-old events, the one mile Grand Criterium at Longchamp. For a long time it looked as if she was going to be beaten by Tarquin, but in the final furlong she battled on with the utmost resolution and got her head in front literally in the very last stride to win by a matter of inches. Cherasco was third, two and a half lengths behind Tarquin. In the French Free Handicap Bella Paola was rated inferior only to Texana, who likewise was owned by M. Dupré and trained by Mathet. A daughter of the American-bred Relic, Texana possessed brilliant speed and won eleven races in succession but she did not participate in the major two-year-old events and in fact never ran beyond five furlongs. From the English point of view it was ominous that in the French Free Handicap Bella Paola was rated 2 lb. superior to Neptune II, who had run the leading English colt, Major Portion, to half a length in the Middle Park Stakes.

Bella Paola wintered well and carried complete confidence when she turned out for the one mile Prix Imprudence at Maisons Laffitte on April 11th. This confidence was in no way displaced and she won comfortably by a couple of lengths from Pharstella, who had finished fourth in the Grand Criterium. On May 2nd came the first major objective of her three-year-old career, the One Thousand Guineas. The bookmakers were taking no chances with her and ridden by the twenty-one-year-old Serge Boullenger, who was doing his National Service at that time, she started favourite at 11–8 on. In the paddock before the race she completely dominated her opponents. The hundreds who lined the paddock rails to watch her walk round saw a very big, powerful brown filly standing 16 hands 3 inches. Despite her height, there was not a hint of legginess and she stood over an immense amount of ground. Her limbs were proportionate to her frame, her head kindly and intelligent and adorned with big, slightly lopped ears of the type that so often denote an admirable racing temperament. Her girth measured 72 inches; from hip to hock she was 43½ inches and she had 8 inches of bone.

In the race Bella Paola always held a handy position and at the top of the hill two furlongs from home Boullenger allowed her to stride on. She at once accelerated and overtook the leader, Alpine Bloom, coming into the Dip. Manny Mercer, Alpine Bloom's jockey, observed afterwards: "When Boullenger shook her up, she put five lengths between us in no time."

Inside the final furlong Prince Aly Khan's Amante, ridden by Massard, put in a strong challenge and got within a length of Bella Paola who just for a moment appeared to be feeling the ground, which was distinctly firm. However Boullenger felt no necessity to draw his whip; he just rode her out with his hands and she won comfortably by a length and a half. Alpine Bloom was five lengths away third. The time of 1 minute 38¾ seconds was fractionally faster than that of Pall Mall in the Two Thousand Guineas two days previously.

Bella Paola did not run again before the Oaks in which she was ridden by Garcia, Boullenger having found the military authorities unsympathetic over the question of leave. The going at Epsom was perfect and Bella Paola won so easily that the race was somewhat lacking in excitement. She was sixth into the straight, travelling very easily on the bit, and when Garcia asked her for her effort approaching the final furlong, she quickened in effortless fashion and won with her ears pricked by three lengths from the French-bred Mother Goose, with Cutter a further three lengths away third. Her time was ⅖ths of a second faster than that of Hard Ridden in the Derby.

Bella Paola was not engaged in the King George VI and Queen Elizabeth Stakes so M. Dupré decided to run her nine days later in the Prix du Jockey Club, the French equivalent of the Derby, at Chantilly, despite the somewhat discouraging fact that no filly had won that event since Saltarelle in 1874. Nevertheless in a field of seventeen Bella Paola started favourite at 9–4. There was little support for M. Ramon Beamonte's Tamanar whose price was 59–2.

At the entrance to the straight Launay, Près du Feu and Wallaby were the leaders with Bella Paola still in a distinctly unpromising position near the tail end of the field. Tamanar soon began to make rapid headway down the centre of the course whereas Boullenger, with a wall of horses in front of him, felt compelled to switch Bella Paola to the wide outside in order to obtain a clear run. In the meantime Tamanar struck the front and headed for home as hard as he could. The filly did everything she could to get on terms, but gamely as she struggled, Tamanar was still three-parts of a length ahead of her when the winning post was reached. Peplin le Bref was two lengths away third. It was generally agreed that Boullenger had ridden an indifferent race. There seemed no point in having kept Bella Paola so far behind early on, while he elected to switch her to the extreme outside just when the field was most widely spread across the course. Because of this she had to travel considerably further than the winner, who also secured the advantage of first run and a lead of several lengths.

Undoubtedly Bella Paola had a hard race in the Prix du Jockey Club and she was given a rest until September when she won the Prix Vermeille at Longchamp very comfortably by three-parts of a length from V.I.P. She was accompanied to the post by M. Dupré's Dushka, who made the running for her. Dushka was an unusually distinguished pacemaker, having won the French Oaks and the Grosser Preis von Baden.

In the Prix de l'Arc de Triomphe Bella Paola, ridden by Garcia, ran her one indifferent race and failed to finish in the first six behind the great Irish four-year-old Ballymoss. This was not her true form by a long way as V.I.P., whom she had beaten without trouble in the Prix Vermeille, was fourth. It seemed then as if she had trained off, and although she had not yet gone in her coat, she looked noticeable lighter than she had done at Newmarket and Epsom.

Nevertheless, it was decided to give her one more race and on October 16th, one of those cold, blustery autumn days when Newmarket Heath is at its least attractive, she took part in the ten furlong Champion Stakes. Because of her failure in the Prix de l'Arc de Triomphe, she was easy to back at 4-1, 6-1 having been offered early on. The favourite was Mr. H. J. Joel's Major Portion at 9-4. Bella Paola soon showed that she was anything but a spent force, and ridden by Lequeux, she won very smoothly from the Irish Derby winner Sindon, with Major Portion, who failed to stay the distance, third. Fourth came London Cry who later in the month won the Cambridgeshire with 9 st. 5 lb. Bella Paola's victory was very well received and it certainly represented a fine effort on the part of this tough, courageous filly who had been fighting fit early in the spring and only eleven days previously had had a hard losing race in the "Arc".

This was Bella Paola's final appearance. She had won £35,004 in England and 21,398,280 francs in France. She had certainly demonstrated to some purpose the merits of German blood. So far at the stud the best of her offspring has been Pola Bella, by Darius. As a two-year-old Pola Bella was second to Sir Ivor in the Grand Criterium at Longchamp, while as a three-year-old she won the French One Thousand Guineas and was second in the French Oaks.

Arkle

On October 9th, 1968 came the announcement from Anne Duchess of Westminster, that Arkle's countless legions of admirers had been half dreading, half hoping for: "It has been decided not to race Arkle again. Having given the matter a great deal of thought and after lengthy discussions with Mr. Tom Dreaper and Mr. Maxie Cosgrove, M.R.C.V.S., I have decided that this is the wisest and correct thing to do. Mr. Cosgrove is satisfied that the broken bone in Arkle's hoof is completely healed and that he is sound and well.

"However he has been off the racecourse for nearly two years and is eleven years old, and I feel that possibly even Arkle with all his immense courage could not be expected to reproduce his old brilliance. He has been retired to my home in County Kildare."

So ended the long period of suspense that had lasted since Tuesday, December 27th, 1967, when Arkle pulled up lame at the finish of the King George VI Chase at Kempton Park with a fractured pedal bone—twenty-two months during which the full blaze of modern publicity, of Press, television and radio, had been turned on him to a degree unprecedented in the history of the thoroughbred, let alone of steeplechasing. Hopes of an eventual return to the racecourse had been raised several times. In October 1967 it was stated that, if progress were maintained, he might be able to have a quiet race or two in Ireland after Christmas, and then travel to Cheltenham for the Gold Cup, the race in which he had demonstrated his supremacy in the three years from 1964 to 1966. On March 6th, 1968, a special flat race, the Saval Beg Stakes over two miles three furlongs, was staged at Leopardstown to provide him with a suitable opportunity for his comeback, but as the date approached his reappearance was postponed. On the Tuesday after Easter, April 16th, the executive at Fairyhouse, just down the road from

Tom Dreaper's stables at Kilsallaghan, put on a special hurdle race, the Mosney Hurdle over 2½ miles, for a like purpose. This time an Arkle comeback which would have packed the Fairyhouse enclosures even more tightly than when he gained his Irish Grand National victory there four years earlier was really on the cards. But the weather turned sour during the vital period of preparation. The early spring was bedevilled by hard night frosts and bitter east winds. The going at Kilsallaghan and on the racecourse became unseasonably firm, unsuitable for a big horse recuperating from a serious injury. There were anxious consultations between Nancy Westminster and her advisers. In the end the expert view of Cosgrove, who had argued all along that time, more time and still more time was essential for full recovery in such cases, could not be gainsaid. Arkle was withdrawn from the Mosney Hurdle, and an announcement was made to the effect that he would have a further period of convalescence during the summer and go back into training in the autumn.

So the final announcement of Arkle's retirement was received with mingled disappointment and relief. To have seen Arkle just once more in full form and in full cry would have been a joy not to be missed; but an ageing Arkle struggling to beat, or worse still not to beat, mediocrities that he would have brushed aside contemptuously in his prime would have been an indignity not to be borne. Not a single voice was raised to question the propriety or the wisdom of his owner's decision.

No one who was present will ever forget the drama of that bleak December day when Arkle ran his last race. It was surmised that he sustained the injury when he failed to rise enough at the fourteenth fence, an open ditch, and hit the guard rail hard with his forefeet. From that moment he was clearly in trouble. He was locked in a duel with Woodland Venture when that horse fell at the second last fence, and when Dormant came out of the blue to challenge him after the last fence he could produce none of the dazzling speed for which he was famous, and was beaten by a length. For a few moments in the winner's enclosure Doris Wells-Kendrew, who naturally had eyes only for her own horse Dormant in the final stages of the race and as they pulled up, was jubilant. Dormant had beaten Mill House when he won the Whitbread Gold Cup two years earlier, and now he had done his giant killing act again. Then in an instant her sense of elation was dashed as a Pressman told her:

"Arkle has broken down." At once she left her own horse and crossed to the crestfallen group of Arkle's connections to express her sympathy. Admiration for Arkle linked the whole National Hunt community and transcended the emotions normally inspired by victory and defeat. There could be no fairer measure of his greatness.

In the months that followed evidence of the hold that he had gained on the imagination of the public in Great Britain and Ireland and much further afield piled up. It piled up literally in the form of "Get Well" cards and letters (many of them addressed simply to "Arkle, Ireland") so numerous that he required a social secretary to answer them; figuratively in the form of hordes of visitors who arrived to pay their respects when he had recovered sufficiently to be moved back to Kilsallaghan from Kempton Park. He held court every Sunday; or perhaps it would be more correct to say that his box was an object of pilgrimage for his faithful fans. Every aspect of his life, every stage in his recovery, was newsworthy. He was the subject of a full-scale biography by Ivor Herbert, an hour-long television programme, and a song written and recorded by Dominic Behan which made the charts. No thoroughbred had ever known such fame, and the spontaneity of many of the tributes to him proved that he did not owe everything to the pressures of the mass media of communication.

Arkle was incomparable. He was the greatest chaser that has ever lived or is ever likely to live. His greatness easily surpassed all the renowned chasers of the past, including the mighty Golden Miller. Even Golden Miller did not achieve such supremacy as to necessitate a change in the National Hunt Rules. Arkle did, for the authorities were compelled to extend the range of weights for valuable steeplechase handicaps so that, if he were entered and did not run, all the runners would not be congregated on the lowest weight mark. Probably in no country where the sport of horse-racing is practised in fully developed and sophisticated form has any individual established more complete supremacy in his own category. Arkle may have been no greater, relatively speaking, than St. Simon, for example. But in terms of endurance and physical exertion there is no comparison. St. Simon ran about twelve miles in his nine races. Arkle covered $95\frac{3}{4}$ miles in his thirty-five races, and jumped nearly five hundred fences of 4 feet 6 inches in height and varying degrees of stiffness.

The racing career of Arkle has been so amply chronicled that it would be superfluous to trace it in detail. It will suffice to recall some of the moments of high drama and to comment on certain of the more controversial aspects of his career. His chasing career falls naturally into two parts, of which the first comprised his challenge to and humiliation of the reigning champion Mill House, and the second comprised his period of consolidation. Exported Irish jumpers are regularly labelled "the finest horse that ever came out of old Ireland", and the label is as regularly discredited. In the case of Mill House, the "Big Horse" as he was known, it was accepted as true when he trounced Arkle's stable companion Fortria in the Cheltenham Gold Cup in 1963. Mill House was only six years of age, and there were predictions that he would equal or surpass the record of Golden Miller, who won the Gold Cup five years in succession in the nineteen-thirties. Yet, in the hour of his triumph the seeds of his downfall were present as surely as in a Greek tragedy. Two days earlier Arkle, who was exactly the same age, had won the Broadway Novices Chase, annihilating the opposition to win by twenty lengths, and Arkle, emerging swiftly from the novice grade, saw to it that Mill House never won the Cheltenham Gold Cup again.

Nevertheless the Mill House and Arkle issue was not settled at one stroke. Their first meeting was in the Hennessy Gold Cup over $3\frac{1}{4}$ miles at Newbury the following November when Mill House, with top weight of 12 st., was set to give 5 lb. to Arkle in the handicap, and was made favourite to do so. By that time Arkle enjoyed a tremendous reputation in Ireland and Mill House, though Irish-bred, was regarded as naturalized English. For this reason there was a strong flavour of international rivalry in this and their subsequent encounters, and the first round went to England when Mill House won by eight lengths and Arkle was not even second, losing that place to Happy Spring. But, unnoticed by all but the most observant of the watchers on the stands, Arkle had landed on a greasy patch at the last open ditch and skidded almost to a halt before making one of those miraculous recoveries that were to save him from disaster on several occasions. There was jubilation in the English camp, and when Pat Taaffe, Arkle's partner in all his twenty-six chases and two of his hurdle races, tried to explain what had happened he was received with polite scepticism. Not long after Pat remarked to Betty Dreaper, the trainer's wife, that he would beat Mill House whenever and wherever they met again, a prophecy which was fulfilled to the letter.

Their next meeting was in the Cheltenham Gold Cup four months later. The two horses were unbeaten in the meantime, Mill House enjoying an easy passage through the King George VI Chase at Kempton Park and the Gainsborough Chase at Sandown Park, Arkle facing and readily accomplishing more exacting tasks in the Christmas Chase at Leopardstown, the Thyestes Chase at Gowran Park and the Leopardstown Chase. The Irish were brimming over with confidence by the time they arrived at Cheltenham, while English faith in Mill House was undiminished. The starting prices were 13–8 on Mill House, 7–4 against Arkle, and long odds against the other two runners, who were disregarded in the market and inconspicuous in the race. What followed was an epic of steeple-chasing, unforgettable in its dramatic impact. Mill House, ridden by Willy Robinson, led from the start of the three miles two furlongs and 130 yards race, and for a long time his supporters were happy. But in the last mile Arkle began to cut down the lead relentlessly. This was the race that was the subject of Dominic Behan's song, and as Arkle delivered his challenge after the second last fence the song reached its climax with the words; "Look behind you, Willy Robinson! And what are you about?" Behan's lyrics may have caught the drama of the event, but in terms of jockeyship he was far astray. Robinson was too experienced a rider to be looking round when the pressure was on, and what he was about was driving Mill House for all he was worth. But his efforts were to no avail. Mill House had no more to give, and Arkle had taken the lead before reaching the last fence and then sailed up the hill to win by five lengths.

Unlike many victories that are so called, this victory was decisive. The connections of Mill House were aghast at their champion's dethronement, but Arkle's superiority was even more overwhelming a year later when he beat Mill House by twenty lengths in the Cheltenham Gold Cup, and in their meetings in the Hennessy and Gallaher Gold Cups. Some said that his first Cheltenham Gold Cup broke Mill House's heart, but the fact is that the "Big Horse" still managed to give some magnificent performances, as when he carried a lot of weight to victory in the Whitbread Gold Cup at Sandown Park in April 1967. It was surely more charitable to recognize that Mill House was a top class chaser, probably one of the dozen best of all time, but Arkle was a paragon, a class and a half better than any other chaser that ever lived.

Arkle still had not attained full maturity when he won his first Cheltenham Gold Cup. He reached his peak during the next two seasons when he won his second and third Cheltenham Gold Cups and a whole string of other important races including, besides those already mentioned, the Whitbread Gold Cup. Nevertheless Arkle, or rather his connections, could not escape altogether the sniping of those ungracious critics who are never silent for long in the world of racing. Arkle, those critics complained, was not committed to tasks worthy of his steel; he should have emulated the achievement of Golden Miller, the only horse to have won the Cheltenham Gold Cup and the Grand National; he should have tried to win the French Grand National; gone to America; tackled jumpers of various types of expertise in the Champion Two-Mile Chase or the Champion Hurdle; and to confine him to the "Park" courses of England and Ireland was like confining Hunt and Hillary to the slopes of Snowdon. But the critics are seldom consistent, and in the case of Arkle they condemned his connections almost in the same breath for asking too much of him by running him in the Massey Ferguson Gold Cup, in which he was beaten by Flying Wild and Buona Notte, only a week after he had carried 12 st. 7 lb. to victory in the Hennessy Gold Cup at Newbury in December 1964.

It may be regretted that Arkle was not allowed to have just one go at winning the Grand National. His bold style of jumping would have provided a thrilling spectacle over the Aintree country, and his combination of cleverness, intelligence and brilliance would probably have enabled him to win without undue effort. But his owner was adamant, stating that there was always a big field for the Grand National and so an increased risk of serious accidents. Arkle was always a member of the family as much as an earner of prize money, and his owner's humane consideration for his safety should inspire nothing but respect. As for the rest of the criticism, there might of course have been some entertainment to be derived from Arkle in the role of travelling circus performer, but it is entirely false to suggest that he was given an easy life free from the strains of vigorous competition. On the contrary, he had some very hard races indeed—notably when he gave 35 lb. to Scottish Memories and 42 lb. to Height o' Fashion, horses of first-class speed and infinite resolution, and beat them by narrow margins after tremendous struggles in races for the Leopardstown Chase; and when he wore down the gallant and enterprising Brasher, to whom he was conceding 35 lb., in the three miles five furlongs Whitbread Gold Cup; and when he failed by only half a length to concede 35 lb. to the grey Stalbridge Colonist, who was to run Woodland Venture to three-quarters of a length at level weights in the Cheltenham Gold Cup four months later, in the Hennessy Gold Cup in November 1966. No, there is no substance at all in the accusation that Arkle earned an easy living.

Yet it may still be fascinating to speculate how Arkle might have fared if he had been called to other spheres of racing activity. How good, for example, would he have been if he had been trained to race regularly on the flat? The only time he ran on the flat, except in two "bumper" races at the outset of his career, was in a maiden race over 1¾ miles at Navan in October 1963, when he cantered away from moderate opponents. The speed possessed by top-class chasers is often not fully appreciated. Cottage Rake, another winner of the Cheltenham Gold Cup three times, won the Irish Cesarewitch and the Naas November Handicap, two of the most important long distance races in Ireland. It is well within the bounds of possibility that Arkle might have won the Queen Alexandra Stakes and the Goodwood and Doncaster Cups—geldings are ineligible for the Ascot Gold Cup—if he had been given the chance.

On the other hand, Arkle was bred for the job he actually performed. It is true that his sire Archive (by the unbeaten Nearco out of the St. Leger winner Book Law) had a top class flat-racing pedigree if negligible ability; but his dam Bright Cherry was a good chaser over 2 and 2½ miles. She was by Knight of the Garter, who got many useful chasers, and her dam Greenogue Princess was by My Prince, one of the best sires of chasers there has ever been, with the Grand National winners Reynoldstown, Royal Mail and Gregalach, and two other outstanding chasers in Easter Hero and Prince Regent to his credit.

Yet Arkle's life did not begin auspiciously. As a foal on his breeder Alison Baker's farm in County Dublin he galloped into wire and had to have forty stitches in the wound, and after Anne Duchess of Westminster had bought him for 1,150 guineas at Ballsbridge as a yearling, he seemed quite an ordinary young horse during his early days with Tom Dreaper. Those who knew Arkle in his prime, with his exceptional depth of body and his muscular, perfectly shaped quarters positively bursting with power, and witnessed the speed and sureness of his jumping, may find it hard to believe that he was ever in danger of being taken for a nonentity. But nonentity he might have remained if he had not fallen into the right hands; of Anne Duchess of Westminster, a noted rider to hounds and in Point-to-Points in County Cork in early days; of that consummate trainer of jumpers Tom Dreaper; of Pat Taaffe who, for all his untidy finishing, was a lovely horseman over fences.

Arkle has been described as the most conceited of great horses. The charge was not unfair, as anyone may testify who saw him strutting round the parade ring or savouring the applause after one of his victories. All that needs to be said by way of mitigation is that he had plenty to be conceited about. To a degree achieved by few other great horses, he influenced the course of racing history. For the adulation with which he was regarded was the most potent single factor in popularizing National Hunt racing and gaining it a reputation as one of the most thrilling of outdoor spectacles. If he was a chaser of unprecedented greatness, he was also a publicity agent of genius.

Sea Bird II

Exactly one hundred years after Gladiateur, nicknamed "The Avenger of Waterloo", had scored the first French success in the Derby, Sea Bird II won the Derby for France in such brilliant style that he must surely be rated one of the outstanding winners of that race during this century. Moreover his form in France, in particular his astonishing triumph in the Prix de l'Arc de Triomphe, stamped him beyond any shadow of doubt as a truly great racehorse.

Sea Bird was bred and owned by M. Jean Ternynck, a well-known personality in French racing who had won the Prix du Jockey Club and the Grand Prix with Sanctus, the One Thousand Guineas with Camaree. Sea Bird is by the American-bred Dan Cupid out of Sicalade, by Sicambre. He is thus yet another example of that combination of American speed and toughness and French stamina that has proved so successful in recent years. In actual fact, judged on his pedigree, Sea Bird hardly appeared likely to leave any appreciable mark on Turf history since not one of his five immediate dams had managed to win a single race under the rules of a recognized flat-racing authority in any country. However, his third dam, Couleur, bred Camaree, and Couleur was descended from the good English mare Donnetta, dam of Diophon and Diadem, winners of the Two Thousand and One Thousand Guineas respectively.

Dan Cupid is by the famous American horse Native Dancer, a male line descendant of Hyperion's half-brother Sickle, out of Vixenette, by Sickle. When in training Dan Cupid was a stocky, close-coupled colt that looked a typical sprinter. Trained, like Sea Bird, by Etienne Pollet at Chantilly, he ran second to Masham in the Middle Park Stakes. The following year he was sixth in the Two Thousand Guineas and well down the course in the Derby. The best performance of his career was to run close up second to a really good horse in Herbager in the Prix du Jockey Club, thereby demonstrating that he was by no means deficient in stamina. His subsequent races suggested he had trained off and he was retired to the stud at the end of the season.

As a two-year-old Sea Bird was obviously a good colt but at the same time there was no clear evidence that he was likely to become a great one. He certainly did not possess the precocious brilliance, for example, of a Tudor Minstrel and in general he indicated that staying was his game and that he would probably need a mile and a half to be seen at his best as a three-year-old.

Pollet wisely did not hurry him and he only ran three times as a two-year-old. He gave proof of his speed in making a winning debut in the five furlong Prix de Blaison and was then submitted to a sterner test in the seven furlong Criterium de Maisons Laffitte. He duly won, defeating among others Carvin, who had been second to Sea Bird's stable companion Grey Dawn, rated the best two-year-old in France, in the important Prix Morny at Deauville.

Sea Bird's final outing as a two-year-old was in the one mile Grand Criterium at Longchamp on October the 11th. Pollet also started Grey Dawn, who was the more fancied of the two and was ridden by the stable jockey T. P. Glennon, Sea Bird being partnered by M. Larraun. Grey Dawn, a grey colt by Herbager, was very quick into his stride and soon was leading the field. He increased his advantage coming down the hill and ran on to win unchallenged by two lengths from Sea Bird.

Sea Bird, drawn on the outside, had been slowly away. He did not come at all smoothly round the final bend but once into the straight he ran on with admirable determination, overhauling all his opponents with the single exception of Grey Dawn. Not a few people who saw that race considered that Sea Bird had been unlucky and that with different tactics he might well have run Grey Dawn very close indeed. He certainly looked a good prospect for 1965 and in the French Free Handicap was rated equal second with the English colt Double Jump below Grey Dawn.

Whereas Grey Dawn disappointed as a three-year-old, Sea Bird went from strength to strength and in what was beyond argument a vintage year for French three-year-old colts, he proved outstanding, winning all his five races with consummate ease. At the start of the season he was, in appearance, a tall, rangey, chestnut with a white

blaze and two stockings behind, rather spare and lacking in substance. He certainly did not make a particularly favourable impression on the Epsom paddock critics before the Derby. As the season
progressed, though, he filled out considerably and at Longchamp in
October it was noted that he had put on a lot of weight and acquired
a general air of well-being. Early in the year there had been
whispers that he was highly strung and that his temperament might
prove unsuited to the Epsom crowds, but in the event these
aspersions proved unfounded.

Sea Bird's first appearance in 1965 was at Longchamp in April in
the ten furlong Prix Greffulhe, in which event he was opposed by
eight three-year-olds who had all been rated inferior to him in the
French Free Handicap. His task, therefore, was not one of undue
severity, but he won with such singular ease that it was clear from
that moment that whatever race he ran in, he was going to be a
force to be reckoned with. A month later he faced a sterner test at
Longchamp in the ten furlong Prix Lupin. Among the runners were
Cambremont, who had beaten Grey Dawn in the French Two
Thousand Guineas; and Baron Guy de Rothschild's Diatome, who
had won the Prix Noailles and later in the year was to win for France
the Washington International at Laurel Park. Sea Bird proceeded to
win in the most brilliant style imaginable. With a furlong to go he
moved up on the bit to join Diatome and when Glennon asked him
to go he fairly flew, winning as he pleased by half a dozen lengths.
Diatome was second and Cambremont third.

It had long been decided that Sea Bird was to go for the Epsom
Derby and on the strength of his scintillating victory in the Prix
Lupin he started a hot favourite at Epsom at 7–4. Seldom can the
Derby have been won so easily and it is hardly an exaggeration to
say that Sea Bird treated his rivals as if they were weary hacks from
some local riding school. Moreover it was not a mediocre Derby
field by any means, the runners including Meadow Court, who
subsequently won the Irish Derby and the King George VI and
Queen Elizabeth Stakes; I Say, who a year later won the Coronation
Cup; Niksar, who had won the Two Thousand Guineas; and Silly
Season, who was to win the Champion Stakes.

The going was good and the gallop a fast one. At Tattenham
Corner the outsider Sunacelli held the lead, followed by Niksar,
Meadow Court, Gulf Pearl, I Say and Sea Bird. A furlong later
Sunacelli was in trouble and was headed by I Say. Sea Bird, though,

was travelling very smoothly and with less than a quarter of a mile to go he moved up on the bit and swept past I Say as if I Say had conveniently agreed to mark time. In the final two hundred yards Sea Bird began to idle and look around whereupon Glennon roused him to such purpose that he opened up a four lengths lead. Glennon was able to drop his hands before the winning post was reached, at which point Sea Bird was again on the bit. It was an electrifying performance and most experienced racegoers agreed that never had they seen the Derby won with such contemptuous ease. The victory earned Sea Bird's owner £65,301. It only remains to add that Meadow Court, running on strongly, was second, two lengths behind Sea Bird, and I Say third.

After a month's rest Sea Bird, favourite at 5–1 on, took the field in the £38,000 Grand Prix de Saint-Cloud run over a mile and a half. This was the first time that he had taken on horses older than himself but he was fully equal to the occasion, winning on the bit by two and a half lengths from Couroucou.

It was now decided that Sea Bird should have one more race that season, the Prix de l'Arc de Triomphe run over a mile and a half at Longchamp on October 3rd. The field for the "Arc" that year was an international one of quite exceptional strength. Besides Sea Bird, France had Reliance, a full brother of Match III and a half-brother of Relko, that had won the French Derby, the Grand Prix and the French St. Leger; Blabla, winner of the French Oaks; Diatome, who subsequently won at Laurel Park, and Demi Deuil, who had won the Grand Prix du Printemps. Meadow Court, Anilin and Tom Rolfe had won the Irish, Russian and American Derbys respectively. Marco Visconti was one of the best stayers in Italy, while England was represented by two four-year-olds, Oncidium, winner of the Coronation Cup, and Soderini, winner of the Hardwicke Stakes. Sea Bird was a hot favourite at 6–5 and Reliance, hitherto undefeated, second favourite at 9–2.

It proved to be one of those wonderful races that can never be forgotten by those who were fortunate enough to see it. At the turn for home Marco Visconti and Anilin were in the lead, while Meadow Court was hard on their heels and so were Sea Bird, Reliance and Tom Rolfe. In fact at that point any one of those six could have won. Meadow Court was unable to keep up the pressure, though, and with two furlongs to go the great French pair, Sea Bird and Reliance, swept past their foreign opponents and it looked as if there was going to be a tremendous battle between those two. The battle, though, never materialized. Quite suddenly Sea Bird accelerated and in a trice, despite a tendency to veer towards the stands, he had opened up a gap of several lengths. To the exultant cheers of thousands of his admirers he passed the post six lengths in front of Reliance, who was himself five lengths in front of Diatome. Free Ride was fourth, Anilin fifth and Tom Rolfe sixth. It was a fantastic victory that stamped the winner as one of the best horses ever to be bred in France, an out-and-out stayer with fabulous acceleration that was capable of making even a great horse like Reliance look like a plater.

Unfortunately, though Sea Bird was perfectly sound and had certainly not been over-raced, his owner decided to retire him. Sea Bird's seven victories had earned M. Ternynck just on £225,000, a European record. Sea Bird would no doubt have proved a wonderful asset for European breeders, but alas, the lure of the dollar proved too much for M. Ternynck, who agreed to lease Sea Bird for five years to the American breeder, Mr. John W. Galbreath, for a sum reported to be $1,350,000. It may be remembered that Mr. Galbreath originally leased the mighty Ribot for a five year period, but in fact the great Italian horse has never returned to Europe. It remains to be seen what happens to Sea Bird at the end of the five year period if his first American runners show signs of living up to their sire's reputation.

Vaguely Noble

The scene was the Park Paddocks at Newmarket, the time early in the first week of December 1967. Two of the most distinguished trainers in Europe were standing on the straw-covered grass discussing the December Sales catalogue—Cecil Boyd-Rochfort, the trainer of a dozen English Classic races and shortly to be knighted for his services to the sport, and Etienne Pollet, the gifted master of a stable of fifty hand-picked horses at Chantilly. Inevitably the conversation turned to the forthcoming sale of two-year-old Vaguely Noble, the brilliant recent winner of England's richest two-year-old race, the Observer Gold Cup, and widely tipped to break all records for a horse at public auction in Great Britain. "I am told he'll fetch £100,000," said Boyd-Rochfort. The tall, red-haired Pollet demurred. £100,000 for a colt who had no Classic engagements—it was ridiculous. Pollet shook his head in disbelief. For this reason there was sweet irony in the fact that ten months later Pollet, grouped with the Société d'Encouragement president Marcel Boussac and the joint owners Robert Alan Franklyn and Nelson Bunker Hunt, was facing the cameras in the Longchamp parade ring and giving a victory smile after training Vaguely Noble to win the Prix de l'Arc de Triomphe and raise his value above the £2 millions mark.

In the meantime, a couple of days after Boyd-Rochfort and Pollet had conversed and a few minutes after 6.00 p.m. on Thursday, December 7th, Vaguely Noble had been sold for 136,000 guineas, a price which left remotely far behind the previous auction record for a horse in training of 37,500 guineas paid by the Frenchman Edmond Blanc for the Triple Crown winner Flying Fox sixty-eight years earlier. The sale itself was one of the most dramatic events in Turf history. Every seat in every tier of Tattersall's spacious sale-ring building was taken twenty minutes before Vaguely Noble was due to be sold. The stairs and gangways were packed like the foyer of a theatre on a star-studded first night. There was such a crush of spectators in the entrance gateway that Kenneth Watt, the senior partner of Tattersall's who occupied the rostrum for the occasion, had to beg people to stand back as Vaguely Noble was led in, lest someone should be hurt. The bidding opened at 80,000 guineas, and rose rapidly into six figures. Bidders dropped out one after the other, until only two were left. At 135,000 guineas an abrupt wave of the catalogue from far up on the right and opposite the rostrum left the bidding with the French agent Godolphin Darley. There was a pause; then Watt took one more bid on his left, Godolphin Darley did not respond, and that was the end. The tense silence that had fallen on the ring during the sale broke up in excited chatter.

At first the purchaser was announced as the Anglo-Irish Agency, but it soon became known that the actual purchaser was Albert Yank and the World-Wide Bloodstock Agency, names completely unfamiliar in the English racing community. And within minutes Yank, a swarthy and flamboyant little American who had chosen a suitably turgid title for his agency, was telling the Press that he had bought the colt for Doctor Robert Franklyn, a plastic surgeon who specialized in the art of making Hollywood's beautiful ladies even more beautiful.

So perhaps the most fantastic gamble ever in bloodstock was launched. For Vaguely Noble, deprived by omission from the Classic races of the chance to run in any of the races which normally determine top thoroughbred values, had virtually one race, and one race only, that he could win which would enable him to retain, let alone enhance, his sales price; and that was the world's richest and most prestige-bearing race, the Prix de l'Arc de Triomphe. That he did win it, and that he won it from a field of all the European talents with an authority that left him undisputed champion of the world, was proof principally of his own greatness but also, in no small measure, of the genius of the trainer who had so undervalued him at the December Sales. But the extraordinary story of Vaguely Noble began long before the December Sales, before he was even foaled, and to seek its origins we must go back four years, to the time when his sire Vienna first went to stud.

Vienna, who had the bright chestnut colour and the white legs of his sire, the Queen's famous stallion Aureole, was bred by Sir Winston Churchill. He was lightly and unsuccessfully raced as a two-year-old, but carried the pink and chocolate Churchill colours with distinction during the next three seasons. He won seven races altogether, gaining his most important victories in the Blue Riband Trial at Epsom and the Prix d'Harcourt at Longchamp, and was third to St. Paddy in the St. Leger. Then he retired to the Airlie Stud of Captain Tim Rogers near Dublin, with the reputation of being a good and stout-hearted horse who, like so many of the horses trained at Epsom by Walter Nightingall, loved to run along in front in his races, but who was not absolutely top class. Indeed he was the kind of horse that breeders with Classic ambitions wonder whether to patronize or not. Major Lionel Holliday, who strove only to breed horses of the highest class at his studs in England and Ireland, found himself in two minds. One morning at Newmarket he was discussing his matings with the local trainer Teddy Lambton and asked whether he should use Vienna. "I think you should," Lambton replied, and accordingly the fifteen-year-old mare Fragilite was sent to Vienna in his first stud season. The result was disastrous. Fragilite slipped a headless foal. The hot-tempered Holliday, as impatient of frustrations as he was determined to breed the best and race them to win, suffered instant disenchantment with Vienna. The horse had been worth trying; now, after one failure, he must be discarded. But already his mare Noble Lassie, a great granddaughter of the 1931 Oaks winner Brulette, was booked to visit Vienna in the 1964 season. The mating took place as arranged, but for the future the name of Vienna was struck off the list of possible mates for Holliday mares. The result of this unwanted, never-to-be-repeated union was Vaguely Noble.

Lionel Holliday did not live to share even a first instalment of the success of the horse destined to become the world's best. The old Yorkshireman, crotchety to the last but strangely mellowed and respected in the racing community during his final years, died at his home, Copgrove Hall, near Harrogate, on December 17th, 1965, when Vaguely Noble was just seven months and two days old. Vaguely Noble, who was reared at the Holliday Irish breeding establishment, the Cleaboy Stud near Mullingar in County Westmeath, became the property of Lionel Holliday's executors, along with the rest of his bloodstock interests, but was to race in the name of Lionel's son Brook when he was sent to the Holliday private trainer, Walter Wharton, at Lagrange Stables at Newmarket in the autumn of 1966.

Wharton, a Yorkshireman who had moved down from Wetherby to take charge of Lagrange two years earlier, found Vaguely Noble a gangling baby, even more backward than normal for a May foal, when the colt arrived. The following February, when the entries for the 1968 Classic races had to be made, the decision was made to leave out Vaguely Noble. His somewhat unprepossessing appearance at that stage did not encourage the belief that he would measure up to Classic standard; nor did his breeding, for his dam Noble Lassie, despite her illustrious ancestry and her own victory in the Lancashire Oaks, had failed to distinguish herself in the Oaks at Epsom. Providentially he was entered in the Observer Gold Cup, England's most richly endowed two-year-old race, for which the entries had to be made about the same time. In the past good Holliday two-year-olds had lost their form by the time the Observer Gold Cup was run in late October, and it was felt there was a slender chance that Vaguely Noble, who certainly would not be ready for serious training in the first half of the season, might be showing worthwhile form, and above all stamina, in the autumn. Big issues often hang by the most tenuous of threads in the world of bloodstock, and the almost casual decision to put Vaguely Noble in the Observer Gold Cup enabled him to collect a £16,944 prize for Brook Holliday and acquire a reputation in his first season which made him a record-breaker at the sales.

To Wharton, during the early months of 1967, Vaguely Noble revealed himself as "a real Christian of a horse". On the gallops it was difficult to know what to make of him. He would work, on terms of unpretentious equality, with a moderate plater or a horse of fair class. Unlike Albert Yank, he had nothing flamboyant about him. Yet he was so immature it was impossible to predict a great future for him. The Sandgate Maiden Stakes over six furlongs at Newcastle at the end of August was chosen for his first race and Doug Smith, who was shortly to retire after a career in the saddle which had brought him the champion jockey's title five times, was given the mount. His opponents, who numbered a dozen, were not high class, nor were they of the lowliest grade. Vaguely Noble was able to keep a place among the leaders the whole way and finished second, a neck behind Sweet Thanks. Afterwards Smith told Brook Holliday that he thought Vaguely Noble could have won if he had given him a tap with the whip, but had not liked to touch such a backward colt first time out. "I am glad you did not," Holliday replied. Smith had been pleased with the way Vaguely Noble had carried him, because long experience had taught him that any two-year-old of class ought to show speed even if he was backward; nevertheless he received no impression, so he confessed more than a year later, that he had ridden a world-beater to be.

Nor did the performance of Vaguely Noble in his next race, the seven furlongs Feversham Maiden Stakes at Doncaster the next month, prove much more revealing. Ridden by Bill Williamson, he again finished second, this time three-quarters of a length behind Saraceno. Ribero, who was to win the next year's St. Leger and Irish Derby, was fourth, but was running for the first time. Vaguely Noble showed himself in an entirely different light in his third race, the seven furlongs Sandwich Stakes at Ascot in October. The course had been drenched by torrential rain which fell almost incessantly all day, and by the time Vaguely Noble went out to run at 2.30 p.m. the ground was only one degree away from being waterlogged. The favourite was World Cup, who had come over from Paddy Prendergast's stable in Ireland with the reputation of being something out of the ordinary. But in the race World Cup bogged down, whereas Vaguely Noble, seemingly indifferent to the saturated state of the turf, settled easily into a relentless stride that carried him steadily further ahead of his struggling rivals in the last quarter mile so that he passed the winning post with twelve long lengths to spare.

Vaguely Noble's superiority that day was overwhelming, and the performance, in the absence of any other two-year-old of suitable qualifications, secured for him the right to carry the Holliday white and maroon colours in the Observer Gold Cup two weeks later. Yet many of the pundits remained unconvinced that he was top class. They argued that he alone of the eighteen runners in the Sandwich Stakes had been able to gallop freely in the appalling conditions, and that the others were of no account. Even Wharton, as he made his evening rounds at Lagrange, used to ask himself whether a colt who still looked so weak and undeveloped could be expected to succeed in the toughest test of a two-year-old. The market on the Observer Gold Cup reflected these public and private doubts; Connaught, who was to be second in the Derby, was favourite, with the Irish candidate Hibernian and the north-country colts Chebs Lad and Doon next in the betting. Vaguely Noble was only fifth favourite at 8-1. The result was an eye-opener. Vaguely Noble settled comfortably in the wake of Doon and Lorenzaccio, who led round the bend and up the straight of Doncaster's round mile. For a time Vaguely Noble seemed to be shut in, but Williamson was unruffled. As they entered the last furlong a yawning gap opened in front of him, and the tall bay colt surged through it. There was no sudden acceleration, rather a purposeful, irresistible forward move. The issue was settled in a second or two as Vaguely Noble went ahead with every stride and passed the post with seven lengths to spare from the gallant Doon.

It is a pity that the times of English races are not recorded furlong by furlong. Vaguely Noble's overall time for the race was unremarkable, as was inevitable in the soft conditions, but he gave the impression of covering the last furlong at top-class sprinter's pace.

The season was over and Vaguely Noble was officially reckoned the second best two-year-old of 1967, conservatively placed 1 lb. below the Gimcrack and Middle Park Stakes winner Petingo in the Free Handicap. But death duties and taxation are facts of life and not to be denied. Lionel Holliday's executors decreed that Vaguely Noble must be sold in December. So it was that Vaguely Noble, supreme product of English and Irish breeding, passed into American ownership. After the sale he was consigned to the stable of Paddy Prendergast and, on account of foot-and-mouth regulations, had to spend a quarantine period in Dublin before proceeding to the Curragh. Meanwhile there were moves behind the scenes. Bunker Hunt, the oil tycoon from Dallas, Texas, who had been the underbidder for Vaguely Noble through the agency of Godolphin Darley, felt burning regret that he had not persevered. He negotiated successfully, through Albert Yank, for a half share, and insisted that the colt should be transferred to Pollet's stable where he would be poised for the all-out assault on the Prix de l'Arc de Triomphe which must be his exclusive objective in 1968. The horse was to run in the name of Franklyn's wife Wilma.

Within a few months of his arrival Pollet, who had had charge of another world-beater, Sea Bird, three years earlier, was talking of Vaguely Noble as "a phenomenon". Owing to his lack of big race engagements Vaguely Noble had to begin his French career in races of secondary importance. First he gave a smooth if not supercharged performance in the Prix de Guiche over nine and three-quarter furlongs at Longchamp, in April, and followed with a more scintillating victory in the Prix du Lys over the French Derby course of one and a half miles at Chantilly on French Derby day. The Grand Prix de Saint-Cloud in July was his first real test on French soil. By then the French crowds had granted him heroic stature and made him an odds-on favourite, but the result was a sharp setback to the hopes of his admirers. He never looked like winning. At halfway in a fast-run race he was in a bad position far down the field. Having swung wide into the straight he began to catch the leaders rapidly, but was much too late to catch Hopeful Venture, carrying the colours of the Queen of England, and Minamoto. After a close struggle in the last furlong Hopeful Venture, ridden by Sandy Barclay and trained by Noel Murless, beat Minamoto by a neck, and Vaguely Noble was two lengths further behind in third place.

What had gone wrong? Few were prepared to accept that Vaguely Noble was less than a super horse, so the explanation for his defeat had to be sought elsewhere. Some said that the ground was too firm for him, others that he did not gallop evenly round the left-handed turns; but most laid the blame squarely on the shoulders of Pollet's stable jockey Jean Deforge. Always prone to overdo waiting tactics, Deforge had committed the cardinal error of ignoring his own pacemaker, Admiral's Boy, and giving the leaders too much start. Vaguely Noble's owners insisted that Deforge must be replaced by Bill Williamson in future.

The imperturbable Williamson resumed his old partnership when Vaguely Noble had his preliminary outing before the Prix de l'Arc de Triomphe in the Prix de Chantilly over eleven furlongs of the Long-champ course in September. Horse and rider matched each other in quiet efficiency, and Vaguely Noble stretched out in the straight to beat Felicio, who had nearly caught the limping Royal Palace in the last strides of the King George VI and Queen Elizabeth Stakes at Ascot in July, just as he liked. So Vaguely Noble arrived at his make-or-break test in the Prix de l'Arc de Triomphe on October 6th. Seldom since its foundation after the first world war had the greatest European international race attracted a field of such all-round high quality. The runners included no fewer than eight individual Classic winners—the French-trained Roseliere, La Lagune, Samos III and Dhaudevi, the Irish-trained Sir Ivor, the English-trained Ribero, the German-trained Luciano and the Russian-trained Zbor. Interest in the race was both intense and widespread. English visitors came by the plane-load on package outings. Most of them had not seen Vaguely Noble since the Observer Gold Cup or the December Sales and were astonished by the transformation in his appearance as he paraded in the autumn sunshine. He had been quite an ordinary horse as a two-year-old. Now, with his sleek bay coat shining and his air of panache, he looked a champion. And a champion he proved in the race. Luthier and the dashing filly Roseliere, accompanied by Zbor for the first half mile, made the running, but Williamson and Vaguely Noble were always lying handy in fifth or sixth position. As the leaders swung into the straight a gap opened between the tiring Luthier and Rosaliere, and through it surged Vaguely Noble with the same long, relentless strides that had gained the day at Doncaster. Sir Ivor came after him, and for a moment or two there were visions of Lester Piggott conjuring the same kind of acceleration from Sir Ivor that had snatched his sensational victories in the Two Thousand Guineas and the Derby. But horses do not accelerate when in pursuit of machine-like gallopers like Vaguely Noble. Struggle as he would, Sir Ivor could not close the gap, and at the winning post the merely hand-ridden Vaguely Noble was three lengths in front of Sir Ivor, who was even further ahead of the third horse Carmarthen and the rest of the field.

Vaguely Noble had fulfilled his mission and justified his purchase in the grand manner. Within months his valuation in the United States was five million dollars. Immediately after the race Dr. Franklyn gave an impromptu Press conference on the gravel forecourt of Longchamp's severely neo-classical weighing room. Blandly he gave thanks to the late Major Lionel Holliday for breeding Vaguely Noble, to the late Sir Winston Churchill for breeding the colt's sire Vienna, to Her Majesty the Queen of England for breeding the colt's great grandsire Aureole, and to British breeding in general for giving him the greatest horse in the world.

Nor did impartial critics fail to echo Franklyn's boast. For example the French racing journalist Maurice Bernardet wrote: "The best thoroughbred in the world won the Prix de l'Arc de Triomphe. He did it in a manner that permits no argument. He absolutely outclassed his rivals." Outclassing eight Classic winners takes some doing.

In 1968 the international form slotted neatly into place just as it had done three years before when Pollet had his previous world-beater. Diatome, third to Sea Bird in the Prix de l'Arc de Triomphe, had crossed the Atlantic a month later to win the Washington International at Laurel Park; and Sir Ivor paid his own tribute to Vaguely Noble by beating the picked field for the same race.

Perhaps it was a pity that Vaguely Noble himself did not run at Laurel Park. No one could say that he was tired or over-raced. But Pollet advised that the left-handed turns and the sharp American course would not suit him. Vaguely Noble, after all, had done enough that sunlit autumn day at Longchamp to establish his greatness for all time.

Index

N2830 ✱ 95¢ ✱ A BANTAM NINETY-FIVE

JAMES A. MICHENER
HIS FIRST NOVEL SINCE HAWAII
TREMENDOUS! MAGICAL! MAGNIFICENT!

CARAVANS

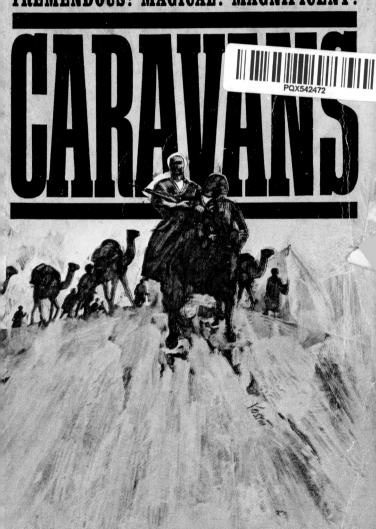